Gail,
Best Wishes
for a healthier
future!
  Andrea Munger

Food Allergies, What Do I Eat Now?

Donna Pilgrim, R.N., B.S.N.
Prudence Munger, R.N., B.S., D.C.

Sandi Fitterman, Editor

Food Allergies, What Do I Eat Now?
Coping and Cooking Day to Day

By
Donna Pilgrim
Prudence Munger

Published by:
Food Allergy Solutions, Inc.
2995 Johnson Ferry Road, Suite 250-802
Marietta, GA 30062

E-mail: food_allergy_solutions@yahoo.com

All rights reserved. No part of this book may be reproduced or transmitted in any form or by any means, electronic or mechanical, including photocopying, recording or by any information storage and retrieval system without the written permission from the authors, except for the inclusion of brief quotations in a review.

This book is not intended as medical advice. Its purpose is to inform and educate the reader. This book is not intended as a replacement to medical guidance. Consult a medical professional for advice on your individual needs and medical conditions.

The authors tested the recipes in this book. Nutritional values were calculated by a computer program and may vary depending on the quality of the ingredients used. Nutritional status and needs of each individual should be assessed by a doctor or qualified nutritionist.

Copyright© 1998
by Donna Pilgrim and Prudence Munger
Printed in the United States of America
Library of Congress Cataloging-in-Publication Data
Pilgrim, Donna and Munger, Prudence

    Food allergies, what do I eat now? Coping and cooking day to day.
    by Donna Pilgrim, and Prudence Munger --1st edition.

    Includes bibliographical references and index.
    ISBN 0-966606-8-1

Editor, Sandi Fitterman
Cover Design by Prudence Munger and Donna Pilgrim
Cover Art by Prudence Munger

Printing, Industrial Printing Service, Inc.
Canton, Georgia, 1998

Food Allergies, What Do I Eat Now?

Table of Contents

	Page

Chapter One
Introduction to Intolerances and Food Allergies — 3

Chapter Two
Prudy's Experience with Food Allergies — 5

Chapter Three
Donna's Experience with Food Allergies — 8

Chapter Four
How Do You Know You Have Food Allergies?
- Frequently Asked Questions — 11
- Signs and Symptoms — 15

Chapter Five
What Common Foods Provoke Reactions?
- Reading Labels — 20
- Wheat — 21
- Milk and Dairy — 27
- Corn — 31
- Soy — 34
- Eggs — 36
- Sugar — 38

Chapter Six
Methods of Testing
- Medical Testing — 41
- Self Testing — 43
- Food Diary — 45
- Sample Food and Reaction Diary — 46

Chapter Seven
Children and Food Sensitvities — 48

Chapter Eight
Cleansing and Elimination — 56

Chapter Nine
Food Classification — 61

Chapter Ten
Five Day Rotation Plan — 70

Food Allergies, What Do I Eat Now?

Chapter Eleven   Page

- **Eating Away From Home**
  - Special Considerations — 87
  - Traveling — 89
  - Camping Out and Reaction — 90
  - Brown Bagging Lunches — 93

Chapter Twelve

- **Tips for Hectic Lives** — 98

Cookbook

- **Introduction to Cookbook** — 104
  - Appetizers and Dips — 107
  - Beverages — 125
  - Breads and Baked Goods — 139
- **Introduction to Breads and Bake Goods** — 140
  - Breakfast — 169
  - Campfire Cooking — 187
  - Desserts — 205
  - Fruits, Salads and Dressings — 265
  - Main Dishes and Entrees — 305
  - Sauces — 387
  - Soups — 403
  - Vegetables — 433

Appendix — 457

- Product List — 458
- Food Product List — 459
- Trademark List — 465
- Bibliography — 466

Index — 468

Chapter One

Introduction to Intolerances And Food Allergies

It seems that during the last few years, the consumer conscious public has readily accepted the trends and fads toward convenience foods. Your ever increasingly busy lives have made it necessary to take the shortest path toward meal preparation: getting your nutrition from fast foods, convenience meals, and foods lacking in nutritional value. These factors can affect your lives in a negative, silent manner that you would probably, not knowingly, choose. This trend can cause the premature onset of disease or, worse yet, stifle the normal development of your children. The old adage, "You are what you eat," may be far more true than ever imagined. Consuming foods that you do not realize are enemies to your body may have long-term adverse effect.

We and our families have suffered through physical symptoms and depression not knowing what the cause could be. Through the help of friends who recommended books, an allergist and his wife, and our own investigation and research, we have learned how to cope with our sensitivities to foods.

Not all our days are without food-related problems; but, now that we know what foods cause our problem, we can investigate and track our eating habits to find causes. We hope that we can give you some of the tools to help you adapt your diet and live well in spite of your food allergies.

Perhaps, you have been diagnosed with food allergies and are trying to find a way to live with this condition. Or, you may be assessing the cause of unexplainable symptoms. Whatever your reason, this book can help.

Food Allergies, What Do I Eat Now?

We hope this book can help the estimated 20 percent of you that have food and preservative sensitivities, and, hopefully, another 20 percent with other types of allergies. If you have one allergy, you are likely to have other sensitivities as well. Unless you make the necessary changes in your diet now, the likelihood of developing other sensitivities will increase as you age. It could be that your child's asthma might be more manageable with dietary changes, giving the child a more normal life. It may even make the difference whether or not your child can play sports. Screening the diet for possible allergies and sensitivities may prevent that child from the drawbacks of starting Ritalin™ therapy.

We designed the information in this book to help you and your family. The cookbook section provides numerous tasty recipes to help you in your search for a healthier you. For more information on food allergies, please consult the reading list in the bibliography section. Use the following list of goals to help you realize the value of this book:

- To educate about diet, food allergies, intolerance and sensitivities.
- To help you detect food allergies, intolerance, and sensitivities sooner.
- To demonstrate how you can make the transition to start the needed dietary changes.
- To give simple hints for cooking, baking, and making life with allergies and food intolerance easier.
- To provide delicious recipes, directions and nutritional content for each recipe.
- To increase awareness about labeling methods, and educate you on how to understand label information.
- To demonstrate alternative methods to achieve optimum diet and nutritional needs.
- To answer questions and dispel myths about alternative foods.
- Finally, to help you make a transition to a new and healthier life.

Chapter Two

Prudy's Experience With Food Allergies

I want to describe to you the specifics of a few real life situations that may help in giving you a better understanding of what can happen. Understanding more will help increase your awareness and add vital insight so you can help yourself or your loved ones.

A friend has allergies to many common allergic foods, but her symptoms are very different than mine. When she eats foods she is allergic to, the weaker areas of her body are affected. She experiences visual changes due to swelling of the macula (the posterior area of the eye) that blurs vision in one eye. She saw an ophthalmologist who diagnosed and treated her for macular edema, a condition for which she needed to seek treatment. Some time later she realized the visual changes were always worse when she allowed herself to go off her diet. Swelling in various parts of the body is a common occurrence when you are sensitive to certain foods. The swelling is more visible in some individuals. The swelling can be very noticeable, in joints similar to an arthritis, or it can intensify the swelling of a weakened and not so obvious location like the eyes, only detectable by the medical professional. She also experiences mood changes, irritability, and severe drowsiness about 20 minutes after ingestion of wheat or foods containing wheat. The drowsiness is severe enough that she can go to bed and sleep 10-14 hours.

Another friend had bright red, scaly patches on her knees and elbows. They were large and unsightly and she was very self-conscious about them. Over a six-month period of time the patches had spread to her face. She told me the skin patches were eczema caused by food she ate and that she was seeing a toxicologist for the problem. I was in disbelief at the suggestion that diet could cause this eczema. She described a diet plan that eliminated dairy products. It was several months before I saw her again. This time I was in shock. She had followed her diet completely and every patch had disappeared. I had to grab her arms to look closer at her elbows to see that the patches truly were all gone. What a difference it made in her confidence, she once again felt good about her appearance.

Throughout grade school and high school, I struggled to stay awake in even my most favorite classes. This made test taking very difficult and my grades suffered. As an adult I experienced headaches. The headaches grew worse over the years. I went to several doctors and no one could find the problem. An endocrinologist gave me several medications. I could see the medications only covered the symptoms and did not address the cause. Eventually, at the suggestion from a friend, I sought help from a rheumatologist. I was experiencing severe joint pain and swelling all over my body. I was diagnosed with fibromyalgia and put on medications that, at least, made me more comfortable. Still the cause had not been addressed.

In college, I began to learn more about how the body functioned. I could not learn enough! I went to see a toxicologist and was tested for food sensitivities. I learned I was highly allergic to wheat, dairy, and eggs, and mildly allergic to tomatoes, lobster and almonds. I started the detoxification process by eliminating all the allergic foods. After using the diet for several days, I had more energy, slept better, and could think clearly for the first time in years. Even the drowsiness I had experienced in the past had disappeared.

It was not until several years after learning the cause of my symptoms that I realized that I always felt the best when I would diet to lose weight. When dieting for weight loss, I eliminated all breads and dairy.

My husband had been bothered with a persistent cough and sinus problem for many years. He wanted me to be successful with the elimination diet and thought it would be easier if he followed the same elimination diet. We were surprised when we realized within a few days he had stopped coughing and the sinus problems had dramatically improved. We were careful to reintroduce foods into Tim's diet one at a time. It quickly became evident that he was sensitive to dairy, corn, and wheat. He has eliminated these foods from his diet. The symptoms are gone.

My son, in his teens, experienced severe headaches. I finally convinced him that it was possible that he had the same allergies as myself. He eliminated tomatoes from his diet for two weeks. He had been without a headache for more than a week when he ate some convenience foods containing tomatoes and catsup. The next two days he experienced a severe headache, abdominal cramping, and diarrhea. He again eliminated the tomatoes for another two weeks.

Food Allergies, What Do I Eat Now?

Then, he tried adding them back into the diet again. The headaches returned. He no longer eats tomatoes and does not have headaches.

I have seen many patients in my office with a variety of back and neck pain complaints that were aggravated by food sensitivities. A patient came to me about a year ago with chronic severe head and neck pain that she could no longer tolerate. She tried prescription pain medications and didn't like how they made her feel. This patient was very active, running, swimming, working out lifting weights, and she continued in spite of her pain. She responded very well to Chiropractic care, but it seemed something just wasn't quite right. At times, her skin was very ruddy. I noticed it was worse on some days, and there was no obvious pattern to the coloration as with the butterfly rash of Lupus. One day, she came into the office clearing her throat, and continued to do so several times. It was frequent enough that she apologized for doing so. She explained that she had just eaten a particular brand of cookies - her favorite. On a later visit the conversation came to diet, and she was frustrated about how her muscles hurt especially in her neck. Diet was discussed, and the possibility of food allergies was broached. She described having food allergies as a child, without follow-up and adherence to avoiding these allergens. She eliminated wheat and dairy products from her diet. Her total well-being soared to a new level. Her skin tones returned to a normal color and her muscles improved. Now she knows when she has been negligent with her diet; she feels ill and the symptoms return. Many of the symptoms are muscular in nature, and of course with this patient it is always obvious at a glance when she has strayed from her diet, the ruddy skin returns.

As a rule, in caring for patients with biomechanical and musculoskeletal problems, food sensitivities can delay progress and improvement in their condition. I find they require more intensive care when they stray from their elimination diet.

These personal experiences, as well as those some of my patients have experienced, have compelled me to help others understand more about food sensitivities.

Chapter Three

Donna's Experience With Food Allergies

My experience with food allergies actually involves three personal stories.

Story 1:

It began about 22 years ago. My husband has always been a health conscious long distance runner. On a day-to-day basis, we did not notice a problem. However, just before every important race he would begin carbohydrate loading, a common practice with runners. Eating large amounts of complex carbohydrates prior to a race offers one of the most efficient ways to obtain and store energy needed for long distance running. The complex carbohydrate most runners choose is wheat in the form of pasta and breads. The morning of the race, he would have severe cramping and gastrointestinal distress. The diarrhea brought about fluid and electrolyte imbalance that was complicated by the demand that running the race normally placed on his body. He would have muscle cramps and spasms due to potassium, sodium, and fluid depletion. It was a potentially dangerous situation, and it would take days for his body to recover. This went on for about a year before we realized that wheat was the problem. He eliminated wheat and milk from his diet. During the elimination period, we also discovered that other related grains evoked similar symptoms, so we eliminated those grains as well. We were able to use other complex carbohydrates prior to races that served his purpose just as well.

Now, he can tolerate wheat occasionally without problems. After 22 years, he still enjoys long distance running. He manages about nine miles five days each week.

Food Allergies, What Do I Eat Now?

Story 2:

As a toddler, our daughter developed a rash on the back of her knees that was diagnosed as eczema. It spread up her thighs and down her calves. We used creams and ointments prescribed by our pediatrician to no avail. The condition became worse during hot summer months and would even leave scarred areas when it improved for whatever reason. This scenario went on for about 11 more years.

Finally, at age 13 she began to complain of severe stomach cramps, nausea, and gastrointestinal distress. These symptoms always happened after meals. Our pediatrician tested for parasites, and the results were negative. He suggested it might be a food-reaction, and told us we could see an allergist or begin eliminating foods one by one. We decided to try eliminating foods. We were lucky; the first one we eliminated was milk...bingo! The cramps and other intestinal symptoms dramatically improved. As a bonus, the rash on her legs <u>completely</u> disappeared, and the scarring has slowly been replaced by healthy skin.

She did well for about one year. Then, the cramping, nausea, and intestinal distress began to slowly return. She also began to lose weight. We eliminated two of the most common allergens, wheat and corn...bingo, again!! Immediate improvement, but she would still occasionally have recurring symptoms. We decided that she had many food allergies that were going to be difficult to diagnose in this manner. (Now, I know that only eliminating one food at a time is a very inefficient and unreliable method to use if an allergy to more than one food is the problem.) She continued to lose weight, and I felt that her nutritional status had been compromised too long. We decided to seek the help of a long-time friend, H.S.Dixon, M.D. in Rome, GA. He suspected multiple food allergies as well as a latex allergy. Her results to IgG and IgE tests were positive for wheat, corn, soy, cane sugar, milk, tea, and Type I for latex. She also has a sensitivity to legumes (beans) that did not show a positive reaction. You will read later how this can happen. Dr. Dixon explained that "delayed reactions" are common among food sensitive patients.

After receiving the test results, she began the elimination phase. On the fourth or fifth day, she felt better than she had in years. We were encouraged by the results and moved on to the next phase--rotating the non-allergic foods to help avoid developing allergies to them. We have been successful with this phase and continue to enjoy the variety of foods available. We have found substitutions that work well in place of the allergic foods.

Food Allergies, What Do I Eat Now?

Story 3, my own:

One and one-half years ago, I was diagnosed with fibromyalgia, a painful swelling and inflammation of muscle tissue and joints. My right hand became swollen and so painful to move that I could not write at times. I did not want to just treat the pain; I wanted to treat the cause. Unfortunately, that can be difficult and sometimes impossible to do. Prudence (co-author of this book) suggested, from her personal experience, that food preservatives could be causing some of the problem. She questioned me about my eating habits of late and any changes in my diet. At that time, I had begun a business and found myself rushing from one appointment to another with no time to eat a balanced lunch. I had become dependent on "fast-food" restaurants for many lunchtime meals. She told me to try eliminating the fast food to see what the result would be. I had improvement of symptoms in about two weeks. I had even eliminated the aspirin I had been taking regularly for the pain. Within two months, the swelling and pain were completely gone. Being a skeptical person by nature, I conducted a test; I ate fast-food French fries two days in a row and the pain was back 36 hours later. I was convinced. I pack my own lunches and snacks and try very hard to avoid fast-food restaurants.

Since that time, I have been tested for food allergies and am allergic to cane sugar and common mushrooms. I have eliminated them from my diet, and when I challenged them (tried them again after a six month elimination period), they still provoked nausea and headaches. I will continue to eliminate them and challenge again in about three to six months. I have found a good substitute for both and do not miss them in my diet at all. Dr. Dixon suggested challenging exotic mushrooms in place of the common ones, and I have found that I can tolerate a variety in my diet once a week. In the place of cane sugar, I have found a multitude of sweeteners.

I have also suffered from migraine headaches since my early teens. They are classic migraine headaches and respond well to medications recently developed specifically for migraine headaches. Neurologists have known for decades that, for some patients, certain foods can trigger migraine attacks. New medications, such as Imitrex™, have brought new hope to migraine sufferers. I have had good results preventing the onset of migraine headaches with Imitrex™, but still must avoid the foods known to trigger the headaches. If I eat a raw banana, I have a migraine that nothing will help. Since avoiding these foods, my headaches have decreased in number, but they still occur sometimes for no apparent reason. More information on foods that trigger migraine can be found in "Signs and Symptoms".

Chapter Four

How Do You Know You Have Food Allergies?

Frequently Asked Questions

When diagnosed with food allergies, there are so many questions that run through your mind. The allergist, who diagnosed my daughter, also suffers from food allergies, and pointed me in the right direction. I read everything I could get my hands on and received direction from the allergist's wife. She gave me helpful hints about foods related to common allergens and where I could shop in my area for alternate food items. She even gave me access to their private office library to help me gain some insight. I was lucky to have such guidance; many people are not. When trying to diagnose food allergies through a self-test, the need for information and answers to questions is paramount.

When people found out that we were writing a book, they all seemed to have questions, even if they do not have food allergies. Comments run from "What made you decide to write a book on allergies?" to "I do not believe there is such a thing as food allergies." Many times, the last response came from medical professionals with whom we work. We have been encouraged and discouraged by persons in the medical profession.

The questions frequently asked by people that we meet who have food allergies have a great deal in common. Some of the most frequently asked questions are:

1. "What am I supposed to cook for my allergic child (husband or myself)?"
   Cooking for the allergic family member can be a real challenge. First, cook as many fresh, non-processed foods as possible. Next, learn about food classifications and what foods may

be related to the allergic foods you are avoiding. Also, learning to read labels is important in avoiding allergic foods. Additionally, you can cook many of your own recipes with substitutions, and you can try some of the new recipes in the cookbook section!

2. "Can I still shop at my local grocery store?"

Absolutely! Fresh fruits and vegetables are available in all grocery stores, and many grocers' butcher shops can order natural meats and poultry that have been raised free from hormones and antibiotics. If pesticides are used on the fruits and vegetables, you may want to look for a source of organically grown items. You, also, may need to find a mail order source for alternative grains or a health food store that can meet your needs.

Some grocers will begin to order and stock these items if they feel there is a market for them. Assure them that there is and ask your allergist and friends for their support in this endeavor. They can call and ask for these natural items, also.

3. "I cannot find these nonallergic specialty items at my store, where do I get these unusual foods?"

Many large grocery store chains are beginning to carry healthier foods made with no or few preservatives and additives. However, some items can only be found at specialty stores, nutrition centers or by mail order. Some grocery stores even carry certified organically grown fruits and vegetables. If you cannot find a source for special flours and grains, we have supplied a shopping section with addresses of suppliers. You can write to these sources for a complete price list of items that you may not be able to find in a smaller town. Some internet addresses are included in the resource and shopping guide in the back of the book.

4. "Will I ever be able to eat the foods I am allergic to?"

There is a good chance that you will be able to rotate the allergic foods into your diet after a six-month elimination period. After that time, some of the allergic foods can be tolerated once a week in small amounts.

5. "My child buys his lunch at school. Since he is only allergic to wheat, can he just avoid the bread that comes on the lunch tray?"

School lunch programs rely heavily on wheat, corn, soy, and sugar. They use many processed foods in preparation of a meal that is usually standard to the whole school system. This is the most efficient way to feed large numbers of children and supply a "nutritionally balanced" meal. "Nutritionally balanced" however, should not include dyes and other preservatives and additives. The meat patties may contain meat extenders that may come from wheat, corn or soy. Most of the vegetables and fruits that are not prepared fresh are processed with additives, preservatives, and sugars. Therefore, wheat may be present in more items on his tray than just the bread. The effects of these preservatives are discussed in Chapter Seven, Children and Food Sensitivities.

6. "What kind of bread can I eat if I am allergic to wheat?"
There are many types of breads available made without wheat flour. Almost all health food stores and many grocery stores carry alternative grain breads, but read the label carefully for hidden wheat. There are also some bread recipes in this book that do not contain wheat.

Another problem sometimes associated with wheat allergy is gluten intolerance. Gluten is a natural part of the wheat grain. Allergies to gluten are usually associated with Celiac Disease or Celiac Sprue. The section on wheat discusses this condition further.

7. "What is the difference between a food allergy and food intolerance?"
A food allergy involves a reaction to a food protein at the cellular level. It provokes an immune response by the body and can actually be measured by antibody/antigen reactive tests.

A food intolerance/sensitivity can evoke very similar reactions as allergic responses. Food intolerance/sensitivity usually cause gastrointestinal problems, but are not limited to the intestinal tract. Any food intolerance can cause the same symptoms as allergies.

Intolerance to preservatives/additives can cause muscle and joint pain, swelling, hyperactivity in children, and inability to concentrate just to name a few symptoms. Food intolerance is more difficult for the allergist to diagnose because there is not a test that can be conducted to prove that a food sensitivity or intolerance exists. Only through diligent dietary elimination and challenging can you diagnose the intolerance. (Food challenging is a method of eliminating a specific food for a period of time, then reintroducing it to the diet. This is discussed in the chapter on testing.)

The bottom line is that a specific food is causing a problem and needs to be addressed. However, the management on a day to day basis remains the same. So, for simplicity, it is best if we collectively refer to these dietary challenges as food sensitivities.

8. "How do I learn more about food allergy/sensitivity?"
Reading this book is a good place to start! When we realized that we had food allergies, we started on the long journey of collecting information. The more information we collected, the more evident it became that there was a correlation between our experiences and the foods we were eating. It is often up to the individual to gather more information, raise their own suspicions, and seek help from a medical source that frequently deals with these types of problems. The focus of this book is to give you the tools to cope with food allergies, <u>not</u> to take the place of proper diagnosis.

There are many sources of information and support: your local library (many have computers with Internet accessibility), healthcare professionals, web-sites, and Internet support groups. Our reference section lists some of these.

9. "My doctor says I may have a gluten intolerance, can your book help me?"
Yes, gluten intolerance is a sensitivity to all products and food items containing gliaden protein. The recipes and information in this book will help you successfully manage your intolerance-coping and cooking day to day.

10. "I don't have time to cook complicated meals for my allergic family member. How can I make this work for the whole family?"
Bear in mind that your entire family will benefit from these changes. We have included quick and easy menus and meals which can be prepared with foods from your local grocer. (Special breads and flours may need to be purchased from health food stores or ordered through the mail, but most items can be purchased from you current food source.) You will find helpful hints to make meal preparation simple and convenient.

11. "How do I know what foods to choose since I don't understand the ingredient names listed on labels?"

Labeling is very misleading. We have included basic label reading information, which you will find helpful in making food selection.

12. "I don't think I can give up the foods I've become accustomed to and enjoyed all my life. Do I have to give up my favorite foods?"

We love steaks, ice cream, desserts, loaded baked potatoes, and sensuous, sinful sauces! We <u>still</u> enjoy them, and this book will show you how you can, too. With the rotation food plan, these foods don't have to be sacrificed. Eventually, as you learn to manipulate the recipes and ingredients and become comfortable with this new way of cooking, you will create your own delightful varieties of delicacies that will tantalize your taste buds.

Signs and Symptoms

One of the first questions you might ask if you suspect that you or a family member are sensitive to foods is, "What is the symptom of an allergy to milk (or whatever food you suspect)?" Many people are under the misconception that one food will evoke one specific symptom. In reality, a food can elicit a reaction from nausea to anaphylactic shock (a life threatening condition).

Manifestations of symptoms of food allergies can be different for every person. Wheat may cause chronic fatigue for one person, while another person may suffer from severe intestinal distress. The symptoms may be immediate or delayed. For some allergic persons, the symptoms may have been so subtle that the person has a difficult time recognizing when the symptoms actually began. Some symptoms, such as headache and fatigue, become chronic and are accepted as a part of life. Life does not have to be like that. Through careful testing, food sensitivities can be identified and managed.

The following list of common food reactions are by no means a complete list of symptoms caused by food allergies, and food allergies are not the only cause for these symptoms. The purpose of the list is to show the wide range and variety of conditions that can be caused by food sensitivities. A thorough assessment of your symptoms should be made by your physician to rule out other pathological possibilities.

Allergic reactions to foods are as varied as the persons who suffer from them. Symptoms can include:

Food Allergies, What Do I Eat Now?

General symptoms:
Headache
Joint pain
Swelling
Dizziness
General fatigue
Drowsiness
Insomnia

Gastrointestinal symptoms:
Nausea   Weight loss
Vomiting   Weight gain
Stomach cramps   Food cravings
Diarrhea
Mouth ulcers
Gas
Heartburn

Skin conditions:
Hives
Itching
Facial edema (puffiness)
Eczema
Skin rashes
Increased sweating
Increased flushing

Respiratory symptoms:
Congestion   Asthma
Runny nose   Coughing
Itchy nose
Post nasal drip
Chronic ear infections in children

Mood alterations:
Confusion – brain fog
Mood swings
Depression
Irritability
Hyperactivity

Cardiac symptoms:
Increased heart rate
Mild arrythmias

Musculo-skeletal symptoms:
Fibromyalgia - pain caused by inflammation and swelling of the muscle fibers.

Food Allergies, What Do I Eat Now?

The reaction time to a food can be very quick or latent, and symptoms can be subtle or severe. Many resources give in-depth descriptions about hypersensitivity reactions. A summary of different reactions follows.

Type I – (Immediate type) This type can produce a response in less than 15 minutes! You suddenly feel warm, heart rate increases and can go above 100 beats per minute while you are at rest. Your skin may suddenly become reddened.

Type II – (Cytotoxicity) This type affects the cells in tissue. Cell and tissue function is changed due to reactions caused by an allergen. This particular type can affect the shape of the blood cell as well as shorten the life of the blood cell. It also can affect the filtration system of the kidneys. Our kidneys are very complex and need to function efficiently to rid the body of the toxins and byproducts of metabolism.

Type III – (Deposit of immune complex in vessels or tissue) This results in the release of an enzyme and permeability factors in tissue which produces an acute inflammatory reaction.

Type IV – (Delayed hypersensitivity) The delayed reaction lends mystery to all our efforts to understand reactions to foods. It may take 48-72 hours for the delayed reaction to occur. This is why it is so difficult to connect the wheat you had three days ago with the migraine you have today. Headaches are a common delayed reaction. It is not normal to have headaches, and the cure is not in a medicine bottle. The only cure is to discover and deal with the cause.

Allergies and sensitivities can cause a multitude of symptoms, but they can also cause symptoms of other conditions to worsen. Conditions such as arthritis, eczema, and Celiac Disease can be made unbearable by eating some foods to which you may or may not be sensitive. With these conditions, an allergy to the food is not required for the foods to cause symptoms to worsen.

Arthritis is not caused by an allergic reaction, but certain foods may worsen the pain and swelling. Vegetables from the nightshade family can cause arthritis symptoms to worsen. These vegetables include: potatoes, tomatoes, eggplants, sweet peppers (red, green, yellow and orange), banana peppers, chili peppers, cayenne pepper, tobasco, paprika, tobacco, and pimiento. You could have adverse reactions to this plant family even if no true allergy to the specific vegetable is apparent. According to Dr. John Mansfield, *Arthritis, the Allergy Connection*, the studies on the correlation of allergies and arthritis are producing convincing results that the medical profession can no longer ignore. Many arthritis patients have found that pain and swelling may decrease when certain foods are eliminated from the diet. Foods that also may trigger increased pain and swelling for arthritis sufferers are milk products and caffeine.

Diseases of the skin can be troubling, especially when the effected area appears on the face and hands. Pain associated with the lesions is compounded by the psychological distress of a possibly disfiguring condition. Many who have eczema have had dramatic improvement and even complete remission of the skin lesions when the allergen was removed from the diet. Usually, the allergic food is milk (lactose or casein). When milk and all milk products are eliminated from those diets, the skin lesions may completely go away in about one to two months. Removing all lactose containing products requires that every label be read diligently. More information on what products contain milk and "hidden milk" in foods will be discussed in Chapter Five.

While no one food can be attributed to all gastrointestinal problems, one common factor seems to be milk, milk products, and foods containing the milk sugar lactose. Lactose intolerance usually does not cause permanent damage to the lining of the intestinal tract, but it can cause severe distress that can effect activities of daily life. Weight loss and a general decline of your nutritional status may result if the sensitivity is not properly diagnosed. Other common foods that can cause gastrointestinal distress are tomatoes, corn, eggs, soy, coffee, and tea just to name a few.

Another condition that is directly related to food sensitivities is Celiac Disease. With Celiac Disease, intolerance for gluten causes severe gastrointestinal distress. Gluten, a naturally occurring substance in wheat and a few other grains, cannot be tolerated even in small amounts and can even damage the cilia in the intestinal tract. Elimination of gluten containing grains from the diet and any other allergens is usually all that is necessary for the Celiac patient to lead a normal life.

The medical profession has known for decades that certain foods can trigger migraine headaches. Migraines are vascular headaches characterized by severe pain usually on one side of the head. Other symptoms include nausea and vomiting, sensitivity to light and sounds, and inability to concentrate. These symptoms can also be signs of more serious neurological and vascular conditions. Any severe or unusual headache needs to be evaluated by your medical doctor to rule out more serious medical problems.

Food Allergies, What Do I Eat Now?

Some foods that are known to trigger migraines are:

<u>Dairy products</u> (especially aged and ripened cheeses - blue, Boursault, brick, Brie, Camembert, cheddar, Emmenthaler, Gruyere, mozzarella, Parmesan, Romano, Roquefort, Stilton, Swiss, Gouda, Provolone)

<u>Seafood</u> - caviar, pickled or dried fish

<u>Fruits</u> - figs, bananas, citrus fruit, raisins, papaya

<u>Vegetables</u> - onion, avocado

<u>Beverages</u> - caffeine, alcohol, some teas

<u>Breads</u> - any hot yeast breads

<u>Beans</u> - peanuts, navy beans, pinto, lima beans

<u>Cured meats</u> - bacon, hotdogs, lunchmeats, pepperoni, pork, and sausage

<u>Misc</u> - pickled foods, excess salt, MSG, some vinegar, chocolate

Check with your physician for a complete list of foods and medications that can trigger migraine headaches. Then, investigate what foods may contain that item. You may be able to eliminate or reduce the number of migraine episodes that occur by avoiding those foods and medications.

Thorough testing is necessary to determine the foods causing a reaction. A physician who specializes in allergy treatment can do this, or it can be done by the "self-test" method. A thorough discussion of self-testing can be found in the next chapter. It provides the necessary tools to begin the road to optimum health.

Chapter Five

What Common Foods Provoke Reactions?

Reading Labels

Your chances of being able to avoid an allergen increase exponentially when you have all the information about that particular allergen. As you will see, some of these foods are listed on labels as a component or chemical rather than the food itself. Even if you are not allergic to a particular food listed in this chapter, it will benefit you to read that section anyway. You may be surprised by some of the information.

Reading a label can be an adventure in chemistry! Have you ever tried to read a label for a list of ingredients on a product and wondered "Why is stearoyl-2-lactylate in my food?" An even more perplexing question is "What in the world <u>is</u> stearoyl-2-lactylate? The Food and Drug Administration (FDA) does not require food labeling to include the source of these types of chemicals. It is up to you, the consumer, to find out for yourself where these unfamiliar and unpronounceable additives come from.

According to Stephanie Bernardo Johns, *The Allergy Guide to Brand-Name Foods and Food Additives,* the FDA does not require the food manufacturer to include a list of items that are not directly a part of the ingredients, but are a part of the food due to processing techniques. These additives are called indirect additives. For example, a food manufacturer may put wheat flour or cornstarch on their conveyor rollers to prevent the product from sticking to the roller. This sounds harmless enough – except to the persons allergic to wheat and corn. Incidental ingredients are added to non-food products as well. In the packing process, paper and plastic cups may be dusted with cornstarch or "food starch" to prevent them from sticking in the package. Latex and plastic gloves are dusted with undisclosed powders for the same reason.

At this time, until guidelines change, the best you can do is contact each manufacturer and ask what exactly the food source is for the item in question. **Another piece of advice is that if you cannot read the label and make sense of it, do not buy it.**

The best source for food additive in brand name products is the book, *The Allergy Guide to Brand-Name Foods and Food Additives*, by Stephanie Bernardo Johns. She lists common name brands, their additives, and their food source. At this time, her book is no longer in print, but many libraries have copies.

Included in this book, on the last page, is a form to petition changes in laws that would require manufacturers to include food sources for chemicals and other additives in their ingredient lists. Please take time to read it, sign, and mail or fax it to your state and federal representatives. You can make a difference.

Wheat

Wheat is one of the four most commonly grown grains in the world. It stands to reason that its prominent place in the diet would cause it to become an allergen for many. Wheat can be found in almost every type of processed food. If you suspect you have food allergies, wheat should be one of the first choices for testing.

Many patients have an intolerance for gluten. Gluten is found in many grains used for raised breads (yeast). It provides a protein matrix that helps hold in air and gases produced by the yeast reaction and allows the dough to rise and become light. Since it is not present in all available flours, there are alternatives to use in cooking. Celiac Sprue is a condition of gluten intolerance; the gluten not only brings about severe gastrointestinal distress, it also may damage the lining of the intestine. It is imperative to learn what grains, other than wheat, contain gluten. They are barley, oat, rye, teff, spelt, triticale, and Kamut™. These grains are further explained in this section. Some genetically changed corn may contain gluten.

"Non-gluten" breads are available made with wheat-free flours. Gluten-free breads are usually made with fast rising leavening agents such as baking powder and baking soda. Gluten-free/yeast-free breads can be found at health food stores, and some large grocery stores carry a line of these breads in the frozen health-food section. Some non-gluten grains and flours include most corn (some corn is being genetically altered to contain gluten), amaranth, buckwheat, arrowroot, cassava, millet, potato, quinoa, rice, soy, and chickpea flour. Some exotic flours are also available, but they are pricey.

Food Allergies, What Do I Eat Now?

Many times, manufacturers will not list wheat as a source when, in fact, wheat may be present in varying amounts. Wheat flour is an inexpensive and very versatile ingredient widely used in foods and medicines. Often, wheat cannot be found listed on the label, but it is there in one of its many forms. Some processed foods that list chemical names can be misleading because food sources are not divulged. The best advice is to avoid over processed foods. If you need a degree in chemistry to understand the label, don't buy it. Find a simpler product or make it yourself. Health food stores offer a wide selection of foods that are prepared with no additives or preservatives.

Obvious wheat products:
Breads, crackers, cookies, cereals, pastas, sauces and gravies (thickened with wheat), meats with a coating or crust, prepared meats, and some ice creams and puddings. The labels on these products usually list wheat flour as an ingredient.

Less obvious wheat products:
(These products may contain wheat) Flavored coffees, Postum™, Ovaltine™, some beers and ales, malted drinks, alcoholic beverages (some gin, whiskey, etc.), graham, durum, bran, semolina, rolls, muffins, buns, biscuits, pancakes, waffles, pretzels, cookies, cakes, pastries, wheat cereals, farina, cream of wheat, pasta, egg noodles, cous-cous, triticale, malt cereal, ice creams, sherbet, cones, custard, pie crust, pudding, chocolate, candy, candy bars, stuffing, croquettes, meat loaves (some), sausages, lunch meat, hot dogs, meat extenders, fast food hamburgers, some salad dressing (thickened with food starch), gravies, sauces, bullion, soups, soy sauce, tamari, and steak sauces with soy.

Many allergists, researchers, and dietitians disagree on the subject of what part of an allergen will cause an allergic reaction. Some believe any part of a food protein can trigger a reaction while others believe that when an allergic substance is broken down to its chemical components it will no longer trigger a reaction. However, many people react to MSG with varied symptoms, but is it a reaction to the MSG or to the food source? Since MSG can come from wheat, corn, soy, or a number of other sources, you may not know whether you are reacting to the MSG as a chemical additive or to its food source. Just consider it to be one of the many food additives to avoid. Listed below are some chemical names for wheat source chemicals.

May have wheat as a food source:
Confectioners' sugar (used to prevent caking), MSG, alcoholic beverages such as Bourbon, whiskey, gin, rye, Scotch, and vodka, beta-amylase, caramel coloring, dextrin, ethanol, ethyl alcohol, flour, food starch, glutamates, gluten, hydrolyzed vegetable protein, malt, barley malt, malt syrup, malted milk, malto dextrin, maltol, maltose, modified food starch, modified vegetable protein, soy sauce, vanilla extract, vinegar, vitamin E, chocolate, and cocoa. These food additives may come from many sources other than wheat; they may come from soy or corn, for example.

VARIETIES OF GRAINS CLOSELY RELATED TO WHEAT:
Wheat and its relatives may cause cross-reactions.

Wheat: (contains gluten) There are several varieties of wheat: durum, semolina, whole wheat, unbleached flour, and most of the flours found in the grocery store baking section.

Spelt: (contains gluten) Close relative of wheat. Spelt is an ancient wheat that has not been genetically changed. Some people are able to tolerate spelt in a rotation diet after carefully eliminating wheat from the diet for six months. It can be found in health food stores and is a good substitute for wheat.
Substitute for wheat in recipes: 1-cup for 1-cup

Kamut™: (Contains high gluten) Another ancient wheat not genetically changed. When adding wheat back into the diet after a six-month elimination period, spelt and kamut are good choices to try.
Substitute for wheat in recipes: 1-cup for 1-cup.

Teff: (contains gluten) Closely related to wheat. You may be able to tolerate teff in the diet later. Teff is similar to wheat in every way.
Substitute for wheat in recipes: 1-cup for 1-cup.

Barley: (contains gluten) Closely related to wheat. Used in the production of malt for brewing beer. Pearled barley has the hull and outer bran removed. You may be able to add to the diet in a rotation plan after the six-month elimination period.
Substitute for wheat in recipes: 1-cup for 1-cup.

Rye: (contains gluten) Very close relative of wheat and likely to cause a similar reaction. Rye is, also, used for distillation into grain alcohol spirit. Be cautious when trying to add rye back into the diet. Rye is a heavier grain and works best when combined with another lighter grain.
Substitute for wheat in recipes: ¾ -cup rye + ¼ -cup other flour= 1-cup wheat.

Oats: (contains gluten) Oat is in the grass family with wheat, and some people have a cross-reaction with oat. You can test to see if oat can be tolerated. Use the method of adding a food when you are in the challenging phase of the elimination diet. If tolerated well, oat is a great grain to substitute for wheat in baking. If not tolerated, wait six months and try again.
Substitution for wheat flour in baking: 2/3 cup oat flour + 1/3 cup other flour.

Rice: (does NOT contain gluten) Although rice is in the grass family, it usually does not provoke a reaction. It is a good grain to help supply fiber, and vitamins in your diet. Use whole grain brown rice as a side dish, in casseroles, as a morning cereal, in baking as flour, and as a milk substitute.
Substitute for wheat flour in baking: ¾ cup rice flour + ¼ cup other flour = 1 c.

NON-RELATED SUBSTITUTES FOR WHEAT

Amaranth- (non-gluten) A seed from the amaranth family, it has a mild nutty flavor. You will find it in the health food stores as a cooked morning cereal, cereal flakes, or as flour for baking. Check labels on the cereal flakes; it is sometimes mixed with corn.
Substitute for wheat: ¾ cup amaranth flour + ¼ cup other flour = 1 cup

Food Allergies, What Do I Eat Now?

Potato starch flour: (non-gluten) A member of the nightshade family, potato starch flour works best for baking when combined with other flours. Adds lightness to baking with heavier flours. It works well as a thickener, but a little goes a long way. It does not add a noticeable flavor to what is being thickened.

Substitute for thickening agent: 1-tsp. potato starch flour per 1-cup liquid.

    For thicker gravy: 2-tsp. potato starch flour per 1-cup liquid.

Substitute for wheat in baking: 1/3 cup potato flour + ¾ cup other flour= 1 c.

Arrowroot: (non-gluten) Marantaceae family (a tuberous root). A good substitute for cornstarch. Has a bland flavor similar to cornstarch. To use as a thickener: 2-tsp. per 1 cup of liquid to be thickened.

Substitute for wheat in baking: 1/3 cup Arrowroot flour + ¾ cup other flour = 1 cup wheat flour.

Buckwheat: (low gluten - contains a gluten analog - use only a small amount in your diet to test for sensitivity) Not related to wheat at all. It is in the same family with rhubarb. Dark buckwheat flour has a bitter taste that gets stronger with age. Light buckwheat is milder in flavor and is better substituted for wheat in baking. Refrigerate the package whether it has been opened or not. This will help to prevent the bitter taste from forming. It is best when mixed with other flours.

Substitute for wheat in baking: 2/3 cup buckwheat + 1/3 cup other flour =1 cup wheat flour.

Tapioca flour: (non-gluten) From the spurge family, tapioca comes from the cassava plant. When tapioca is ground to a fine powder, it can give lightness to baking with heavier flours. It is similar to cornstarch and can also be used for thickening. Use 2-tsp. tapioca flour per 1 cup of liquid to be thickened.

Substitute for wheat flour: 1/3 cup tapioca flour + ¾ cup rice, amaranth, or buckwheat flour = 1 cup.

Quinoa: (non-gluten) pronounced keen-wa. Quinoa is a seed from the goosefoot family, and is cultivated in South America. It is delicious and probably the most nutritious of all grains. It is extremely high in protein and is a complete protein; it contains all the essential amino acids. Quinoa reminds me of sweet creamed corn when prepared with chicken stock. I prepare it in

my recipes that call for cous-cous (wheat). It has a similar texture to cous-cous. It can be added to casseroles, soups, or chopped vegetables to prepare as a pilaf. Quinoa seeds need to be rinsed and drained to remove a natural bitter coating. Ground into flour, it can be substituted very well for wheat flour or corn meal. In a batter, quinoa flour has the texture of cornmeal. In the recipe section you will find a recipe for Quinoa "Corn"bread that tastes similar to cornbread.
Substitute for cornmeal: 1 cup quinoa = 1 cup cornmeal.
Substitute for wheat flour: ½ cup Quinoa flour + ½ cup rice flour = 1 cup wheat flour.

Millet: (non-gluten) It is related to wheat, so, there may be a chance of cross-reaction. Millet flour has a coarse texture similar to cornmeal with a nutty flavor. If you do not react to millet, you may place it on your rotation diet. There are two different forms of millet, finger millet and pearl millet. Pearl millet looks like birdseed.
Substitute for wheat: ½ cup millet flour + ¼ c. rice flour + ¼ c. potato flour = 1 cup wheat flour.

Soybean flour: (non-gluten) A member of the legume family. Since soy is one of the most common allergens, it is not recommended that you rely heavily on this flour. If you do not react to soy, or have been tested and proven not to be allergic, you may want to add this flour to your 5-Day Rotation Plan.
Substitute for wheat flour: ½ cup soy flour + ½ cup rice flour = 1 c. wheat flour.

Exotic flours: There are many exotic flours available at a substantial expense. Some of them are Jerusalem artichoke flour, banana flour, chickpea flour, lima bean flour, lotus root flour, malanga flour, nut flours, seed meal flours, sesame flour, water chestnut flour, and sweet potato flour. It might be fun to experiment with some of these flours, especially if you have multiple food allergies. Your health food store manager will probably order one of these for you, but be prepared to pay more.

Food Allergies, What Do I Eat Now?

Milk And Dairy

My allergist says, "Cow's milk is great…for baby cows." Milk has become a staple of the American diet. For most, it is a part of the diet from birth. According to Dr. James Braly, *Dr. Braly's Food Allergy and Nutrition Revolution,* "…a fetus begins to form antibodies against allergic substances as early as 11 weeks into the pregnancy". It is the opinion of many allergists that a mother's intake of cow's milk while breast-feeding should be limited. The lactating mother may obtain calcium requirements from vegetable, seed, and grain sources or supplements in the diet.

Milk is one of the most common allergens worldwide. The responses vary from true allergic (immunologic) responses to lactose (milk sugar) intolerance. In the case of lactose intolerance, the enzyme required to digest the sugars in milk is missing. Undigested lactose in the intestine can provide an ideal breeding ground for bacteria.

Milk allergies are one of the most common causes of upset stomach, indigestion, bloating, nausea, vomiting, diarrhea, and stomach cramps. The most common symptoms involve the digestive tract, but can also include skin rashes, eczema, itching skin, headache, "sluggish" feeling, irritability, fatigue, congestion, chronic otitis media (ear infection), "runny or itchy" nose, watery eyes, cough, and thickened mucus in the mouth. These symptoms may be immediate or delayed. Most allergists believe there is a direct relationship between milk sensitivities and chronic rhinitis and otitis media in children. Chronic swelling of the Eustachian tube in children will prevent drainage of the middle ear and facilitate the growth of bacteria in that area.

Symptoms caused by milk sensitivity can be dramatically improved with avoidance. My daughter has severe gastrointestinal symptoms whenever she ingests any milk product. After two months on a milk-free diet, the intestinal symptoms from milk disappeared, as did the eczema on her legs she had suffered with for over ten years.

Many allergists are asked, "If you are sensitive to cow's milk, will you be sensitive to other animal milks?" The answer varies among allergists. The bottom line is that since lactose is present in all animal milk, you <u>may</u> react to all animal milk in the same way. After eliminating all animal milk from your diet for six months, try adding goat's milk or other milk into your rotation diet. You may or may not react. If you cannot tolerate any milk after six months, continue to use the nut milks, rice milk, or soymilk (if you are not sensitive to soy). You may want to add a calcium supplement to your diet.

Infants who are sensitive to cow's milk present a different problem entirely. Their nutritional status is vital to growth, both mentally and physically. Consult your pediatrician if you suspect that your child's fussiness or physical symptoms are caused by problems with milk. Diarrhea, excessive spitting-up or vomiting is a serious condition for infants. Their health status can be effected in a matter of hours by fluid and electrolyte imbalances. You may be under the impression that breast-fed children are immune to this problem, but many studies show that infants can react to what the mother is eating in her diet.

Obvious foods that contain milk:
All animal milks, cream, cheeses, yogurt, cottage cheese, cream cheese, sour cream, butter, ice creams, sherbets, and margarines (even those made from vegetable oils).

Less obvious foods that may contain milk:
Augratin dishes, biscuits, most breads, some corn breads, bisque, butter sauces, milk chocolate, chowders, creamed soups, sauces, gravies, custards, cakes, milk frosting, doughnuts, processed meats (hot dogs, sausages, lunchmeats), muffins, omelets, scrambled eggs, pancakes, waffles, pudding, mashed potatoes, scalloped dishes, kefir, curds, some salad dressing, pancake mixes, biscuit mixes, cookies, and pies.

Chemical names that can have milk as the food source:
Casein, caseinate, sodium caseinate, lactose, lactalbumin phosphate, "curds," whey, lactalbumin, lactoglobulin, lactic acid, Beta-carotene, calcium lactate, calcium stearoyl-2-lactylate, caramel color, lactic fermenting agent, lactylated fatty acid esters, malted milk, mystristic acid, peptones, sodium lactate, starter culture, starter distillates, maltose-milk sugars, milk derivatives, and milk solids.

Note: Any Kosher product marked "pareve" does not contain milk. The symbol K also indicates that a food is pareve.

Food Allergies, What Do I Eat Now?

Some patients who are lactose intolerant may not react to casein. If you react to it, read labels carefully and try it again after six months.

Substitutes for milk:
Fruit juices and fruit purees can be substituted for milk in some recipes.

NUTQUIK™ - from Ener-G Foods is a dry product, made from almonds, that can be reconstituted with water, strained and used in recipes, as a beverage or over cereal.

Nut milks can be purchased at most health food stores, or can be made by using ¼ cup nuts (any variety will do), 1-tsp. honey, and 2 cups boiled water. Blend on high for 2 minutes. Strain through cheese cloth or fine mesh strainer. Keeps in the refrigerator for about five days. Making small batches is recommended for use in the Five Day Rotation Plan.
The nut milks are, in my opinion, the best tasting and creamiest of all the substitutes.

Sesame seed milk is made by blending ¼ cup sesame seed with 1-cup water for 3-4 minutes. Strain, use in cooking for a milk high in calcium.

Soymilk can be a good substitution if you are not sensitive to soy.

Substitutes for Margarine:
Clarified butter (butter that has been heated so that the milk solids separate from the butterfat) may be tolerated by some. After heating butter, pour the top layer of fat into a container and discard the solids in the bottom of the pan. Place the container in the refrigerator and use as you would butter.
A variety of oils may be used instead of butter, margarine or shortening (usually comes from corn or animal fats).
Rice margarines, canola margarine, and other oil margarines can be found at health food stores. Be sure to read the label carefully for other allergens that may effect you. Many contain soy or casein (a milk protein that may cause problems for some individuals).

Food Allergies, What Do I Eat Now?

<u>Substitutes for sour creams:</u>

Mock sour creams are usually made from soy products. Check recipes or labels if you are sensitive to soy. You can make many creamy casseroles by adding 1-teaspoon potato starch flour to 1 cup of milk of the day to thicken the milk to the desired consistency. Adding 2 teaspoons lemon juice will give it tartness similar to sour cream. Use your imagination and whatever you have on hand.

<u>Substitutes for cheeses:</u>

Some persons can tolerate some hard cheeses because much of the whey has been removed. Cheese made from rice milk is available at most health food stores, but it usually contains casein and cornstarch.

Nut Cheeses are available at health food stores; most of them contain casein. We can tolerate these without problems in our Five-Day Rotation Plan. The almond mozzarella is especially good on pizza. It tastes and melts like the real thing. The almond cheese with herbs and garlic is especially tasty! Read labels for soy, casein and corn.

Food Allergies, What Do I Eat Now?

Corn

Corn is a member of the grass family, subfamily: Panicoideae. It is native to the Americas and is one of the most common food allergens. Corn is one of the most common crops grown worldwide, so, it is understandable that its frequent use would make it high on the allergen list. It is low in protein but high in starch and contains moderate fiber. It contains no gluten, which makes it a good grain for those with gluten intolerance (unless you also have an intolerance for corn). In the future, hybrid corns may contain gluten.

Beware of any foods that have the word "corn" on the label. They obviously have corn as an ingredient. **You must train yourself to read labels diligently.**

Some obvious foods that contain corn are:
Corn fritters, creamed corn, popped corn, corn syrup, corn sweeteners, corn flakes, corn bread, stuffing, corn oil, vegetable oil, corn starch, grits, hominy, corn chips, corn noodles, corn cakes, succotash, most breakfast cereals, biscuit mixes, and other baking mixes, tortillas, taco shells, some salad dressing, and battered or breaded foods that have cornmeal as an ingredient.

Some of the less obvious foods that might contain corn are:
Hotdogs, puddings, pastries, confectioners sugar (uses corn starch to prevent caking), sauces, beer, ales, lagers, hard liquors, wine, sparkling wines, soft drinks, frosting, margarine, deep fried foods, baby foods, bacon, ham, processed cheese, pickles, sausage, canned soups, some chocolate, caramels, chewing gum, cough drops, hard candies, malted foods, ice cream, canned fruits, jelly, jam, preserves, toothpaste, syrup, Aspartame™, saccharin, soy milk, some medications (especially in tablet form), adhesives, laundry starch, restaurant salt shakers, vitamin C supplements, sweetened peanut butter, canned and frozen peas, stamps, and envelopes. Some manufacturers use cornstarch to dust conveyor rollers to prevent sticking. Since cornstarch would not be an ingredient "in" the food, it is not required to be listed on the label. This dusting of cornstarch may be enough to elicit an allergic reaction in some people. Products such as paper cups, plastics, and latex gloves may have cornstarch added to prevent sticking.

Food Allergies, What Do I Eat Now?

Some additives to foods that can be from corn as the food source are:

Dextrose, dextrin, glucose, invert sugar, sorbitol, mannitol, alcohol, bourbon, corn whiskey, gin, Holland gin, rye, Scotch, vodka, whiskey, ascorbic acid, baking, powder, beta-carotene, brominated vegetable oil, calcium citrate, calcium lactate, calcium stearate, calcium stearoyl-2-lactylate, caramel color, cerelose, citric acid, diglycerides, erythorbic acid, ester gum, ethanol, gluconic acid, glucono delta lactone, glutamates, glycosides, glycerol, glyceryl monostearate, hydrogenated vegetable shortening, hydrol, hydrolyzed vegetable protein, isomerose, lactic acid, lactylated fatty acid esters, lecithin, levulose, malic acid, malt, malt flavoring, malt syrup, malto-dextrin, maltol, maltose, modified cornstarch, modified food starch, modified vegetable protein, monoglyceride citrate, MSG, polydextrose, polysorbate, potassium gluconate, propylene glycol monostearate, sodium citrate, sodium erythrobate, sodium gluconate, sodium lactate, sodium stearoyl-2-lactylate, sorbitans, sorbitol, starter distillate, stearic acid, tocopherols, vanilla extract, vegetable oil, xanthan gum, and zein.

The best advice we can give is to purchase food items whose labels are easy to read or buy fresh, unprocessed foods. If you have no clue what in is a food from reading the label...don't buy it!

Substitutes for corn:

Many items can be used in the place of corn in recipes. Try some of these in your recipes and you will be surprised at how well these substitutions work.

Cornstarch - use arrowroot (health food stores usually sell this in bulk), potato starch flour or tapioca flour.

Corn syrup - use honey, maple syrup or rice syrup.

Cornmeal - a great substitute for cornmeal in recipes is quinoa (keen-wa). It has a sweet corn taste and has a texture almost identical to cornmeal.

Batter and breading - Use any other flour substitute and season as usual. Some good choices are mixes of potato starch flour, tapioca flour, quinoa flour, oat flour, chickpea flour, Buckwheat flour, and rice flour.

<u>Corn oil</u>- You may use any of the variety of oils. Experiment with the different flavors that some oils can add to foods. Good choices are canola oil, olive oil, sesame oil, sunflower oil, safflower oil, palm oil, peanut oil (if you are not sensitive to peanuts), and coconut oils. Some of these oils contain higher amounts of cholesterol than others. This may be a significant factor in your diet.

<u>Vinegar</u>- since most vinegars are made with corn, a good substitute is apple cider vinegar, lemon juice or rice vinegar.

Food Allergies, What Do I Eat Now?

Soy

The soybean was originally found in China and is a member of the legume family. Surprisingly, the U.S. is now the leading producer of soybeans. It is a good source of protein and oil, but its frequent use as extenders and fillers in many foods has caused it to be a leading allergen. You may be under the impression that you rarely eat soy, when in reality you probably consume it almost everyday.

<u>Some obvious soybean products are</u>: Soy sauce, tamari, soy milk, coffee substitutes, protein drinks, baby formulas, miso, teriyaki marinade, tofu, some baked goods (check labels closely), soy flakes in cereal, boxed cereals, some mayonnaise, salad dressing, some vegetable oils, bean curd, and vegetable oil sprays.

<u>Some less obvious products with soy are:</u> Crisco™, Worcestershire sauce, some margarines, lunchmeats, hamburger extenders, commercial meatloaf, meat balls, meat substitutes, veggie burgers, some ice-cream and sherbets, processed cheese, most milk substitutes (check labels), some cheese substitutes, butter substitutes, and ice-cream substitutes.

<u>Some additives to foods that may come from soy</u>:
"Partially hydrogenated vegetable protein," lecithin, "emulsifiers," TVP, beta-amylase, beta-carotene, brominated vegetable oil, calcium stearate, calcium stearoyl-2-lactylate, diglycerides, disodium guanylate, ester gum, fatty acid, fatty alcohol, glutamates, glycerides, glycerol, glyceryl monostearate, hydrogenated vegetable shortening, hydrolyzed vegetable protein, lipoxidase, maltose, miso, modified vegetable protein, MSG, natto, peptones, polysorbates, propylene glycol monostearate, sodium stearoyl-2-lactylate, sorbase, sorbitans, soya lecithin, soya protein, stearic acid, tempeh, tocopherols, urease, Vitamin E, and other multivitamin supplements.

If you frequently eat at fast food restaurants, chances are you are consuming soy in the meat products.

Substitutes for soy:

Soy as a filler - is easily replaced with grains such as oatmeal, rice meal, and buckwheat. Almost any grain can be used as a filler substitute. Quinoa would be my first choice since it is even higher in essential amino acids than soy. Ground rice crackers are a great extender for meat dishes.

Milk: rice milk or any of the nut milks can replace soymilk. In cooking, it is difficult to tell the difference. Over cereal, we prefer almond milk's flavor to soy.

Soy sauce: Unfortunately, the flavor of soy sauce is hard to mimic when cooking Chinese dishes. If soy is not a problem, but wheat is, try a wheat-free soy sauce (available at most health food stores).

One flavor enhancer you can try is to add sesame oil to the recipe. It cannot replace all the oil in the recipe due to its strong flavor. Try using 2 tsp. of sesame oil mixed with 2 TBS. of other oil when stir-frying vegetables and meats. Fresh chopped gingerroot and lemon grass can impart a fresh new flavor in oriental cooking. Both gingerroot and lemon grass are available at oriental stores or larger grocery stores. When replacing soy or Worcestershire sauce in other recipes, turn to spices and herbs to give more flavor to the dish.

Homemade "veggie" burgers are flavorful and high in grain protein. Our soy-free/wheat-free Veggie Burgers are wonderful on wheat-free breads or as a main dish. Look for them in the recipe section of the book.

Food Allergies, What Do I Eat Now?

Eggs

For purposes of allergy discussion, we will consider that all eggs are alike since they all share the same basic protein. However, there is a difference in parts of the egg, for example, egg whites and yolks. An allergy to egg whites and eggs yolks can make a big difference in your diet. If your allergists tested for whole egg, and you had a positive reaction, then, you had best avoid all eggs and egg products. If you are allergic to egg whites only, you may separate the egg when baking and use only the yolk. Likewise, if you are allergic to the yolk, you may separate the egg components and use the white when baking.

Since few products or recipes use only the egg white or egg yolk, you must assume that a whole egg may have been used in the processing of store bought products. For instance, it is true that meringue is made of egg white, but the pie or custard beneath it was probably made with the whole egg or the yolk. Unless you prepare a recipe yourself, suspect that the whole egg was used. If you are allergic to only one component of the egg, as stated before, you can use the other in cooking and baking. Eggs are great for binding flour mixes in baked goods. If you are allergic to the whole egg, all is not lost. There are egg substitutes on the market that work well in recipes. A good egg substitute that is 100% egg-free is Egg Replacer™ by Ener-G Foods, Inc.

A homemade substitute for eggs in baking is 1 tsp. wheat-free and corn-free baking powder (hard to find) for each egg. One cereal free baking powder is Featherweight Baking Powder™ by Chicago Dietetic Supply, Inc. I, personally, have not been able to find a distributor for it in my area, so I make my own.

Do not substitute "Egg Beaters" or any other egg substitutes found in grocery stores. Almost all contain eggs. They are great for use if you are trying to lower your cholesterol or fat intake, but they are not meant as a substitute for persons with egg allergies. **Always read the labels carefully!**

<u>Foods that obviously contain eggs are:</u>
Eggnog, French toast, and omelets.

Food Allergies, What Do I Eat Now?

Less obvious products that may contain eggs are:

MMR Vaccine!!!!!(these vaccines are grown in eggs), malted drinks, Ovaltine™, root beer, wines (many are cleared with egg white), cakes, cookies, doughnuts, macaroons, meringues, pastries, pancakes, waffles, pretzels, muffins, bullion, baking powder, some frosting, croquettes, fritters, pastas, egg noodles, mayonnaise, hollandaise, tartar sauce, salad dressing, Caesar dressing, breaded foods, battered foods, fast food burgers, prepared meats (sausage, hot dogs, lunchmeats), puddings, custards, marshmallows, chocolate bars, cream pies, sherbet, soft candies, ice cream, nougat, creamed soups, noodle soups, and commercial egg substitutes.

Chemical terms for eggs:

Any chemical that begins with "ova" or "ovo" probably contains egg since these prefixes mean "egg." Albumen, albumin, con albumen, lecithin, livetin, ovalbumin, ovomucin, ovomucoid, peptones, vitellin, ovamalt, yolk.

If eggs are a highly reactive problem for you: when the time comes for immunizations, always ask if the serum was cultured in egg (albumin). Many are grown in eggs, and people sensitive to eggs have been known to react. If your health care professional is uncertain, have them contact the pharmaceutical manufacturer of the vaccine to ask if eggs were involved in the vaccination preparation. It is a frequently asked question, and the manufacturer is usually prompt in their response. Drug companies have employees whose job is to answer questions from pharmacists, doctors, nurses, and patients. They are readily available with accurate answers. Waiting 10 minutes for phone verification from the pharmaceutical company is well worth the benefit of knowing that you or your child will not react adversely to the injection.

Food Allergies, What Do I Eat Now?

Sugar

The term "sugar" may refer to almost any type of sugar source depending on which geographical area the product was manufactured. In the southern United States and in Central America, the predominant sugar source is cane sugar and corn sweetener. In the mid-western, northern, and western states the source may be beet sugar, corn sweeteners or cane sugar. Worldwide, the types of sugars vary greatly: cane, beet, corn sweeteners, maple sugars, honey, rice sweeteners, sorghum, and date sugar to name a few.

Not only do the types of sugars vary from one region to another; but also, when more than one sweetener is available, the producer may change the recipe to allow the less expensive sweetener at the time of production. For instance, a cola made in the South may state on the label "corn syrup and/or cane sugar" as the sweetener. This, usually, means that whichever sweetener was less expensive or more readily available at the time of production is what went into their product, or it could be a combination of the two. A potato chip maker will, usually, list two or more oils on the label for the same reason. Unless stated, you cannot be certain whether canola oil, peanut oil, soybean oil, or whatever is listed on the label may have been used. Many times, I have purchased potato chips that tasted like peanuts. The label stated "canola oil and/or peanut oil;" obviously, that batch was made with peanut oil or a combination of the two. Always read labels carefully, and it is best to assume that any or all of the ingredients listed went into the product.

Allergists test for specific sugars used in your area, so, tell him which sugar you use in your normal diet. The most common sugars and sweeteners used in the U.S. are cane, beet and corn.

<u>Forms of sugars you may have been using in your diet:</u>
Cane sugar - comes as granulated, confectioners' (has wheat or cornstarch added to prevent caking), brown sugar (has molasses added for color), flavored sugars, and sucrose.
Maple sugar - granulated or syrup.
Beet sugar - granulated or confectioners' (also has cornstarch or flour added to prevent caking).
Molasses - liquid (a form where the whole sugar has had crystals removed leaving the liquid). Can come from many sources, including cane and corn.
Honey - Product of bees. Sensitivity can develop depending on the source of the pollen collected.

Brown sugar - can come from many sugar sources. Usually from cane or beet- molasses added for color.

Confectioners' sugar - comes from cane or beet. Usually has cornstarch or wheat added to prevent caking.

Sorghum - a dark syrup, from many sources, usually corn.

Date sugar – dehydrated dates that have been ground.

Flavored sugars - usually cane or beet granulated with various flavorings added.

Sucrose - usually cane sugar or sugar beets.

Fructose - from fruits or honey, dahlia, Jerusalem artichoke or other tubers.

Glucose - fruit sugars, corn or honey.

Dextrose - corn sugar, glucose, dextroglucose or grape sugar (usually corn).

Obvious products that may contain sugar:

Candies, sodas, sweetened fruit juices, instant teas and coffees, chocolate milk, chocolate syrup, chocolate candies, chocolate chips, cookies, cakes, frosting, puddings, pastries, doughnuts, juice boxes, sweet crackers, breakfast cereals and bars, processed sweetened coconut, sweetened can milk, frozen desserts, ice creams, sherbets, popcicles, whipped topping, flavored yogurt, flavored gelatin mixes, caramel, candied orange peels and other candied fruits, dried berries and fruit, alcohol, jelly, jam, preserves, sweet corn muffins, and any muffin.

Less obvious products that may contain sugars:

Ketchup, mustards, mayonnaise, lunchmeats (packaged and deli), bacon, marinades, wines, beers, meringues, hotdogs, toothpaste, teriyaki sauce, worcestershire sauce, hashbrown potatoes (packaged), BBQ sauce, steak sauce, sweetened canned fruits, canned vegetables, salad dressing, tomato sauce, breads (yeast needs sugar to rise), baby foods, flavored potato chips and corn chips, pickles, and medications (especially children's liquid medications for colds, congestion and fever).

Sugar chemical names:

Sucrose, refined syrups, cane syrups, cane sugars, caramel, caramel coloring, Rum, mannitol, dextrose, glucose, and fructose.

Alternatives and substitutes for sugar:

Avoid artificial sweeteners and diet sweeteners if possible.

Honey- moistens baking product. When substituting honey in a recipe, decrease the other liquids used in the recipe to adjust for the liquid of the honey.

Maple syrup- use maple sugar in the same proportions as granulated cane or beet sugar.

Rice syrup- Use rice syrup in baking the same way you would honey. Sometimes, it leaves an aftertaste when tasted straight from the jar.

Beet sugar- Being from the South, I had never used beet sugar in cooking. It is used in the same manner as granulated cane sugar and is now part of our diet plan.

Apple juice concentrate- It can be used in baking in the same manner as honey. The recipe may not be as sweet as you are accustomed, but it will be an acceptable substitution in your Rotation Plan. Reduce the amount of liquid in the recipe by ½ cup for each ¾ cup apple juice concentrate. This type of sweetener is much preferred for children with hyperactive symptoms, but any sugar in excess will cause problems.

Example:

If your recipe calls for:	You will use:
1 cup milk	½ cup milk of the day
½ cup sugar	¾ cup apple juice concentrate

If the batter is too moist, add about ¼ cup more flour to the recipe. If you add more than ½ cup flour over what the recipe calls for, be sure to add another ¼ tsp. leavening.

Do not be afraid to experiment.

White grape juice concentrate-Can be used like apple juice.

Chapter Six

Methods of Testing

Testing

When your physician tells you that the symptoms you have been experiencing are not pathological in origin (they are not caused by a disease which alter the body's function), you breathe a sigh of relief. But, you are left wondering what could be causing the bothersome or even debilitating symptoms. If your physician has not suggested food testing, let us suggest it. There are several avenues of testing available. All have certain advantages and disadvantages.

What follows is a discussion of testing methods available and their pros and cons.

Note: if you have disturbing symptoms such as difficulty breathing or rapid heart rate when you eat certain foods, you should not attempt challenge or self-test. These symptoms can be life threatening, causing a condition known as anaphylactic shock. R A S T testing should be conducted by a board-certified physician specializing in the treatment of allergies.

Laboratory testing or physician testing:

When signs and symptoms warrant, physicians draw a blood sample to test for "antibodies" or conduct a skin scratch test to determine if food allergies are present. These two tests are very different, can yield different results, and must be conducted by a physician/allergist. A third type of test is the "self-test," which is explained later in this chapter.

R A S T or IgE (IgG) test:

The most accurate test currently used is the IgE (IgG) R A S T test. The physician draws a blood sample, and sends the sample to a laboratory. The laboratory tests for "tags" known as antibodies on cells. These identifying markers on the cell instruct the immune system to react to a foreign invader. As a normal function of the immune system, it is how our bodies fight bacteria and viral invaders. When the body begins to react to normal nutrient sources as invaders, the result is allergic responses to the triggering foods. Simply put, the immune system now sees specific foods as a target it must attack. You become a victim of your own immune system.

The IgE (IgG) R A S T test identifies specific antibodies and indicates the degree to which that person is allergic to that food or environmental substance. The test works especially well when the patient suspects which specific foods might be causing a reaction. The R A S T test targets specific tags to specific foods to which the patient is sensitive. Therefore, you, as the patient, can tell the physician that every time you eat corn you have severe abdominal cramps or whatever symptoms are provoked. The physician/allergist will know that corn needs to be one of the primary foods to test.

If the patient has no idea which foods might be causing symptoms, the physician/allergist has to take an educated guess as to which antigens (foods) to test. He tests for the most common allergens that research and experience show are most likely to cause a reaction. Your allergist may have you choose from a list of foods that you consume on a regular basis. Regular consumption of foods increases the chance of allergy development. Occasionally, an obscure, infrequently consumed food can cause a reaction. You and your allergist have to investigate the possibilities of this if you continue to have reaction symptoms.

The antibody/antigen (R A S T) test also has some shortcomings. While it is probably the best and most reliable test available, it shows immediate reaction to allergens. If you have a reaction known as "delayed or masked," the IgE (IgG) R A S T may not show a positive reaction. Allergists realize this and are likely to investigate further, and diagnose and treat by symptomatic history. The allergist may come to the conclusion that the reaction is an intolerance for a specific food and not a true allergy. Intolerance to foods can elicit the same symptoms as an allergy; the difference between the two is allergies trigger a reaction by the immune system while intolerance reactions do not involve the immune system. Intolerance symptoms can be as severe as allergies, but may not be proven through conventional testing.

For instance, my daughter did not have a positive reaction to certain legumes (beans) on the R A S T, but she cannot tolerate legumes without severe gastrointestinal upset. Her symptoms could be a delayed or masked reaction or an intolerance to specific beans. Whatever we call it, she is sensitive to legumes. The conclusion is that it is probably a delayed reaction, because she tested positive to soy (a legume).

While the R A S T test is more accurate and reliable than skin test, they can be very expensive. Most insurance plans cover these tests, but check with your carrier first. Ask the allergist what the cost will be for the package of tests. The cost may range from $500 to $1000 or more depending on the number of items tested.

Skin testing:

Skin testing is the other type of allergy test. This test has been around for decades and is still used by some physician/allergists. The main drawback to this method is that some reactions may show a false negative. A small amount of allergen is injected under the skin to elicit an allergic response in the form of a reddened, swollen area. A positive reaction may not be evident because your symptoms may be delayed until after you leave the doctor's office, or your reactions for that food may be, for example, stomach cramps, diarrhea or post nasal drip. These symptoms may not be triggered by a skin test.

Self-testing:

The third method of testing for food allergy and intolerance is to self-test. This method is exactly what the name implies. You take control of the testing process, and if done properly, this method can be very accurate. There are many ways to conduct self-testing, and accuracy depends on the method used. The following is the method we recommend, because it is nutritionally sound and results can be accurate due to the way in which foods are reintroduced. The only expense will be groceries that are unprocessed and without preservatives and additives. Medical testing gives results usually within a week or two, while self-testing can be a long process depending on how many foods you test and how many of those foods evoke a reaction.

The process consist of four basic steps:
1. Keep an accurate "Food Diary." This is discussed later in this chapter.
2. Perform cleansing and elimination, which lasts five to seven days.

3. After cleansing and eliminating common foods, add foods that are not likely to cause a reaction, which can take two to three days per food addition.
4. Perform challenge testing (a sequence of eliminating a suspected allergen for a specified period of time and adding it back into the diet while keeping detailed records of reactions). Include individual foods that you suspect may cause a reaction. This step can take up to three days per food addition. **Again, we stress that challenge testing should not be done if you have experienced a severe reaction to a suspected food in the past.**

Each step is equally important and cannot be eliminated or cut short. You must be committed to the self-testing process to be successful. The urge to quit or cheat is tempting, especially in step two of the test.

Before beginning a self-test, you need to consult your physician, allergist or other healthcare professional, such as a licensed nutritionist experienced with food allergy therapy, and tell him of your plans to begin an elimination diet to identify food allergies/sensitivities. Be prepared; the physician may not be supportive, unless your physician is an allergist. We continue to be amazed by the number of healthcare professionals who do not believe that foods can be the cause of symptoms other than gastrointestinal distress even in the light of extensive research and decades of successful treatment of individuals. Your health status needs to be addressed before beginning any diet. You will most likely go through several days of withdrawal-like symptoms such as headache, irritability, nausea, shakiness, and lack of energy. These symptoms should last only three to four days, but you should begin to feel much better on or about the fourth day.

One very inefficient and unreliable self-test method is one where the patient continues on the same diet and eliminates one food at a time. That specific food is reintroduced into the diet after a week or two, and any adverse reactions are noted.

This method is unreliable because most people with food allergies rarely are allergic to only one food. Eliminating only one food and introducing it again at a later time can give misleading results. The other allergic foods may continue to provoke symptoms during this entire scenario, and any relief of symptoms from eliminating only one food may go unnoticed. You may know or suspect what other foods are causing symptoms; then again, you may be sensitive to foods you do not think possible. *You will get more reliable results only by eliminating all the foods you eat regularly and those foods most commonly known to be allergens.*

Food Allergies, What Do I Eat Now?

Food Diary

A food diary is one of the most important tools in diagnosing food allergies. Since some reactions may not occur for 48-72 hours after eating the food, a diary can be the only way to see what caused the reaction or at least begin to eliminate possible causes.

Perhaps, the term Food diary is not the most accurate term; it includes a record of medications, alcohol, chewing gums, mints, and any other thing that passes the lips. Every item that goes into the mouth must be documented. The diary includes the date, the time, the item eaten, the amount, any immediate reactions, and your general health that day. If you have a fever that day, note it because an illness could possibly change or even mask an allergic reaction. For best interpretation of data, the diary should be within a period of time when you are free from fever or cold and flu symptoms. If you contract a cold or flu during the food diary period, make a note of this. Some cold symptoms such as a runny nose and itchy, watery eyes can be symptoms of allergic reactions to foods rather than just cold symptoms. Therefore, you can see how this data, during a period of illness, could be misleading and should be noted on the food diary.

Simple foods are easiest to keep track of on the diary. Accuracy is the key, but if a food is covered in an unknown sauce, it will be impossible to note the ingredients on your diary. Should a reaction occur, it might not be apparent what caused the reaction. Initially, the best way to determine what you have eaten is to prepare the food yourself. And keep it simple!

We have included a sample food diary. This diary is one my allergist, Hamilton S. Dixon, M.D., gave to me. You might need more space or a different format. Feel free to customize it to fit your own needs.

After keeping an accurate diary for a two-week period, it may be possible to see patterns of cause and effect. It may become apparent what foods are causing a reaction. Sometimes, the connection may not be clear. The symptoms from a specific food may not appear for 48-72 hours. In that case, making the connection between the symptom and the food that was the culprit might be next to impossible. When this happens, some form of testing is required.

7 Day Diet Diary

Patient's Name _____
Date

	1st Day	2nd Day	3rd Day	4th Day	5th Day	6th Day	7th Day
BREAKFAST	egg hash browns wheat toast orange juice coffee	Cream of wheat fresh fruit coffee-black	grilled grapefruit rice cereal, milk coffee-black	toast and apple jelly coffee	juice and coffee	orange juice oatmeal coffee	1 egg mini omelet with turkey sausage and green pepper onion and tomato orange and grapefruit hot herbal tea
Symptoms	runny nose	woke with headache diarrhea after eating	headache gone no diarrhea	tired, woke with headache, swollen	tired, woke with headache, swollen	tired, woke with severe headache	woke rested, headache nearly gone
Medication	none	none	none	none	none	none	none
LUNCHEON	chicken salad apple ice tea	tossed salad with tuna Italian dressing croissant water	lunch Wok Restaurant Shrimp tempura egg roll fried rice (egg & veg with soy sauce)	chicken rice soup biscuit	ham and cheese and cracked wheat crackers hot tea	spinach salad, boiled egg, tomato, onion, green pepper, brown rice, cider vinegar canola oil dressing iced herbal tea	turkey and veggie casserole. contains cheese and turkey broth with peas, carrots, broccoli
Symptoms	none apparent	diarrhea, headache decreasing	increased heart rate, sleepy, 2 hr cramping	can't concentrate, severe headache, sick like flu, diarrhea	can't concentrate, severe headache, sick like flu, diarrhea	feel better, headache slightly decreased, no increase in heart rate	no headache, cramping, increased heart rate, or diarrhea
Medication	none	none	none	none	none	none	none
DINNER	broiled shrimp baked potato steamed green beans homemade bread sliced mango	Steamed broccoli, carrots asparagus roast pork brown rice cut up celery, applesauce, unsweet decaf coffee	pizza crust from a box with ground beef pepperoni green pepper tomato sauce ham cola drink	breaded chicken scalloped potatoes creamed corn fruit salad with mayo carrot & celery sticks ice tea	Beef tips and noodles carrot raisin salad brussels sprouts cola drink	grilled salmon basted with margarine, lemon and herbs veggie kabob without marinade: pineapple, tomato, onion, mushroom ice herbal spice tea	steak, mashed sweet potatoes, toss salad, honey mustard dressing, baked apple
Symptoms	increased heart rate, runny nose sleepy		sleepy, runny nose, headache, increased heart rate, generalized swelling cramping before bed	cramping and increased heart rate, ate less than usual with GI distress. headache bad	cramping and increased heart rate, ate less than usual with GI distress. headache bad	diarrhea gone, loose formed stool, mild headache, alert. no cramping, or increased heart rate after eating	none
Medication - none		none	none	none	none	none	none

7 Day Diet Diary

Patient's Name _____
Date _____

	1st Day	2nd Day	3rd Day	4th Day	5th Day	6th Day	7th Day
BREAKFAST							
Symptoms							
Medication							
LUNCHEON							
Symptoms							
Medication							
DINNER							
Symptoms							
Medication							

Chapter Seven

Children And Food Sensitivities

Why is it that in the years from 1990 to 1996 sales for health food items, vitamins, food supplements, and home remedies soared to record highs? During this period, Ritalin™, an artificial and potentially unhealthy drug, was prescribed for a record number of 11.3 million children, a 400 % increase. It is shocking that we as adults consume supplements of this proportion, yet, our children rarely obtain the nutrients so crucial to their proper mental and physical development. The chemical warehouse within you can only function properly with adequate supplies of nutrients. The optimum situation is to allow our biochemistry to work as intended without interruptions or road blocks in the normal chemistry pathways by providing these essential nutrients.

Convenience foods have been in existence now for some 40 years such as frozen dinners, pot pies, meals in a box, and fast foods. Manufacturers reduced spoilage and lost revenue by adding preservatives to extend the shelf life of as many products as possible.

Our bodies were not made for preservatives . Our bodies are massive natural chemical factories, and when in proper working order, need very little save for water and other nutrients. We have been eating foods with additives, preservatives and items not reflected clearly on the label for years. These additives and preservatives have no function in the body; they only help *to increase the pollution stress on your body and make you more likely to develop allergy type sensitivities.*

Food Allergies, What Do I Eat Now?

From a consumer standpoint, the introduction of food additives and preservatives have compounded the problem of identifying food allergies. For many individuals this practice has created problems for your bodies.

It certainly becomes a very complex and difficult task to be a good advocate for our children's diets. With the soaring problems our young are experiencing, it seems we are not doing a very good job. The incidence of behavioral, and serious medical problems in the young is growing with alarming rate. Are these related to food additives and preservatives? Many researchers believe so. Any nutritional expert will have stacks of research data that shows a correlation between food additives and increased behavioral problems.

As a society, we were taught to treat the symptom rather than take advantage of our natural feed back system and see the symptoms as warning signs. If we have a headache, we take something to make us more comfortable, take the pain away and ignore the origin. A baby can only cry. They hurt, too.

How do you know when a food sensitivity is present?

There are a few simple guidelines that can help you identify if a food sensitivity exists. A diary seems a bother at best, but is crucial to discovering or ruling out the suspicious food item(s). When a food sensitivity is suspected you must keep a diary. You may think a diary is a bother but it is crucial to discovering suspicious food items. Since many signs and symptoms can also indicate some medical problems, you should always consult with your pediatrician to be sure the sign and symptoms are not related to a medical condition.

You have to recognize the red flags observed in behavioral changes and a multitude of other symptoms before you can correct the problem. Identifying food and additive sensitivities in children a difficult, and you may not notice the small and sometimes subtle signs.

A child is unable to explain why she or he cannot concentrate, cannot sit still, or stares off into the distance as if in a trance. A normal child does not experience a headache, yet the numbers of children experiencing headaches increases. Without understanding the **reason** for the headache we are too quick to give a pill. Ignoring a headaches may slow the early recognition and medical diagnosis of a serious illness. So, when it comes to children, you must be particularly observant.

One major obstacle in realizing a food sensitivity is that you can have a delayed reaction. This is why so many food sensitivities have gone unrecognized for so long and in the eyes of some medical professionals, remains controversial. Dr. William J. Rea authored a very interesting and very technical book called "*Chemical Sensitivity*". This book was based on a study of 20,000 individuals with chemical sensitivities. No, that figure was not a misprint. Dr. Rea's research and references were so numerous that each chapter has its own reference section. Hooray, someone understands, has studied this situation, and you are not alone. Since awareness of how a reaction occurs will help you, you should record everything in a diary.

What is a delayed reaction?

A reaction can occur within 15 minutes or can be delayed for as long as seventy two hours. This is why it is so important that you record your child's diet and symptoms: anything and everything from itchy eyes to diarrhea or gas and even a runny nose. A more detailed diary may actually shorten the time it takes to identify the foods to which your child may be sensitive. Review Chapter Four on signs and symptoms and the sample diary to get you started.

Recognition of Food Allergy in Babies

Identification of a food sensitivity in an adult is difficult and more complex in a young person or a baby. Obviously, it is necessary to be a good detective, especially in the case of a young child who can not express themselves. Your goal is to recognize the symptom or behavior that is not normal, and identify the cause; not just attempt to abate the symptoms with a medication. Some medications can actually cover up symptoms.

Breast Feeding

Until the mid 1940s, babies were mostly breast fed, and it was rare that a baby had any kind of noticeable reaction to breast milk unless mom herself ate foods that were observed to upset the baby. Now we are learning that foods consumed by mom on a **daily basis** while pregnant or during breast feeding (or both) can predispose that child to development of allergies to those foods and increase chances of developing other sensitivities. It is necessary for the mother to vary her diet during pregnancy and during breast feeding. Another adage that is worth its weight in gold when it comes to diet is "all things in moderation". Having the same food item on a daily basis may actually be an indication of a food sensitivity. So, the question should be asked "is it the craving whim of pregnancy or is this an indicator of a food sensitivity?" If the mother has a known food sensitivity, eliminating the item or limiting the item to only once every 5 days will help both mother and baby. This is discussed in the Chapter 10 on the 5 Day Rotation Plan. Daily intake of foods you are sensitive to, will make the unborn baby likely to experience the same sensitivity, especially if the sensitivity reaction is of the antigen-antibody type. This is summarized in the Chapter Four on How Do You Know You Have Food Allergies?

Formulas

Over the years popularity of breast feeding declined and babies were put on bottled milk of many kinds. Sometime in the 50s, soy infant formula was introduced. Isn't it interesting that today, something like soy introduced to the commercial foods industry in the 50s is still gaining popularity for multiple uses, while it, too, is one of the top seven foods most likely to provoke food sensitivities. Corn starches (or modified food starches) and sugars in baby formulas and commercially prepared baby foods are adding to the magnitude of the problem. Recent information indicates that the United States is the only progressive country that does not add nutrients to baby formula essential to brain function and development.

Cow's Milk

Frequently, when diarrhea is due to food sensitivity in infants and children, the food often turns out to be cow's milk. The gut wall is altered by the reaction to milk, the gut wall becomes leakier, and allows other food **molecules** through. The body may then react adversely to these as well. This situation has been called many different names but "leaky gut syndrome" is probably most widely used. This is why for the health and welfare of the child you need to recognize the signs and symptoms and not ignore what this little body is trying to tell you.

Diaper Rash and Other Skin Problems

If a prolonged and unexplained diaper rash exists, it may be the result of a food sensitivity. The entire bowel can be irritated, including the anus which appears reddened. Irritation of the anus can occur from diarrhea alone. A medical reason for the irritation should be ruled out by your doctor. Diarrhea in an infant is a serious condition and needs to be evaluated.

According to "*The Complete Guide to Food Allergy and Intolerance*" by Dr. Jonathon Brostoff and Linda Gamlin, symptoms in children can include colic, eczema, asthma, persistent runny nose, glue ear, headaches, migraine, behavioral problems, and can be linked to certain foods or food additives. Dr. Brostoff discusses in detail the hyperkinetic child, in that some of the behavior exhibited may indeed have an emotional origin, but explains that it could be provoked by a food sensitivity.

There are many different types of behavioral syndromes included with attention deficit disorder, ADD. Most of the syndromes can be summarized as, <u>inattention</u>, <u>impulsive</u>, with or without <u>hyperactivity</u>. Hence forward we will refer to hyperkinetic and attention deficit disorder as ADD.

Over the years many have begun to realize the influence of food colorings, preservatives and other additives in children with ADD. Dr. Feingold made this correlation, along with the influence of aspirin-like compounds found in fruits and vegetables. The Feingold Diet eliminates additives and preservatives, and initially the foods with aspirin-like compounds most often found to contribute to ADD. The Dr. Feingold diet has been a significant benefit to families everywhere with "considerable improvement in 70 percent" and a "dramatic difference" in a small percentage of children.

The Feingold Association is a non-profit volunteer organization and support group. The organization is made up of families and thousands of people who have been helped by the Feingold diet. Contact the address below for more information.

Feingold Association of the United States
127 E. Main Street, Suite 106
Riverhead, NY 11901
Feingold Counseling line, 516-369-9340
Membership: 800-321-3287   (800-321-FAUS)
Website: www.feingold.org

<u>ADD, Nutrition and Ritalin™</u>

There is hope for the parent who is not willing to indiscriminately relinquish control and resort to giving your child Ritalin™. Kelly Dorfman, a well known nutritionist, speaker, and founder of the Developmental Delay Registry newsletter, gives hope to many parents who have learned of the drawbacks of giving their children Ritalin™. The side effects of this drug include depression, loss of appetite, weight loss, and about one third of the individuals will develop tics. A tic is a habitual motion like a twitch, or habitual behavior trait. Kelly Dorfman has helped literally hundreds of families through tough times and the frustration that accompanies the disruption of the family with one or more children diagnosed with ADD. She cautions that in some cases the drug may be necessary, and further explains that it is common for children with ADD to have nutritional deficiencies. When the nutritional deficiencies are remedied, the dosage of Ritalin™ needed may actually be less, and, in some cases, the drug can be withdrawn completely with the consult of a medical doctor.

Recently, a patient asked me about the drug Ritalin™. Her child's teacher said her son should be put on Ritalin™. She discussed the drug with the child's pediatrician, and the drug was prescribed. She was still reluctant to give the child the Ritalin™. The topic of possible food sensitivity was discussed. Mom was overwhelmed and didn't think she could effectively and methodically take certain foods away long enough to determine if there was any influence on behavior. She asked if there was any test that could be done. After explaining about the IgE test for food reactions and the IgG test for delayed reactions. I suggested that she discuss it with her pediatrician.

When she asked the pediatrician she was bluntly told, "Absolutely not." The pediatrician was outraged at the suggestion that foods could be a part of the problem. This mom was upset, especially since her child was already taking Ritalin™, and this doctor didn't want to explore the possibility of food influence. Mom wanted the test done to rule out the possibility of food sensitivity. If the IgG and IgE tests results were negative mom knew she would feel better about giving the Ritalin™. The child was tested and found to be very allergic to mustard, dairy, wheat and peanuts. These were all foods he loved and would eat at any meal! He is off the medication for the summer and off the allergic foods. Thus far behavior has dramatically improved without the medication.

In a recent seminar given by Kelly Dorfman, she told her audience how to nutritionally support children with ADD. Many of the people in the room were parents looking for answers. There were many in the audience who had attended a previous seminar. Many gave countless testimonies to the **remarkable** results from changes in diet and nutrition and how it had positively impacted their lives. We recommend and encourage you to attend a Kelly Dorfman seminar if you have a child with ADD, or any developmental disorder. You can contact her through the address included in the list below.

For more information, below is a partial listing of suppliers for various items that may be difficult to find.

NutriChem
1303 Richmond Rd.
Ottawa, Ontario K2B7Y4
613-820-4200   Fax: 613-821-2226

Vitamins

Kirkland Labs
Super Nutera-Pills Powder High B-6
800-245-8282

Vitamins

Pathways
Ron Keach - Pharmacist
800-869-9160

Can obtain some medcations without food colorings or preservatives

Gluten Free Pantry
800-291-8386

Supplier for Celiac, Gluten intolerance foods.

Autism Network
Box 17711
Rochester, NY 1460711

Support group, source of information

Immuno Labs
800-231-9197

Feingold Association of the United States
127 E. Main Street, Suite 106
Riverhead, NY 11901
Feingold Counseling line, 516-369-9340
Membership: 800-321-3287 (800-321-FAUS)
Website: www.feingold.org

Non-profit volunteer organization, support group

Kelly Dorfman, MS, LN
Developmental Delay Registry (DDR)
6701 Fairfax Road
Chevy Chase, Maryland   20815
301-652-2263
Website:
http://funnelweb.utcc.utk.edu/~jroman/ddr.htm

Co-founder of DDR, a newletter. Wealth of information useful in ADD, ADHD, and autism. Support groups, seminars, books and helpful hints for daily living.

Website posts new developments, information.

ADD Action Group
212-769-2457
Website: http://www.addgroup.org

Non-profit organization NY and NJ
Helps people find local resources providing local alternative treatments for attention deficit disorder, learning differences, hyperactivity, dyslexia, and autism

Cognitive Enhancement Research Insitute
415-321-CERI

Newsletter- Smart Drug News

Chapter Eight

Cleansing And Elimination

Cleansing and Elimination

A cleansing or elimination diet serves two purposes. It helps to rid the body of toxins and allergens that may be in the system, and it helps prevent any further introduction of toxins and allergens into the system. Toxins are any substances that the body does not recognize as a nutrient. These can be, for example, medications, allergens, dyes, pesticides, fertilizers, industrial pollutants, food additives not necessary for nutritive purposes, narcotics, alcohol, nicotine, and caffeine. Many toxins are stored in fatty tissue and are very difficult to release. Some industrial toxins, once in the body, bind to tissue at the molecular level and may never be released. This is not meant to scare you to the point of being afraid to live; it is only meant to make you aware that you <u>can</u> make <u>better choices</u> for food consumption.

Another plus to cleansing is that most people will lose a few unwanted pounds during this five to seven day phase. Do not attempt cleansing if you are underweight or undernourished. You may need to seek the help of a nutrition expert to get you in better nutritional shape before attempting step one. This can be a "catch 22", especially, if the reason you are undernourished is because food sensitivities have drastically affected your eating habits.

The best time to start an elimination diet is when your stress level is fairly low. Starting a cleansing/elimination diet in times of celebration or the winter holiday season is asking for certain failure. Temptations are too great!

Schedule your cleansing/elimination diet so the middle of the third and fourth days fall on your off-days. If your normal days off are Saturday and Sunday, then, Wednesday evening would be the best time to begin. The peak of withdrawal symptoms would then fall on Saturday and Sunday.

Plan a quiet weekend with your favorite movies and a good book. Get plenty of rest, and allow for exercise and fresh air. You may be tired and irritable, therefore, you need to get a good night's sleep every night and warn everyone in advance of your possible moodiness. By Monday you should be feeling better. For us, the third and fourth days were the worst. By the end of the fourth day, I could feel a marked improvement. My daughter had a similar experience with cleansing/elimination. The fourth day, for her, was the first day in one year that she did not go to school with an upset stomach, and she was able to concentrate on her schoolwork. In the year since we began this process and determined the foods to which she was sensitive, her grades have improved.

Each person is different, so you may achieve different results. By the seventh day, you should be able to see an improvement in your symptoms. If you do not see a marked change, the foods you selected for cleansing may be causing the problem. Choose different foods, ones that you have <u>never</u> eaten, and begin again.

Failing to stick with the routine will put you back to square one. Reintroduction of allergic reactive foods will send your body back into the old immunologic confusion again. If you found you could not stay on the diet this time, relax and take time to think about why the diet did not work this time. Try again in a week or so.

During cleansing, take your lunch to work or school, and avoid parties and eating out with friends. Cleansing is difficult enough without tempting yourself at a weak moment.

<u>How to cleanse</u>:

There are many cleansing/elimination diets designed to remove allergens from the diet and promote the body healing itself. One method is fasting, which we do not suggest for long periods of time. It is very difficult to fast for one day…forget about seven days! Your body needs nutrition to facilitate healing and to carry out normal metabolic processes.

Another method is the few-foods diet. According to Dr. Jonathan Brostoff , *The Complete Guide to Food Allergy and Intolerance,* on this diet, you are allowed to eat a few of the foods you are certain do not elicit a response. These foods vary with each person.

A variation of the few foods diet is the rare foods diet. You choose from a list of foods that you probably have never eaten. This is a good method if you live near a large farmer's market and have access to a large assortment of unusual foods. As Dr. Brostoff mentions, "Unusual foods do not come cheap."

The method we recommend is one similar to the few foods diet. To begin, eliminate all foods that you eat on a daily basis and ones that you feel may be causing a reaction. By eating foods that you rarely eat or do not eat often, you are less likely to have an allergic reaction.

To begin the cleansing/elimination phase, you must determine what nutritional requirements are necessary to maintain normal metabolic function. You still need the normal servings of protein, calcium, fruits and vegetables, grains, and fats in your diet. Water is also a very important part of cleansing. If possible, drink at least eight to ten glasses of water a day (distilled water enhances the cleansing process).

If possible, select fruits and vegetables that are organically grown. These can be found at health food stores; some large grocery stores are beginning to stock them. Obviously, summer months are the best time to find an abundant selection of unusual fruits and vegetables, but do not put off cleansing and elimination until summertime. Make do with what you can find.

To begin cleansing, make your food selections from the list in the back of this section. Rotate the foods so that you do not eat the same foods everyday. A Five Day Rotation Plan begins when the cleansing process is complete. Keep meat servings to only one or two each day; get the other two protein servings each day from high protein grains such a quinoa. Make a large batch of brown rice and refrigerate to have ready for a quick meal.

We have included many cleansing and elimination recipes in the cookbook. We recommend that you eat sensibly during the cleansing phase. You are more likely to succeed when you feel as if you are not starving yourself!

Make your meals simple, without sauces or spices. Your digestive system as well as your taste buds will be taking a break. Find a vitamin supplement that is all natural and free of soy, wheat, corn, sugar, dairy, and eggs. You can find these at a health food store. If you buy any processed food items, make certain that they are free of additives and preservatives. To be safe, prepare your own food.

Remember to get regular exercise - even if you feel badly. Take 15 minute walks several times a day. Sometimes, the fresh air can revitalize you.

Remember that this is the first step on the road to better health. More recipes appropriate for cleansing are included in the cookbook; they are noted with a "C/E".

Food Allergies, What Do I Eat Now?

Food choices for cleansing:

Protein: Turkey, lamb, and fish are excellent choices for making broths and as main dish servings. These meats can usually be found at large food markets. You should ask the manager of the meat department in your favorite store to make these choices available. Make sure the turkey is not basted and is without additives and preservatives. At large farmer's markets, you can also purchase rabbit and bison. These are excellent choices for cleansing. If you are or know a hunter, venison and rabbit may be more accessible to you. Avoid eggs, soy products, and milk products since these are frequently reactive foods. Some grains are excellent sources of proteins. Quinoa is a complete protein source - it supplies both essential and nonessential amino acids.

Vegetables: There are many vegetables that are available. Most people have only a few vegetables that they eat frequently. Now is the time to experiment with vegetables that you have never or rarely eaten. Some good choices are some of the bean varieties listed in the legume family in the food classification section, sweet potatoes, cabbage, cauliflower, cress, kale, rutabaga, turnips, parsnips, celery, celeriac, asparagus, spinach, Swiss chard, endive, artichoke, jicama, okra, olives, and avocado. If you eat any of these on a regular basis or suspect that you may be sensitive to any, omit them.

Fruits: Melons, pears, raspberry, plum, apricot, cherry, nectarine, grapes (only if you do not eat them regularly), currants, mango, coconut, fig, cranberry, blueberry, guava, pineapple, kiwi, papaya, and passion fruit.

Grains and seeds: Brown whole grain rice, wild rice, millet, oats, quinoa, sunflower seeds, buckwheat, kasha, pine nuts, sesame seeds, amaranth grain, and poppy seeds.

Nuts: Cashew, walnuts, filbert nuts, hickory nuts, pistachio, hazelnuts, and Brazil nuts.

Oils: Olive oil, safflower oil, sunflower oil, canola, and sesame.

Milk substitutes: Rice milk, oat milk, almond milk, coconut milk (these are readily available in health food stores), you can prepare cashew milk, sesame milk, pecan milk, and Brazil nut milk. Instructions on how to prepare these milks are in Chapter Five, in the milk alternative listing.

Sweeteners: Honey, rice syrup, date sugar, beet sugar, and maple syrup are great sweeteners for the cleansing period.

Avoid: All caffeine, alcohol, recreational drugs, refined sugars, additives, and preservatives.

Chapter Nine

Food Classification

Food Classification

All foods are divided into classes and families for identification. The classes that a few foods belong are disputed among botanists and other scientists. Therefore, we have listed the classes of foods that we found to be most commonly accepted in a majority of the research material we found.

Foods, that is, plants and animals, are placed in classes and families based on common characteristics they possess. The plants and animals placed within the same family usually have genetic similarities. These genetic similarities are what make "cross-reactions" so common within family classes. For instance, persons sensitive to one fish often find that other fishes evoke a reaction as well. In the plant kingdom, persons who react to onions may react to shallots and leeks also, because they are in the same family and share similar characteristics.

We have included the Food Classification section for two reasons:
1. Cross-reaction is a possibility, and you need to know the foods to use with caution.
2. The food classes that present no problem for you can be included in your diet. This information shows you the multitude of choices available within a family, so you can avoid constant repetition of any one food. Since you are more likely to become sensitive to foods repeated frequently, this knowledge could save you from new allergy development.

Food Classification

Grass Family: Graminea

Sub families are very important in this family. Many times, foods in one sub family can be tolerated when foods in another sub family may evoke an allergic response.

Pooidae-wheat, triticum, rye, barley, oats, avena.

Panicoideae-corn, sorghum, sugar cane, bulrush, pearl millet.

Bambusoideae-rice, wild rice, oryza, zizania, bamboo shoots.

Chloridoideae-finger millet

Bean and Pea Family: Leguminoseae

Beans-all including black, kidney, lima, navy, pinto, white, butter beans, chick peas, black eyed peas, green beans, snapbeans, string beans, green peas, peanuts, soya beans, lentils, split peas, carob, guar gum, gum arabic, gum acacia, gum tragacanth, kudzu, licorice, mung bean, senna (cassia), tamarind, coffee substitutes, fenugreek spice.

Cross-reaction of peanuts and soya beans is common.

Nightshade family: Solanaceae

Potato (not sweet potato), tomato, bell pepper, sweet peppers (red, yellow, green, and orange), eggplant, paprika, chili peppers, tobasco, banana peppers, cayenne, pimiento, tobacco, cape gooseberry.

Note: poisonous alkaloids are present in minute amounts and can be toxic to persons suffering from arthritic conditions.

Cabbage/Mustard family-Cruciferae (old name), Brassicaceae (new name):

Broccoli, Brussels sprouts, cabbages, canola (rapeseed), cauliflower, collards, cress, horseradish, kale, kohlrabi, mustard, radish, rutabaga, turnips, watercress.

Carrot family-Umbelliferae:

Carrot, parsnip, celery, celeriac, fennel, parsley, anise, aniseed, caraway, dill, cumin, coriander, chervil, lovage, sweet cicely.

Food Allergies, What Do I Eat Now?

Lily family-Liliaceae:

Onion, aloe vera, asparagus, chives, garlic, leek, sarsaparilla, shallot.

Cucumber family-Cucurbitaceae:

Cucumber, melon, watermelon, zucchini, squashes, cantaloupe, honeydew, pumpkin, gourds.

Spinach family-Chenopodiaceae-

Spinach, spinach beet, Swiss chard, beetroot, sugar beet, goosefoot, New Zealand spinach, Lamb's quarter, quinoa.

Daisy family-Compositae:

All lettuces, chicory, endive, Belgian endive, globe artichoke, Jerusalem artichoke, salsify (greens or root), sunflower (seed or oil), safflower (oil), chamomile, dandelion, escarole, tarragon, stevia

Apple family-Rosaceae:

Sub families in this class are divided. Foods in one sub family may be tolerated, while foods from another sub family may evoke an allergic response.

Apple family: Apple, crabapple, pear, quince, and loquat.

Berry family: Blackberry, boysenberry, dewberry, loganberry, raspberry, Saskatoon berry, strawberry, youngberry, and rosehip.

Plum family: Plum, prune, apricot, greengage, cherry, peach, nectarine, sloe, almond, chokeberry.

Buckwheat family-Polygonaceae: Buckwheat, rhubarb, sorrel.

Citrus family-Rutaceae:

Orange, lemon, tangerine, clementine, grapefruit, lime, citron, kumquats, tangelo.

Grape family-Vitaceae:
> Cream of tartar, grapes (all varieties), wines, raisins, muscadine, muscatels, and sultanas. (Some "currants" used in baked goods are raisins.)

Arrowroot family-Marantaceae:
> Arrowroot thickener.

Currant family-Saxifragaceae:
> True currants, black currant, red currant, white currant, and gooseberry.

Walnut family-Juglandaceae:
> English walnut, pecans, black walnut, hickory nut, butternut.

Cashew family-Anacardiaceae:
> Cashew, Mango, pistachio. (These foods are closely related to poison ivy. If allergic reactions to poison ivy have been experienced, avoid this class of foods.)

Palm family-Palmaceae:
> Coconut (milk, oil, and fruit), sago (a form of tapioca), palm oil.

Date family-Arecaceae:
> Dates.

Ginger family-Zingiberaceae:
> Cardamom, ginger, turmeric.

Banana family-Musaceae:
> Banana, plantain, musa (another form of arrowroot).

Mulberry family-Moraceae:
> Mulberry, fig, bread fruit.

Birch family-Betulaceae:
>   Filbert nuts, hazelnuts.

Heath family-Ericaceae:
>   Blueberry, cranberry, huckleberry, bilberry (whortleberry), cowberry, wintergreen.

Mint family-Labiatae:
>   Mint, basil, marjoram, oregano, rosemary, sage, thyme, savory, peppermint, spearmint, and applemint.

Laurel-Lauraceae:
>   Avocado, bay leaf, cinnamon, sassafras.

Mallow family-Malvaceae:
>   Cottonseed oil, okra, Hibiscus (oils used in perfumes and teas), tropical roselle (used in jellies, and exotic sauces.)

Morning glory family-Convolvulaceae:
>   Sweet potato, jicama.

Myrtle family-Myrtaceae:
>   Allspice, cloves, eucalyptus (used in pharmaceutical antiseptics, nasal decongestants, and deodorants.), guava.

Tea family-Theaceae:
>   Black teas, green teas, oolong teas.

Pine family-Pinaceae:
>   Pine nuts, juniper (gin).

Nutmeg family-Myristicaceae:
>
> Nutmeg, mace (used in cooking, perfumes, tobacco, and medicines).

Fungi Kingdom:
>
> Hemiascomycetes-Yeast- Used for baking, wines, beers
>
> Dicomycetes-Morels, truffles
>
> Basidiomycotina-Mushrooms, puffballs

Spurge family-Euphorbiaceae:
>
> Castor oil, cassava (tapioca-commonly used in U.S.)

Arum-Araceae: Poi and Taro

The following families have limited items that are used in foods, but these items are used frequently enough to justify including them in this classification list.

Maple-Aceraceae: Maple syrup, maple sugar

Olives-Oleaceae: Olives (all), olive oils

Peppercorns-Piper Nigrum: Black and white pepper

Pineapple-Bromeliaceae: Pineapple

Vanilla-Orchidaceae: Vanilla flavoring

Sesame-Pedaliaceae: Sesame seeds and oil

Kiwi-Actinidia: Kiwi

Macadamia-Proteaceae: Macadamia nuts

Food Allergies, What Do I Eat Now?

Coffee-Rubiaceae: Coffee beans

Chocolate-Byttneriaceae: Cocoa bean, cocoa butter

Chestnut-Fagaceae: Chestnut, beechnut

Brazil nut-Lecythidaceae: Brazil nut

Amaranth-Amaranthaceae: Amaranth grain and flour

Papaya-Caricaceae: Papaya

Passion fruit-Passifloraceae: Passion fruit

Persimmon-Ebonaceae: Persimmons

Pomegranate-Punicaceae: Pomegranates

Poppyseed-Papaveraceae: Poppyseeds

Water chestnut-Cyperaceae: Water chestnuts

Cactus-Cactaceae: cactus, "prickly pear"

Saffron-Iris-Crocus family: Saffron spice

Flax-Linaceae: flax used as a dietary fiber supplement.

True Yam-Dioscoreaceae: Yams (from Africa) are seldom seen in the U.S. They have brown or black skin with white, purple, or red flesh.

Food Allergies, What Do I Eat Now?

Seaweed-
    Agar-Gelidium-Used as thickeners in ice creams, jellies, soups, and sauces.
    Kelp-Phaeophyta-Used in ice creams and confections.

Poultry and Eggs
    Pheasant-Phasianinae: Chicken, pheasant, quail, partridge

    Guineafowl-Numididae: Guineafowl

    Grouse-Tetraoninae: Grouse and turkey

    Duck-Anatidae: Duck and geese

    Pigeon-Columbidae: Pigeon, squab, dove

    Snipe-Scolopacidae: Snipe and Woodcock

    Ostrich-Struthionidae: Emu and ostrich are now being raised for consumption. They may become more common in the marketplace.

    Eggs-Bird eggs are very similar in the type of protein they contain and are considered the same food.

Meats:
    Cattle family-Bovidae: Cows (beef, veal), sheep (lamb, mutton), goats, bison.

    Pig-Suidae: Pig –Pork, ham, and bacon

    Deer family-Cervidae: All Venison, caribou, etc.

    Rabbit-Leporidae: Rabbit and hare

Food Allergies, What Do I Eat Now?

<u>Milk</u>-cows milk, goat milk, sheep milk, cross-reactions are likely.

<u>Fish and shellfish:</u>

<u>Fish</u>- All bony fish have the same protein in common, parvalbumins and may provoke allergic reactions in sensitive people: herring, sturgeon, salmon, trout, flounder, perch, catfish, etc. Patients with other fish allergies may tolerate cartilaginous fish such as shark and rays, but caution should be used when eating these fish.

<u>Crustaceans-Crustacea</u>: Crab, lobster, crayfish, shrimp, and prawn. Many patients react to all crustaceans regardless of family.

<u>Molluses-Mollusca</u>: Mussels, cockles, winkles, oysters, clams, scallops, squid, cuttlefish, octopus, snails (escargots). People allergic to one have and increased incident of allergy to others.

Chapter Ten

Five Day Rotation Plan

Five Day Rotation Plan

The Rotation Plan introduces you to using the food classifications on a 24-hour cycle once every five days. This plan uses the rotation of foods to avoid allergic reactions and to help prevent the development of new food allergies. Omit any other foods that may provoke an allergic reaction for you.

Changing the components of the diet or substituting is simple to do. For instance, if your favorite recipe calls for beef and tomatoes, simply exchange the "vegetable" nightshade group from Day One with the "vegetable" cucumber family on Day Two. Be sure to exchange those two families of food in <u>all</u> categories for that day, and do not repeat that food for the next five days.

A tip suggested by Marilyn Gioannini in her book, *The Complete Food Allergy Cookbook,* is to begin the day's diet with the evening dinner to take advantage of leftovers for lunch the following day. An example would be to roast a chicken for dinner on night one, and serve leftovers in a chicken sandwich or salad the next day for lunch. These two meals will still fall within the same 24-hour period.

This Rotation Diet is prepared for persons allergic to corn, wheat, cane sugar, eggs, soya (soybean), and milk. If you are not sensitive to all of these, include the non-allergic foods on the day where that food family is located. Corn and cane sugar belong to the same grass subfamily as pearl millet (Day 2), and wheat is in the same grass subfamily as oats (insert on Day 1 if you are not sensitive to wheat). Soya is a legume (Day 4), and eggs belong to the poultry section (Day 1). Milk stands in a class all its own, but if you are not allergic to milk, you can also include cheeses and other milk products in one day's diet plan.

If you do not use a meat or vegetable family on its assigned day, you may use it on another day during that week. Be careful not to repeat it again for four or five days. I recommend that you not make this a habit, because it becomes confusing where that food actually belongs on the Rotation Plan. It is nice, however, to have special dinners that may cause you to change the plan around. There should be enough variety in this schedule that you will not have to change it for about six months.

Changing the diet is a snap. One method I believe works well is to use a large piece of paper and write down the categories that we have on each day (protein, vegetables, fruits, and grains). Then, with a pencil, begin to move the categories around one at a time, until you come up with a schedule change that meets your recipe needs. I only recommend doing this about once every six months.

Five Day Rotation Plan
Day One

Protein: Poultry- Chicken, quail, pheasant, partridge, eggs

Vegetables: Night shade family- Potatoes, tomatoes, bell peppers, sweet peppers (red, yellow, orange), chili peppers, pimiento, eggplant
  Fungi family- Yeast, morels, truffles, mushrooms, puffballs
  Daisy family- All lettuces, chicory, endives, artichokes, salsify, dandelion, escarole. stevia, Jerusalem artichokes

Fruits: Grape family- Grapes, raisins, muscadines, muscatels, sultana
  Cashew family- Mango
  Pomegranate- Pomegranate

Flours and grains: Grass/Pooidae family- Oats and oat flour
  Nightshade family- Potato flour

Seeds and Nuts: Daisy family- Sunflower seeds
  Cashew family- Cashews and pistachios

Sweeteners: Grape family- Concentrated grape juice
  Maple family- Maple syrup and sugar

Oils: Daisy family- Safflower oil and sunflower oil

Milk substitute: Cashew family- Cashew milk
  Grass family- Oat milk

Beverages: Daisy family- Chamomile tea,
  Cashew family- Mango juice
  Grape family- Grape juices, wines

Food Allergies, What Do I Eat Now?

<u>Cooking Spices and herbs: Nightshades</u>- Peppers, tobasco, cayenne, paprika

<u>Crocus/Iris family</u>- Saffron

<u>Daisy family</u>- Tarragon

<u>Day One</u>

<u>Rotation Plan Recipes</u>

<u>Appetizers and Dips:</u>

Chicken Wings

<u>Beverages:</u>

Mango Smooth

<u>Breads and Baked Goods:</u>

Raisin Oat Muffins

Oat Muffins with Cashews

Crunchy Cobbler Topping

<u>Breakfast:</u>

Oat Pancakes with Maple Syrup

Mango Syrup

Maple Raisin Syrup

<u>Campfire Cooking:</u>

Oat Granola with Raisins and Sunflower Seeds

Camping Potatoes

Dry Fruit Mix Day 1

<u>Desserts:</u>

Mango Ice

<u>Fruits, Salads, and Dressings:</u>

Chicken Cashew Salad

Chicken Salad Day 1

Grape Mango Salad

Mixed Green Salad

Food Allergies, What Do I Eat Now?

<u>Main Dish and Entrees:</u>
Sunny Chicken Strips
Cashew Chicken
Chicken Artichoke Casserole
Grilled Chicken and Vegetables with Tarragon

<u>Sauces:</u>
Sun Dried Tomato Paste

<u>Soups:</u>
Chicken Tomato Soup
Chicken Potato Chowder

<u>Vegetables:</u>
Mashed Potatoes

Food Allergies, What Do I Eat Now?

Day Two

Protein: Cattle family- Beef, veal, sheep, (lamb, mutton), goat, bison
    Deer family- All venison

Vegetables: Buckwheat family- Buckwheat, rhubarb, and sorrel
    Laurel family- Avocado
    Cucumber family: Cucumber, zucchini, squashes, pumpkin, gourds
    Olive family- Olives
    Cactus family- cactus "prickly pear"

Fruits: Rose family- Apple, crabapple, pear, quince, loquat, blackberry, boysenberry, dewberry, loganberry, raspberry, Saskatoon berry, strawberry, youngberry, plum, prune, apricot, greengage, cherry, peach, nectarine, sloe, chokeberry, rose hips
    Currant family- All currants, gooseberry
    Cucumber family- Melon, watermelon, cantaloupe, honeydew

Flours and grains: Buckwheat family- Buckwheat and kasha
    Grass family-sub-family: Panicoideae- Pearl millet
    Spurge family- Cassava (tapioca in the U.S.)
    Tapioca flour

Seed and nuts: Rose family- Almonds
    Poppyseed family- Poppyseeds
    Macadamia family- Macadamia nuts
    Cucumber family- Pumpkin seeds

Sweeteners: Rose family- Apple juice concentrate

Oils: Olive family- Olive oils, almond oil

<u>Milk substitutes</u>: <u>Rose family</u>- Almond milk

<u>Beverages</u>: <u>Rose family</u>- Apple, peach, nectarine, strawberry, raspberry, apricot, cherry juices, rosehip tea
<u>Laurel family</u>- Sassafras tea
<u>Mint family</u>- Mint tea

<u>Cooking spices and herbs</u>: <u>Laurel family</u>- Bay leaf, cinnamon, cassia buds and bark
<u>Nutmeg family</u>- Nutmeg and mace
<u>Mint family</u>- Mint, basil, marjoram, oregano, rosemary, sage, thyme, savory, peppermint, spearmint, applemint, and lemon balm

<u>Day Two</u>

<u>Rotation Plan Recipes</u>

<u>Appetizers and Dips:</u>
Savory Meatball with Apricot or Raspberry Dipping Sauce

<u>Beverages:</u>
Raspberry Chill

Peach Strawberry Freeze

<u>Breads and Baked Goods:</u>
Apple Almond Buckwheat Muffins

<u>Breakfast:</u>
Blackberry Syrup

Raspberry Syrup

Buckwheat Pancakes

<u>Campfire Cooking:</u>
Dry Fruit and Nut Mix Day 2

Alternate Fruit and Nut Mix Day 2

<u>Desserts:</u>
Pumpkin Pie Filling

Food Allergies, What Do I Eat Now?

Fruits, Salads, and Dressings:
Melon Cup

Main Dish and Entrees:
Avocado Cucumber Gyro

Beef Burgers with Pesto "Pasta"

Beef Burgers

Sauces:
Pesto Sauce

Soups:
Squash Soup

Pumpkin Soup

Vegetables:
Spaghetti Squash

Stuffed Zucchini Squash

Food Allergies, What Do I Eat Now?

Day Three

<u>Protein: Fish</u>- All fish including: Herring, sturgeon, salmon, trout, flounder, perch, catfish, bass, etc.

<u>Crustaceans</u>- Crab, lobster, crayfish, shrimp, prawn

<u>Molluses</u>- Mussels, cockles, winkles, oysters, clams, scallops, squid, cuttlefish, octopus, snails

<u>Vegetables: Lily family</u>- Onion, aloe vera, asparagus, chives, garlic, leek, sarsaparilla, shallot, scallion

<u>Carrot family</u>- Carrot, parsnips, celery, celeriac, fennel, parsley, anise, aniseed, caraway, dill, cumin, coriander, chervil, lovage, sweet cicely

<u>Mallow family</u>- Okra

<u>Fruits: Palm family</u>- Coconut

<u>Citrus family</u>- Orange, lemon, lime, tangelo, tangerine, clementine, grapefruit, citron, kumquats, mandarin orange

<u>Passion fruit family</u>- Passion fruit

<u>Flours and grains: Amaranth family</u>- Amaranth

<u>Palm family</u>- Sago tapioca

<u>Maranta</u>- Arrowroot

<u>Seeds and nuts: Sesame family</u>- Sesame seeds, sesame paste, tahini

<u>Pine family</u>- Pine nuts

<u>Birch/Beech family</u>- Filbert nuts and hazelnuts

<u>Sweeteners:</u> Honey

Oils: Sesame family- Sesame oil
    Palm family- Palm oil
    Mallow family- Cottonseed oil

Milk substitutes: Birch family- Filbert and hazelnut milk
    Palm family- Coconut milk
    Sesame family- Sesame butter

Beverages: mallow family- Hibiscus teas,
    Tea family- Black and green teas
    Citrus family- All citrus juices listed in "fruit" section
    Comfrey family- Comfrey root and leaves tea
    Ginseng family- Ginseng tea

Cooking spices and herbs: Lily family- Onion garlic, chives
    Carrot family- Parsley, anise, caraway, dill, cumin, coriander, celery seed
    Ginger family- Cardamom, ginger, turmeric
    Ginseng family- Ginseng root

Day Three
Rotation Plan Recipes

Appetizers and Dips:
Sesame Amaranth Crackers

Beverages:
Sunny Shake

Breads and Baked Goods:
Amaranth Bread

Breakfast:
Hazelnut Pancakes with Citrus Sauce

Campfire Cooking:
Dry Fruit and Nut Mix Day 3

Food Allergies, What Do I Eat Now?

Desserts:
Coconut Pie Crust

Crunchy Amaranth Cobbler Topping

Ginger Cookies

Lemon Ice

Fruits, Salads, and Dressings:
Ambrosia

Main Dishes and Entrees:
Lemon and Chives Fish Fillets

Salmon with Dill

Ginger Fish Fillets

Sauces:
Citrus Sauce

Soups:
French Onion Soup

Vegetables:
Sesame Asparagus

Honeyed Carrots

Day Four

Protein: Suidae- Pork, ham and bacon
    Rabbit family- Rabbit and hare
    Legumes- Beans and peanuts

Vegetables: Legume family- All beans including: black, kidney, lima navy, pinto, white, butter beans, chick peas, black eyed peas, green beans, snapbeans, string beans, green peas, Soya beans, lentils, split peas, mung beans

Spinach family- Spinach, spinach beet, Swiss chard, beetroot, sugar beet, goosefoot, New Zealand spinach, Lamb's quarters
    Arum- Poi, taro

Fruits: Banana family- Banana, plantain
    Pineapple family- Pineapple
    Kiwi family- Kiwi
    Persimmon family- Persimmon
    Honeysuckle family- Elderberry

Flours and Grains: Spinach family- Quinoa seed, quinoa flour,
    Legume family- Chickpea flour, humus

Seeds and nuts: Legumes- Peanuts
    Walnut family- Walnuts, pecans, black walnut, hickory nuts, butternut
    Banana family- Psyllium seeds

Food Allergies, What Do I Eat Now?

Sweeteners: Spinach family- Beet sugar

    Legume family- Carob as sweetener in baking

Oils: Legume family- Peanut oil

Milk Substitutes: Walnut family- Walnut milk or pecan milk

Beverages: Coffee family- Coffee

    Legume family- Carob

    Banana- Banana shake

    Pineapple- Pineapple juice

    Honeysuckle- Elderberry tea

Cooking spices and herbs: Legumes- Carob, fenugreek, licorice, guar gum, gum arabic, gum acacia, gum tragacanth,

    Orchid family- Vanilla

Day Four
Rotation Plan Recipes

Appetizers and Dips:
Humus and "Bacon" Spread

Quinoa Chips

Beverages:
Tropical Delight Shake

Breads and Baked Goods:
Quinoa Tortillas

Breakfast:
Tropical Syrup

Campfire Cooking:
Dry Fruit and Nut Mix Day 4

Food Allergies, What Do I Eat Now?

<u>Desserts:</u>

Crunchy Topping for Cobblers

Pineapple Cobbler

<u>Fruits, Salads, and Dressings:</u>

Fruit of the Day Salad

Spinach Salad with Chickpeas

<u>Main Dishes and Entrees:</u>

Pork Tenderloin

<u>Sauces:</u>

Pineapple Sauce

<u>Soups:</u>

Smoked Tenderloin and Bean Soup

Vegetarian Bean Soup

<u>Vegetables:</u>

Wilted Spinach with "Bacon"

Day Five

Protein: Grouse family- Turkey and grouse
>Duck family- Duck and geese
>Pigeon family- Pigeon, squab and dove

Vegetables: Cabbage family- Broccoli, Brussels sprouts, cabbages, cauliflower, collards, cress, horseradish, kale, kohlrabi, mustard, radish, turnips, watercress, Bok choy, mustard greens, rutabaga, Savoy cabbage
>Morning glory family- Sweet potato, jicama
>True yam family- yams
>Cypera- Water chestnuts
>Grass family- Bamboo shoots

Fruits: Heath family- Blueberry, cranberry, huckleberry, bilberry (whortleberry), and cowberry
>Myrtle family- guava
>Papaya family- Papaya
>Mulberry family- Mulberry, fig, breadfruit
>Date family- Dates

Flours and grains: Grass family-Bambusoideae sub-family- Rice flour, white rice flour, brown rice flour, white rice, brown rice, wild rice, short grain or long grains, aborio rice

Seeds and nuts: Chestnut family- Chestnut and beechnut
>Brazil nut family- Brazil nut

Sugar substitutes: Grass family- Rice syrup
>Date family- Date sugar

Oils: Cabbage family- Canola oil

Milk substitutes: Grass family-sub-family Bambusoideae- Rice Milk
 Brazil family- Brazil nut milk

Beverages: Chocolate family- Cocoa
 Papaya family- Papaya juice
 Mulberry family- Mulberry juice
 Heath family- Cranberry juice
 Myrtle family- Guava juice

Cooking spices and herbs-Cabbage family- Horseradish, mustard
 Peppercorns- White and black pepper
 Myrtle family- Allspice, cloves

Day Five
Rotation Plan Recipes

Appetizers and Dips:
Beverages:
Red, White, and Blue Freeze

Breads and Baked Goods:
Blueberry Rice Muffins

Cranberry Rice Muffins

Breakfast:
Cranberry Syrup

Blueberry Syrup

Breakfast Rice

Campfire Cooking:
Dry Fruit and Nut Mix Day 5

Desserts:
Rice Pudding

Food Allergies, What Do I Eat Now?

<u>Fruit, Salads, and Dressings:</u>
Rice Broccoli Turkey Salad
Turkey Rice Cranberry Salad

<u>Main Dishes and Entrees:</u>
Quick Turkey Noodle
Roasted Duck with Wild Rice
Turkey Cutlet with Old Fashion "Milk Gravy"

<u>Sauces:</u>
Old Fashion "Milk Gravy"
Gravy From Drippings

<u>Soups:</u>
Broccoli Soup
Sweet Potato Soup
Turkey Cabbage Soup
Turkey Rice Soup

<u>Vegetables:</u>
Baked Sweet Potatoes
Brazil Nut Risotto
Sweet Potato Bake with Cranberries

Chapter Eleven

Eating Away From Home

Eating Away From Home

A diagnosis of food sensitivities does not mean that you have to eat only at home! You can still enjoy dinners with friends, eating out at restaurants, and entertaining friends at home. It does require a little more planning than usual. Entertaining in your home can be delicious and a time for you to showcase new recipes.

When you are invited to dinner at a friend's home, tell them that you are allergic/sensitive to certain foods, and that you must avoid those foods. You could offer to bring a casserole or hearty side dish to serve with the meal. Explain that if they plan to serve a salad, to simply put a serving aside for you before adding the dressing. If your host already has a menu planned, suggest that you bring your own meal, and stress that you would enjoy taking part in the dinner party in that way.

When going to an event where bringing your own food would be unacceptable, eat a large meal before you go. A fresh raw vegetable or fruit platter almost always is available for munching. If you have satisfied your appetite with your non-allergic foods before to the event, you are less likely to give into temptation.

Now that you have successfully identified your food sensitivities and are on the road to recovery, you probably think that eating at a restaurant will be out of the question. Not so! Eating at restaurants presents a different situation altogether. Restaurant food is usually loaded in questionable items such as butter, cream, wheat, corn, eggs, cheese. If you have no idea of exactly what went into the dish, you are taking a chance that a reaction can ruin your evening and set you back in your quest for health. There are ways you can prepare to cope with restaurant dinning. Listed below are a few ways that can help make your dinning out experience a more pleasurable one.

1. Call ahead to ask if the chef will prepare <u>their</u> dish in a simpler way that will be more suitable for your needs. Honestly, I have never been disappointed by the effort put forth by most restaurant personnel. The chef at a seafood restaurant in Pensacola, Florida prepared a feast for my daughter when we dropped in without notice. She ordered her entrée grilled with fresh herbs, and the side dish of carrots was flavored with honey instead of the sauce that covered ours. We provided her dressing for a plain salad without cheese, and her meal was as delectable as any other at the table.

Even with good intentions, some ingredients may unknowingly be used to which you may be sensitive. Ask the chef to prepare your meal as simply as possible, and to sauté vegetables in olive oil (a staple in restaurant kitchens) instead of butter.

2. Take along a card with a list of the basic foods to which you are allergic and send this with your request to the kitchen. For instance, if you are allergic to corn, do not list every thing that contains corn. The list would be so long that the chef would not have time to read it. Below is a list we would give to a chef for our daughter:

    All sauces are to be avoided!

    Allergic to: <u>Wheat</u> (including breadcrumbs) <u>Beans</u> <u>Tea</u>

        <u>Corn</u> (and cornstarch)   <u>Soy</u> (soy sauce)

        <u>Sugar</u> (all sugars)   <u>Milk</u> and all milk products

3. Take one or two slices of your bread, especially if you plan to have a sandwich with your meal. If you have a roll or acceptable dinner bread prepared, slip it into a plastic bag to eat with your dinner.

4. Stress to your waitress or waiter what you can or cannot have on your salad, because they are usually the ones to prepare the salad.

5. Take a small container of your own salad dressing, as salads make a good selection for a simple meal. Plan ahead to be prepared.

6. Take your own sweetener (if applicable) for your tea or coffee.

7. If you are sensitive to milk products, take your own margarine in a plastic bag and dispose of the bag after use. You can use this on bread or a plain baked potato. Potato with butter is my weakness!

8. Order plain grilled, broiled, or baked non - marinated meats, fish and poultry, seasoned only with fresh herbs and lemon.

9. Ask that fresh vegetable side dishes be steamed or baked, and seasoned only with lemon, herbs, and olive oil.

10. Do not order fried foods in a restaurant. Oils for frying usually will be corn, soy, peanut or a combination of oils and may have had wheat coated (battered or breaded) foods fried in it. Deep fryer oils are not usually changed frequently.

11. For dessert, ask for fresh fruit in season without sugar or creams. Strawberries in a bowl make a refreshing dessert and are usually available in most good restaurants.

Traveling with food allergies in tow

Air travel

Long distance trips can be a challenge to the food sensitive person. Most airlines have a number you can call ahead to order special meals. These requests are taken for long flights when a meal is served. You need to have your boarding pass and seat assignment in hand when you call. Ask your ticket agent how much notice the airline needs to provide you with this service. Mix-ups happen, so have a snack on hand just in case someone did not get the order or if it was prepared incorrectly. If they are unwilling to work with you on your meal planning, ask if you can bring along your own snacks. A sandwich that has been frozen for travel can be a lifesaver on a long flight. Prewashed apples also travel well.

Fast food

FAST FOOD IS OUT OF THE QUESTION! Fast food could be the worst thing that you as an allergic person, could put into your system. It is loaded with unknown additives and preservatives, soy, wheat, corn, sugar, and chemicals that you would not want to put into your body. Even the simple, unassuming French fry can put a person allergic to sugar, chemical additives and preservatives into an allergic reaction. Have you ever cut a potato in your own kitchen and observed what happens to it if it is not immediately cooked? It will turn blackish-brown in a matter of minutes unless it is treated in some manner. Well, the fast food industry uses chemicals to slow discoloration. Make a fresh batch at home and taste the difference! If an allergy to peanuts is a problem, beware! Peanut oil or a combination of oils is the primary oil used for frying. There are so many problems with fast food that we could not list them all in this book alone. Just avoid it at all cost.

Automobile travel

Your cooler will become your best friend. I have different sizes for all types of trips: a trip to my sister's house 200 miles away requires the big one, so I can take items such as breads, milks, and juices that might spoil. Freeze nut milks, fruit juices, and water in containers so that you can reduce the amount of ice you need to pack. I also carry nonperishables such as pasta (for meals she prepares for us), our muffins, and cookies so that I do not have to locate a health food store in an area where I am unfamiliar. A day trip requires a small cooler for sandwiches, fresh fruits, veggies, and drinks. A little careful planning makes trip taking less of a chore. You will not be concerned with finding a suitable restaurant along the way if you have planned ahead.

Vacationing, camping and recreation with allergies

When vacationing, we now make sure that we have a kitchenette so breakfast and lunch can be made at the hotel. Even a simple dinner can be handled with flair…if you plan. I take the items that cannot be purchased at grocery stores such as rice pastas, nut milks, cereals, alternative grains, and breads. If you follow this plan, then, a quick trip to the grocery store when you reach your destination to purchase fresh fruits and vegetables, brown rice, and meats is all you have to do. I have found that it is easier to find a grocery store than a natural food market or health food store.

Donna's family is avid campers. We backpack, take canoe trips, hike, and take part in an annual campout in Pisgah, N.C. with about 50 of our friends. We do not let our food allergies limit our fun. And, I do not believe I should be slaving over a cookstove the entire weekend.

These various outings do take a bit of planning and precooking, but it is always worth it. Here are some ideas that I have used on our camping trips. These are only a few common sense things that may make the trip more enjoyable for everyone.

1. Make soup recipes ahead and freeze in meal - sized containers. Freezing the containers of soup helps to keep other items in the cooler cold without adding more ice (this also depends on the time of year and outside temperature). More ice may be needed during the summer months.

2. Instead of serving hot dogs for dinner, prepare "Veggie Burgers" or "Savory Turkey Burgers" recipes ahead and freeze in formed patties to store in the cooler. Remove from the cooler, thaw partially, and cook in a skillet (very little oil is needed).

3. Make homemade trail mix to avoid allergens, preservatives, and additives. Kids love to make trail mix, and there is no supervision needed except to make sure that some is actually left after nibbling. See "Best Trail Mix" recipe.

4. Fast cooking oatmeal (health food store) mixed with your raisins, nuts, coconut, can be a quick, no fuss breakfast. This can be mixed ahead in individual portions and placed in plastic bags so there is no measuring in camp. All an adult has to do is heat nut milk or water and pour. This can also be done with rice cereals for another morning on the rotation diet; use different fruits and nuts that day.

5. Vegetables grilled in foil or directly on the grill are wonderful as a main dish or a side. These are especially good with "Homemade Sausage Patties."

6. Wrap potatoes in foil and place in the hot coals to cook about 1 ½ hours while you hike. Check for doneness; they may need longer cooking time depending on the temperature of the coals and their size. (Do not place directly into fire.)

7. Chicken or fresh-caught fish fillets cook wonderfully in foil pouches with herbs, spices, and vegetables with minimal clean up time!

8. For backpacking, you may want to invest in a dehydrator or learn how to dehydrate foods in your oven. Operating a dehydrator costs less than having your oven on low for a long time. (I purchased my dehydrator for about $20 a few years ago.) For "instant" soups, you may want to precook some "hard" vegetables before dehydrating. Potatoes, carrots, hard squashes, and beans work best for quick meals when they are precooked. Add broth and heat. It's not quite that simple, but look at the assortment of recipes under "Camping Selections." Some friends and colleagues of ours hiked the entire length of the Appalachian Trail and dehydrated a lot of their food for the trip by the slow oven method.

9. For camping, pack a bounty of items such as healthy snacks, rice cakes, oat or rice crackers, muffins, sesame crackers, fresh fruits and veggies (prewashed and cut into finger size for younger children), and trail mix. For some reason, we always are hungry on camping trips. Perhaps it is the fresh air and exercise we get.

10. Finally, do not leave your rotation diet at home just because you are camping, but don't let it rule your weekend. Enjoy the time together as a family and get back to strict rotation when you get back home. If you are camping for a longer period of time, a week or more, stick as closely to the rotation plan as possible.

Food Allergies, What Do I Eat Now?

Brown Bagging Lunches

Making lunches need not be a challenge. Adults and children alike can manage preparing a delicious and nutritious lunch using the Food Rotation Plan. There are three priorities to keep in mind when planning a long-term lunch menu:

1. <u>Avoiding allergic foods:</u> You will have more success avoiding the reactive foods if you plan and prepare your own lunch. Eating out occasionally can be managed. But, when done on a frequent basis, the chances of eating a reactive food, purposefully or inadvertently, increases.

2. <u>Maintaining caloric and nutritional needs of adults and children:</u> Nutritional and caloric guidelines established by the FDA/USDA are very general. Everyone has individual needs to address. For instance, the anemic person needs to significantly increase intake of iron and folic acid. An active athlete's caloric requirements may be significantly higher than the average person the same age to meet the energy needs. Your needs should be assessed by your health professional to maintain adequate metabolic requirements. Since we do not know your individual health status, we can only make general recommendations.

3. <u>Preparing the lunch to insure safe conditions:</u> The crucial point here is to keep food at the appropriate temperature to insure it will be safe for consumption. Keep hot food hot and cold food cold. Sounds simple enough. Your county extension service usually has free information and tips on how to safely transport lunches and picnics. Here are a few ideas we have compiled:

- Freeze juice boxes, rice milks, and nut milks, or water in plastic bottles overnight. They should be thawed or icy when time to drink. They will also keep sandwiches, fruits, and salads cold.
- Some meat sandwiches can be frozen overnight to keep cold.
- An insulated bottle keeps beverages cold, but they do not help keep anything else in the lunch cold. Use cold packs for keeping foods cold in this case.
- Wide mouth insulated containers are great for keeping soups hot and for eating the soup when a bowl is not handy.

Food Allergies, What Do I Eat Now?

Helpful Hints For Success:

<u>Adults - Take an extra snack for afternoon snack time.</u> The vending machines at work become very tempting about one hour before the end of my work day. By taking a small snack or extra piece of fruit, I am more likely to avoid the temptation.

<u>Purchase an appropriate lunch carrier for yourself and your children.</u> Young children need sturdy metal or plastic lunch boxes if the lunch is to survive a school bus ride and the shuffle into the classroom. Older children may want a disposable "brown bag" for lunches so they do not have to keep track of it the rest of the day. As an adult, I have access to a microwave at lunchtime; so, I take leftover "dinners" from the night before to work. A fabric, zippered bag large enough to hold food containers upright suits my needs. Some adults find that a recycled plastic grocery bag works for them. Choose whatever container works for you.

<u>Teaching your child not to swap:</u> The importance of this concept is difficult for children to comprehend, and many adults have a problem with it, too. The adult version of swapping at lunch and snack time is the vending machine, and I am not immune to this, either. We all have weak moments when we think, "That sugary, crème-filled, chocolate covered cupcake looks better than my carrot-raisin muffin; so, I'll swap my quarters for one." I usually end up suffering from that decision for about a week. The headache from the sugar and the mouth ulcers from the chocolate are excruciating. So, why do I do it? Because we usually "crave" many things to which we are sensitive.

Children see sugary treats that other children have and are tempted to swap. There are two ways to combat this. One is education: teaching your child the rationale of good nutrition and reactive food avoidance is the first step. Teaching alone does not do it, however. You must set an example of good eating habits and have the entire family live by it. The second is to pack foods that your child enjoys. Experiment with our recipes, and let your child become involved in planning and preparing their lunch. By all means, do not totally deny treats. Find an acceptable sweetener for cookies, puddings, and fruit-topped cakes and use fruit for dessert. Try to make your child's lunches look appetizing and as normal as possible. Children do not like being different, even at lunchtime.

Food Allergies, What Do I Eat Now?

<u>Menu Samples For Lunch:</u>

Using the Five-Day Rotation Plan from Chapter 10, you can plan lunch menus for the following day using leftovers. If no leftovers are available (a sign that your meals are being enjoyed!), you can use the nuts for that day and make a nut spread and jelly sandwich.

Day One

<u>Sandwiches</u>- Sliced chicken, chicken salad, cashew nut butter with grape or muscadine jelly or jam sandwiches.

<u>Salads</u>- Lettuce or endive salad with tomatoes and chicken chunks, Sunny Chicken Strips salad with tomatoes, egg salad sandwiches (if not sensitive), Chicken-Cashew Salad.

<u>Fruits</u>- Grapes, mango pieces

<u>Soups</u>- Potato soup, Chicken Potato Chowder, tomato soup, Chicken-Tomato soup.

<u>Snacks</u>- Raisins, sunflower seeds, organic potato chips, grape "leather", cashews, pistachios.

<u>Breads</u>- Oat Bread, Raisin-Oat Muffins.

<u>Desserts</u>- Oatmeal-Raisin Cookies, Oat Granola Bars.

<u>Beverages</u>- Grape juice, oat milk, mango spritzer, and cashew milk.

Adults with access to microwave can heat a leftover baked potato.

Day Two

<u>Sandwiches</u>- Roast beef on millet bread, Avocado-Cucumber gyro, almond butter with strawberry jelly on millet or tapioca bread, almond cheese toast, roast beef and almond cheese gyro melt.

<u>Salads</u>- Greek Kasha salad with olives, fruit salad.

<u>Fruits</u>- Apple, pear, strawberries, peaches, nectarine, any melon slices (watermelon, cantaloupe or honeydew.)

<u>Soups</u>- Squash soup

<u>Snacks</u>- fruits, almonds, macadamia nuts, fruit leathers, raw squash rings and cucumber rings with Italian seasoned oils, pumpkin seeds, apple sauce, Cherry Apple Sauce.

<u>Breads</u>- Almond Poppyseed Muffin, Cinnamon Toast

<u>Desserts</u>- Apple-Almond Buckwheat Muffin, Perfect Pumpkin Pie, Pumpkin Cookies, Zucchini Bread.

<u>Beverages</u>- apple juice, pear juice, peach spritzer, almond milk, sassafras tea.

Day Three

<u>Sandwiches</u>- Tuna Fish Salad on Amaranth Bread, Salmon Salad on Amaranth Bread.

<u>Salads</u>- Carrot sticks and celery sticks with Dill Dip, Shrimp Salad with Dill.

<u>Fruits</u>- Oranges, tangelos, tangerines, grapefruits.

<u>Soups</u>- Onion Soup, Asparagus Soup

<u>Breads</u>- Sesame Amaranth Crackers.

<u>Snacks</u>- fruits, filbert and hazelnuts, pine nuts.

<u>Desserts</u>- Carrot Muffins, Coconut Cookies, Ambrosia, Honey Hazelnut Cookies, Ginger Cookies.

<u>Beverages</u>- Citrus juices, black teas, hazelnut milk.

Adults can have left over fish from dinner to heat in the microwave.

Day Four

<u>Sandwiches</u>- Humus and Bacon Spread on Quinoa Tortilla, Ham sandwich on Quinoa rounds, Bacon and Spinach sandwich on Quinoa Bread, Peanut butter and banana sandwich.

<u>Salads</u>- Black bean Quinoa Salad, Spinach salad with bacon, fruit salad.

<u>Fruits</u>- Kiwi, banana, pineapple chunks.

<u>Soups</u>- Ham and Bean Soup, Split Pea Soup.

<u>Breads</u>- Quinoa Bread, Quinoa Rounds, Tortilla, Banana Nut Bread.

<u>Snacks</u>- kiwi, bananas, pineapple, Hummus Dip, Banana Shake, pecans, peanuts, and dried fruits.

<u>Desserts</u>- Southern Pecan Cookies, Banana Boats, Banana nut Bread, Peanut Butter Cookies.

<u>Beverages</u>- Coffee (adults), pineapple juice, pineapple spritzer, pecan milk.

Food Allergies, What Do I Eat Now?

Day Five

<u>Sandwiches</u>- Turkey and watercress on Rice Bread with mustard, Brazil nut butter and blueberry jam or cranberry jam.

<u>Salad</u>- Rice-Broccoli Turkey Salad, Rice Turkey Cranberry Salad.

<u>Fruit</u>- cranberries, dried papaya chunks, and blueberries.

<u>Soups</u>- Broccoli Soup, Turkey Cabbage Soup, Turkey Rice Soup, Sweet Potato Soup.

<u>Bread</u>- Rice Bread, Cranberry Muffins, Blueberry Muffins, Rice Sesame Crackers.

<u>Snacks</u>- dried cranberries, blueberries, Rice Fruit Bars, raw broccoli and cauliflower with Mustard Dip.

<u>Desserts</u>- Sweet Potato Pie, Cranberry Muffins.

<u>Beverages</u>- Cranberry juice, cranberry spritzer, papaya spritzer, rice milk, chocolate rice milk.

When the time comes to change your rotation diet choices and experiment with other recipes as outlined in the Cookbook, you can try:

Carrot-Raisin Salad

Waldorf Salad

Pineapple-Carrot-Raisin Muffins

Lemon Poppyseed Muffins

Savory Rice And Amaranth Bread

Best Trail Mix

Tomato-Cucumber Salad

Gazpacho Soup

Chicken Rice Soup

Beef-Tomato and Rice Soup

Chicken Soup with Spinach

Seven Layer Salad

Mix different fruits and grains for Granola Bars

Chapter Twelve

Tips For Hectic Lives

Tips for hectic lives

We all live in the same hectic world, and the challenge to find time to plan and prepare a nutritious meal is hard enough in itself. Now, you have to find a way to prepare nutritious meals for a food-sensitive person in your life. Both of us (the authors) have been in this situation and have struggled to find a way to use what we know professionally with what realistically can be done by any one human being. Through many years of trial and error (and many inedible concoctions), we have combined our experiences and compiled some (what we hope will be) words of wisdom to help you in your situation.

- <u>Purchase a freezer.</u> I bought mine used for $100, and it has been a faithful servant for many years.
- <u>Shop wisely.</u> - Buy as many items on sale as you can afford and store.
- There are convenience foods to be had for food sensitive persons, but they can be expensive. Look for these on sale; some make excellent additions to lunch packing, such as rice pudding in individual servings: Imagine™ puddings, fruit leathers. Other items to look for on sale, for example, are organic prepared sausages, cookies, and canned broth.
- <u>Prepare fruits and vegetables ahead of time-</u>
- Wash fruit before you put it away in refrigerator or in the fruit bowl.
- Cut carrots and celery into finger size for "raw" snacks and lunches.

- Dice onion, carrots, celery, and peppers for use in recipes and freeze in resealable freezer bags to take out portions when ready to use.
- Purchase berries on sale or in season; wash, dry, and place on cookie sheet in freezer. When frozen, place in plastic freezer bags or containers for later use. Can be used for fruit salads or in cooking.
- Purchase melons in season and make melon balls. Melon balls can also be frozen for later use. These work well when placed in plastic bags or containers and covered with white grape juice.
- Freeze grapes for a treat on hot days. These are as much fun for kids as popcicles. Buy when they are on sale.
- Single servings-
- Cookies, muffins, rolls, and bread slices placed into freezer bags for lunches can help in planning the week's lunch menu.
- Leftovers - Only one serving left? Don't toss it...bag it or wrap it for an adult lunch. Adults usually have access to a microwave and can use leftovers on the rotation plan.
- Double batching - Make double portions when making dishes such as casseroles and breads. Freeze one batch to use later.
- Rotation lunches - Cook dinner with the next day's lunches in mind. Use leftovers for lunches the next day on rotation diet.
- Quick cook recipes – Use quick preparation recipes for meals in minutes on work nights.
- Save complicated recipes and bread making for leisure days. Make double batches to freeze for later.
- Labeling - Label frozen items such as meats, casseroles, individual meals, cookies, breads, and muffins. Freeze them with the name of the item, date frozen, and rotation day number it fits. You now know the rotation day to eat it.
- Rice - Brown rice is the best nutritional value. However, brown rice takes about 45 minutes to cook. Some quick recipes (under 30 minutes) are meant to be served over or with rice. Cook a large batch of rice ahead, divide into large freezer bags that hold enough for one meal for your family. Freeze until needed. Thaw when ready, and microwave. Or, pierce the bag in several places and immerse in hot water. Strain off excess water by holding the bag over sink. Water will run out of holes pierced in the bag.

Food Allergies, What Do I Eat Now?

- Meats--
- Buy turkey breasts on sale and slice into cutlets for meals (½ breast will make two meals for four people at about $3 per meal/recipe).
- To make hamburger patties and sausage mix, combine ground meat and spices. Form into patties, sausages or meatloaf shape. Freeze in marked packages. It is ready to thaw and use as needed. Do this when you bring meats home from the store; it saves time later.
- Boil bones and skins of turkey, chicken, fish or meats to make a rich and inexpensive broth. What would have been discarded can be put to good use and save money at the grocery store. Broth made without preservatives and additives can be expensive. If you do not have time that day to make the broth, place the skins and bones in freezer bags. When you need a broth, take them out and boil them. Freeze broth in ½ or 1 cup portions for use in recipes or in large containers for soups. Label well with type of broth, date frozen, and measurement of liquid.
- Make crock-pot meals on busy days. They are time savers as well as energy savers.
- Eggs - If eggs are not an allergen, buy two dozen instead of 1 doz. when they are on sale. Boil six or so to have on hand for quick lunches with salads, as egg salad sandwiches or for quick breakfasts with toast. Mark boiled eggs "B" with a <u>water color</u> marker so you do not make mistakes.
- Breads -
- Freeze all breads, purchased or homemade. On the rotation diet, you can only eat one type of bread for 24 hours, and you cannot repeat that bread for five days. Freezing will prevent spoilage.
- Dried out bread - Do not discard. Make croutons by spreading the bread with margarine or olive oil, garlic, basil, parsley, and oregano. Cut the bread into small cubes with a knife, place on cookie sheet, and bake at 375* for 10 minutes or until lightly golden. Place in plastic bags and use on salads and as casserole toppings. Or use stale bread for bread crumbs in recipes.
- Use dried out bread for "Classic Dressing" recipe in the Recipe section.
- Milks - Make nut milks only in the quantity you will use in 24 hours; you can freeze any remaining milk. Some rice, oat, and nut milks come in 1-liter containers and can be resealed and frozen for use later. Rice Dream™ comes also in juice box sizes for use in lunch boxes and small recipes. I use this size for campouts.

Food Allergies, What Do I Eat Now?

- Baking mixes - Make your own or purchase one if it does not contain an allergen for you. Many use leavening with corn ingredients. It can be a great time saver for basic mixes such as pancakes, waffles, biscuits, piecrusts, and rolls. (Yeast bread recipe mixes usually cannot be premade.)
- Cookies - Mix cookie dough on off days and divide a regular size recipe into four portions. Cook one portion and freeze three portions by forming into fat cigar shapes and wrap in foil or plastic wrap. Slice and bake on that cookie's rotation day.
- In season – Dehydrator - Summer's backyard bounty of tomatoes are fabulous when dried and placed in plastic, airtight containers or put into jars of olive oil and refrigerated. Used in recipes, they give the flavor of sun-dried tomatoes without the cost. Mushrooms can be dried easily, and when reconstituted with water, make a very rich broth for chicken and meat sauces. Dehydrated fruits and vegetables make great snacks.
- Shopping--
- Always shop with a list in hand and menu in mind.
- Never shop when you are hungry- you will purchase things you do not really need.
- Shop at as few places as possible. One health food store and one general grocery store is ideal if you shop every week or two. Running from store to store for specials does not save when you waste an entire day doing it. If you only shop once a month, shopping for specials may pay off, but not if you shop every week.
- Reuse--
- Heavy duty, resealable freezer bags and storage bags can be washed and opened to dry (do not reuse bags that contained meats or meat sandwiches).
- When plastic spoons and forks make their way back home from lunches, wash and reuse them.
- Have friends save those plate type containers that frozen meals come in. You can use them for your frozen single servings and meals for lunches. Cover with foil or place in freezer bags.
- Breakfast Quickies--
- Shakes make a nutritious breakfast. Try one of our shakes in the beverage section of the book.

- Oatmeal- Quick cook or 1 minute oats can be prepared the same way as instant. Just add boiling water to a bowl with 1/3 cup oats. You could add items such as raisins, nuts, coconut, honey or sweetener of the day.
- Pre - boiled eggs and toast make a very quick breakfast. To reheat the egg, place it in hot water for about two minutes before removing the shell.
- Waffles - Strike while the waffle iron is hot! Make double or triple batches. Freeze four individual waffles or by twos in plastic bags with waxed paper between the waffles. To reheat waffles, place them in the toaster on low heat. Top with honey, maple syrup, rice syrup, or fruit.
- Left over pancakes can be frozen with waxed paper in between each and reheated in the microwave <u>carefully</u> until hot.

Food Allergies, What Do I Eat Now?

Cookbook
To
Health

Food Allergies, What Do I Eat Now?

Introduction to Cookbook

With the recipes in this book, we have tried to show you how to work new recipes into your meals and introduce new products and foods into meal planning. This will facilitate reduction of preservatives and additives as well as incorporating new foods into your diet.

The recipes are simple and are easily changed to meet your dietary needs. Read over each recipe before you prepare it to make sure there is not an allergic food for you. Some recipes contain eggs or an egg replacer. Egg Replacer™ by Ener-G is an egg-free product that substitutes well in recipes where eggs are called for as an ingredient. We actually found that Egg Replacer™ worked better to hold Veggie Burgers together than when we prepared the same recipe with an egg.

If you run across a sensitive food for you in a recipe, use your judgement as to how important it is to the recipe and if it can be eliminated. For example, tomatoes seem to be a problem for a lot of people. Of course, vegetable soup can get by without tomatoes as can any vegetable medley or pasta with veggies, but it is difficult to make Tomato Soup without tomatoes. Simply, move on to another recipe. There are so many to choose from, and many of your own that can be changed to meet your needs. Half the fun of cooking is experimenting and the sense of accomplishment when you have a success.

We have had recipe disasters, but we learn from them and move on. One of the most reliable ways to experiment is to start with a tried and true recipe that requires the elimination of only one or two items. You will probably find the results are quite acceptable.

Have fun, and get the entire family involved in food selection and preparation. Our families have learned the importance of reading food labels, asking questions in restaurants, and our health food storeowner has become a wealth of information for us all when we have questions or need items ordered. Our families help prepare foods for freezing and storage, and come up with new ideas of foods to dehydrate for soups and snacks. We believe we all have begun to look at food in a much healthier way.

Occasionally, you will see the notation C/E beside a recipe name. This means the recipe is appropriate for the Cleansing and Elimination phase.

Some recipes also display a day number beside the recipe name. This notation indicates the recipe's ingredients fall within that day's rotation choices. Do not get bogged down by the rotation diet if one or two ingredients do not fall on that rotation day choice. Use those ingredients, and try not to repeat them within the next five days.

Now that you have the information you need to begin your new allergen-free diet, there are a few tips we feel we need to share with you:

- --Do not become too rigid with your rotation diet. Flexibility will help you to succeed with your diet. You are introducing many new foods, and they may take some getting used to.
- --Use as many of your own recipes as you can. Begin by adapting simple recipes that your family enjoys.
- --If you cannot find a particular food that you need for a recipe, try a substitute from within that food family. Ask your grocer to order special items. Tell him how much of one item you expect to use in one month; this will allow him to order it without having it sit on the self for long periods of time.
- --Start with good cooking tools. Some products work better than others. Choose the best quality that you can afford, but keep in mind that replacing a lesser quality item later will merely double the cost of the product. Pots and pans with heat resistant and tolerant handles will go from the stovetop to the oven with fewer cleanups. Baking vessels made of stone will keep meats juicy while allowing vegetables to retain vitamins. The best single source, I have found, of excellent quality kitchen products is The Pampered Chef (see the listing in the shopping guide). You can host a party and receive free merchandise! Many of the items are exclusive to The Pampered Chef product line and cannot be found anywhere else. Besides the baking stone collection, my new favorite product is the Kitchen Spritzer. Fill it with your cooking oil and spray a fine mist of oil on baking pans and stones. Now you can truly have an additive and preservative free cooking spray in the type oil you need.
- --Make as many meals ahead and freeze. This can be done by "double-batching" or by assigning one "cooking" day every few weeks. This will allow you to have nights free from cooking.
- --Do not be discouraged if your recipe does not turn out as expected. These alternative flours can sometimes be sensitive to humidity in the air. We have had many recipes flop through no fault of our own. My husband is usually the culprit. He is notorious for opening the bread-maker before the bread has completed the rising phase, letting the warm air escape. He can also be very impatient with cakes; he feels he must peek.

- --Follow the substitution guide in the chapter on WHEAT. Experiment with new and exotic flours. They are usually a little heavier than traditional flours, but will yield acceptable results.
- --Read every label diligently! Product ingredients can change.
- --Have your child become a part of the meal planning and preparation. They will be more accepting of the new foods when they have helped to make the food choices.
- --Continue to keep a food diary every time you add a new food or try to add an old one back into your diet.

Nutritional Values are given on all recipes in this cookbook. Many people like to have the calories, fat, sodium, and protein content available. These nutritional values were calculated by computer and are accurate for the ingredients listed. We are not nutritionists and emphasize that the responsibility for interpretation of what constitutes a healthy diet lies with the reader.

Appetizers And Dips

Apricot Dipping Sauce C/E
Serves 8

- 10 ounce jar Sorrell Ridge Spreadable Fruit, Apricot
- 1 Tablespoon apple cider vinegar
- 1/4 cup apple juice

Heat all ingredients and stir until smooth. Do not boil. Serve warm with meatballs, chicken strips, and shrimp.

Variations:
ORANGE DIPPING SAUCE - Use Sorrell Ridge Spreadable Fruit--Orange Marmalade flavored.

RASPBERRY DIPPING SAUCE - Use Sorrell Ridge Spreadable Fruit--Raspberry flavored.

Per serving: 74.8 Calories; 0.0g Fat (0.1% calories from fat); 0.0g Protein; 18.7g Carbohydrate; 0mg Cholesterol; 0mg Sodium

Cranberry Dipping Sauce
Serves 8

- 2 cups cranberries, fresh
- 1/2 cup beet sugar
- 1 small orange, peeled-sectioned
- 2 Tablespoons orange zest, grated

Place orange sectons with juice and cranberries in a medium sauce pan. Heat until fruit begins to boil. Add sugar and turn heat to low. Simmer, sitrring frequently, until berries are popped (about 7 minutes). Add orange zest, stir well. If sauce is too thick for dipping, add 1/2 cup cranberry or apple juice. Place in decorative bowl and serve warm for dipping meatballs, turkey strips, chicken strips, and shrimp.

Per serving: 63.6 Calories; 0.1g Fat (0.6% calories from fat); 0.2g Protein; 17.1g Carbohydrate; 0mg Cholesterol; 0mg Sodium

Honey Mustard Dip
Serves 6

- 1/4 cup canola mayonnaise
- 1/4 cup coarse mustard
- 1/4 cup honey
- 2 Tablespoons orange juice, from frozen concentrate

Mix all ingredients thoroughly and serve with fresh vegetables as dip, or with chicken strips.

Per serving: 128.1 Calories; 8.8g Fat (59.1% calories from fat); 0.9g Protein; 12.9g Carbohydrate; 3mg Cholesterol; 203mg Sodium

Mustard Dip Day 5
Serves 6

- 1/4 cup canola mayonnaise
- 1/4 cup prepared mustard
- 3 Tablespoons orange juice, from frozen concentrate

Mix all ingrdients and stir well. Serve with vegetables or chicken strips.

Per serving: 84.3 Calories; 8.4g Fat (90.5% calories from fat); 0.5g Protein; 1.5g Carbohydrate; 3mg Cholesterol; 192mg Sodium

Cucumber Rounds with "Cheese" and Dill
Serves 20

- 1 medium cucumber
- 4 ounces almond cheese, sliced
- 2 sprigs dill, fresh

This quick and easy appetizer is great for when unexpected guests arrive.
Peel cucumber and slice into 1/3" thick slices. Top with a thin slice of almond cheese. Place a small piece of dill on top of cheese. These can be arranged on a platter as is or placed on slices of bread that have been cut into shapes with cookie cutters.

Per serving: 16.9 Calories; 0.7g Fat (39.4% calories from fat); 1.4g Protein; 1.2g Carbohydrate; 0mg Cholesterol; 58mg Sodium

Hot Wing Dip
Serves 8

- 1 cup canola mayonnaise
- 1 Tablespoon hot pepper sauce
- 1 teaspoon paprika, hungarian
- 1/8 teaspoon white pepper
- 1/4 teaspoon salt

Mix ingredients well until smooth. Refrigerate a few hours to allow flavors to blend before serving.
Serve as dip with Spicy Chicken Wings, and as dressing for Aloha Burger, and sandwiches.

Per serving: 221.1 Calories; 24.0g Fat (99.5% calories from fat); 0.0g Protein; 0.2g Carbohydrate; 10mg Cholesterol; 267mg Sodium

Spicy Chicken Wings
Serves 6

- 3 Tablespoons hot pepper sauce
- 2 Tablespoons canola margarine, melted
- 1 teaspoon paprika, hungarian
- 2 pounds chicken wings, split, without tips

Mix together hot pepper sauce, margarine, and paprika. Set aside. Wash and drain chicken wings on paper towel. Cut at all joints, and discard wing tips. Place wing pieces in large bowl or resealable plastic bag. Add sauce and mix. Marinate for 30 minutes. Cook on grill over low heat or bake at 400 degrees for 20 minutes, then broil until brown and crispy. (20-30 wings)
Serve with Hot Wing Dip.

Per serving: 216.4 Calories; 16.8g Fat (71.0% calories from fat); 15.0g Protein; 0.4g Carbohydrate; 63mg Cholesterol; 100mg Sodium

Shrimp Butter
Serves 24

- 1/4 pound shrimp, peeled, cooked
- 1/4 cup margarine, softened
- 1 teaspoon dijon mustard, natural
- 1 teaspoon lemon juice
- 1/4 teaspoon garlic, minced
- 1 Tablespoon minced parsley
- 1/8 teaspoon salt
- 1/8 teaspoon white pepper
- 1/8 teaspoon celery seed, ground

Chop cooked shrimp very fine and place in a medium bowl. Add margarine and all remaining ingredients. Mix well. Spoon into small decorative serving dishes and cover with plastic wrap. Chill 8 hours. Serve with small toast triangles.

Per serving: 22.3 Calories; 2.0g Fat (80.1% calories from fat); 1.0g Protein; 0.1g Carbohydrate; 7mg Cholesterol; 43mg Sodium

Avocado Dip/Salsa
Serves 8

- 2 medium avocado, ripe
- 2 Tablespoons lemon juice
- 2 cups water
- 1 small tomato, chopped
- 1 Tablespoon onion, minced
- 1/2 teaspoon garlic salt
- 1/2 teaspoon salt
- 1 Tablespoon olive oil
- 1 Tablespoon cilantro, fresh chopped fine

Peel, seed and dice avocado into small pieces. Place in a bowl with water and lemon juice to prevent from turning brown. Soak in lemon water for 1 minute. Drain well. Place in a medium bowl with tomatoes, onion, cilantro (1 teaspoon dried cilantro can be substituted for fresh), garlic salt, salt, and oil. Toss gently to mix all ingredients well without mashing avocado.

Serve with any rice cracker, quinoa chips, or organic potato chips.

This salsa is also great served over baked fish fillets, seafood, and chicken.

Per serving: 79.6 Calories; 7.5g Fat (77.6% calories from fat); 0.9g Protein; 3.9g Carbohydrate; 0mg Cholesterol; 146mg Sodium

Black Bean Salsa
Serves 10

1	can black beans, packed in water
2	cups tomato, chopped
1	medium jalapeno, chopped fine
1/4	cup onion, chopped fine
1/4	cup bell pepper, chopped fine
1	clove garlic, chopped fine
2	Tablespoons parsley, dried
1/4	cup vinegar, of choice
	dash red pepper
	salt and pepper, to taste

In blender, puree 1/2 cup black beans, then mix with all other ingredients. Cover and chill 1 hour. Serve with chips, bite size vegetable pieces, or toasted bread pieces.

Per serving: 79.7 Calories; 0.4g Fat (4.7% calories from fat); 4.8g Protein; 15.2g Carbohydrate; 0mg Cholesterol; 23mg Sodium

Dill Dip
Serves 24

- 1 cup canola mayonnaise, mayo of choice
- 1 Tablespoon prepared mustard
- 1 Tablespoon fresh dill, chopped fine
- dash cayenne pepper
- 4 tablespoons lemon juice
- 1 teaspoon pepper
- 1 teaspoon lemon zest, grated
- 1/2 teaspoon garlic salt
- 1 teaspoon parsley, chopped fine

Combine all ingredients. Stir well. Cover and store in refrigerator for at least 3 hours before serving.

Serve as a dip for chips, shrimp, fresh raw vegetable pieces or toasted bread wedges. Also makes a great dressing for tuna or salmon salads (It should be thinned with 1/4 cup vinegar of choice and 1/4 cup water for use as a salad dressing).

Per serving: 75.1 Calories; 8.0g Fat (97.2% calories from fat); 0.1g Protein; 0.4g Carbohydrate; 3mg Cholesterol; 76mg Sodium

Humus Dip
Serves 8

 1   can chickpeas, drained
 1   clove garlic, minced
 1/2 teaspoon onion flakes
 2   Tablespoons oil, oil of the day
     salt and pepper, to taste
 1   Tablespoon parsley, flakes

In food processor or blender, process all ingredients until creamy consistency. Serve with Quinoa Rounds or toasted bread triangles. If you want to serve this as a dip for chips, simply thin with chicken broth one Tablespoon at a time until desired consistency is achieved.

Variations - For Spicy Humus--1 cup pureed chickpeas
    1 Tbs. Cajun Spice Mix
    1 Tbs. dehydrated onion

94.6 Calories; 1.6g Fat; 5.0 Protein; 16.0g Carbohydrate; 0mg Cholesterol; 91 mg Sodium

Humus and "Bacon" Spread--
    1 1/2 cups pureed chickpeas
    1/4 teaspoon salt
    2 Tbs. peanut oil
    1/4 cup smoked tenderloin, finely chopped

174.8 Calories; 5.9g Fat; 8.7g Protein; 22.8g Carbohydrate; 5mg Cholesterol; 79mg Sodium

Nutritional analysis below is for Humus Dip. Other recipes are as shown above.

Per serving: 123.1 Calories; 4.9g Fat (35.1% calories from fat); 5.0g Protein; 15.6g Carbohydrate; 0mg Cholesterol; 8mg Sodium

Avocado Quesadillas
Serves 6

1	recipe Quinoa Tortillas, prepared
1	large avocado, peeled and diced
1/2	cup onion, chopped fine
1/4	cup black olives, sliced-drained well
1/2	teaspoon cilantro, finely chopped
1	teaspoon garlic, minced
2	ounces almond cheese, grated
1	teaspoon lemon juice
1	cup water

Preheat oven to broil, or use toaster oven. In a bowl, mix water and lemon juice and place diced avocado in lemon water to soak for 1 minute. This will help prevent the avocado from turning brown after cutting. Drain well and pat dry with paper towel. In a large bowl, combine avocado, onion, olives, cilantro, garlic, and almond cheese. Toss to combine ingredients. Place 2-3 Tablespoons of filling on 6 of the quinoa tortillas. Place another tortilla on top of each. Broil in oven or toaster oven until golden. Slice each Quesadilla into 6-8 pieces. Serve with your favorite salsa as an appetizer.

Per serving: 102.0 Calories; 6.3g Fat (53.2% calories from fat); 3.4g Protein; 9.1g Carbohydrate; 0mg Cholesterol; 245mg Sodium

"Cheese" Straws and Crackers
Serves 20

- 8 ounces Rice Slice, or almond cheese
- 1/4 cup margarine, or oil of the day
- 3/4 cup rice flour
- 1/4 cup amaranth flour
- 1/8 teaspoon red pepper
- 1/4 teaspoon garlic salt
- 1/4 teaspoon salt
- 3 Tablespoons water

Makes about 40 crackers or straws.
Preheat oven to 350 degrees.
Grate cheese (yellow Rice Slice or almond cheese works well).
In large bowl, cut together margarine and flours. Add cheese and spices. Stir well to incorporate evenly. Add water one Tablespoon at a time. If oil was used instead of margarine, less water may be needed. Dough should be crumbly and dry. Dough is ready when a small amount placed in your hand and squeezed stays together.
Place about 1 1/2 teaspoons of dough in the palm of the hand and squeeze to form a ball (for crackers) or a 1 1/2" log (for straw shape). Flatten round cracker shape with fingers into the palm of the hand. (Leave in log shape for cheese straws). Place on ungreased cookie sheet or baking stone. Bake at 350 degrees for 15-17 minutes. Do not allow to brown.
These are great for appetizers and snacks. Children love the crackers spread with peanut butter. Pack plain for lunches.
Store in resealable plastic bags or airtight containers.

Per serving: 51.1 Calories; 36.5g Fat (48.7% calories from fat); 68.8g Protein; 17.7g Carbohydrate; 0mg Cholesterol; 3,343mg Sodium

Herbed Savory Bread
Serves 20

- 10 slices bread, of choice
- 4 Tablespoons canola margarine
- 1/4 cup parsley, fresh minced
- 1/4 cup basil, fresh minced
- 1/4 cup green onion, minced

Cut each bread slice into 4 pieces or use cookie cutter for desired shapes. Toast lightly on both sides in toaster oven or under broiler. Cool. Spread each piece of bread with margarine in thin layer on one side. Mix herbs together and spread out evenly on plate. Dip margarine side of bread in herb mix to cover margarine with herbs.
 Serve as an appetizer.
These are especially good with a shrimp placed on top.
This can also be used as a filling for finger sandwiches. Use fresh bread and do not toast when using for sandwiches.

Per serving: 58.1 Calories; 2.7g Fat (41.7% calories from fat); 1.3g Protein; 7.2g Carbohydrate; 0mg Cholesterol; 95mg Sodium

Mini Pizzas
Serves 20

- 1 recipe Individual Pizzas
- 4 ounces almond cheese, grated
- 1 medium tomato, sliced thin
- 1/4 cup black olives, sliced
- 1/4 cup onion, chopped fine
- 1/4 cup fresh oregano, leaves
- dash salt and pepper

Prepare dough according to recipe instructions. Form into 20 balls and flatten into 3" rounds onto lightly oiled foil lined cookie sheets. Allow to rise according to directions and then bake at 400 degrees for 3 minutes. Remove from oven. Top with tomato (may need to cut each tomato slice into 4 pieces and place on paper towel to remove excess water from tomato). Add cheese, onion, olives and oregano leaves. Return to oven for 3-4 minutes just until cheese melts. These are wonderful for snacks or appetizers. Keep covered, as rice pastries dry out quickly.

Per serving: 35.9 Calories; 1.2g Fat (29.9% calories from fat); 1.8g Protein; 4.6g Carbohydrate; 0mg Cholesterol; 98mg Sodium

Quinoa Chips   C/E
Serves 6

- 1 recipe Quinoa Tortillas, makes 12 tortillas
- 1/4 teaspoon garlic salt
- 1/4 teaspoon salt
- dash cayenne pepper, optional

Prheat oven to 400 degrees.
Prepare Quinoa Tortillas according to recipe. Cut into wedges (about 6 per tortilla). Place on a baking stone or thick cookie sheet. Sprinkle with spices. Bake at 400 degrees for 10-12 minutes or until dry and crisp. May take longer depending on the thickness of the baking sheet and tortilla.
Serve with any dip or salsa recipe. This is especially good with Black Bean Salsa.

This treat is low in fat, but high in flavor.

Per serving: 28.5 Calories; 0.7g Fat (21.3% calories from fat); 0.6g Protein; 5.1g Carbohydrate; 0mg Cholesterol; 137mg Sodium

Quinoa Rounds (crackers) C/E
Serves 16

- 2/3 cup quinoa flour
- 1/3 cup tapioca flour
- 1/4 cup margarine, or oil of the day
- 1/4 teaspoon salt
- 1/4 teaspoon pepper
- 1/4 teaspoon garlic salt
- 1/4 teaspoon basil
- 1/2 Tablespoon parsley, dried
- 3 Tablespoons water
- 1/4 cup sesame seeds

Preheat oven to 350 degrees.
In a large bowl, combine margarine and flours. Cut together with fork until crumbly. Add spices and sesame seeds and mix well. Add water one Tablespoon at a time (if oil was used instead of margarine, you may only need to add 2 of the Tablespoons of water). The mix should be very dry, but form a ball when a small amount is placed in the palm of your hand and squeezed together. Place about 1 1/2 teaspoon of dough in the palm of your hand and squeeze together until the dough forms a small ball. Press the ball into the palm with your fingers until very flat. Place on ungreased cookie sheet or baking stone. For best results and a crisp cracker, use a baking stone. Bake at 350 degrees for 15-17 minutes. Do not allow crackers to brown. Remove immediately from sheet and place on a wire rack to cool.
Store in plastic bags or airtight containers.
Makes 32 crackers. This recipe doubles well.
Use these for appetizers, dips and spreads.

Per serving: 67.5 Calories; 4.5g Fat (58.3% calories from fat); 1.6g Protein; 5.7g Carbohydrate; 0mg Cholesterol; 70mg Sodium

Sesame Amaranth Crackers Day 3
Serves 16

- 1 cup amaranth flour
- 1/4 cup margarine, or oil of the day
- 1/4 teaspoon salt
- 1/4 cup sesame seeds
- 1 Tablespoon orange zest
- 3 Tablespoons water

Makes 32 crackers.
Preheat oven to 350 degrees.
In a medium bowl, combine margarine and flour. Cut together until crumbly. Add salt, orange zest, and sesame seeds and mix well. Add water 1 tablespoon at a time (if oil was used instead of margarine, you may only need to add 2 tablespoons of the water). The mix should be very dry, but form a ball when a small amount is placed in the palm of your hand and squeezed together. Place about 1 1/2 teaspoon of dough in the palm of your hand and squeeze together until the dough forms a ball. Press the ball into the palm with your fingers until very flat. Place on ungreased cookie sheet or baking stone. Bake at 350 degrees for 15-17 minutes. Do not allow crackers to brown. Remove immediately from cookie sheet and place on a wire rack to cool.
Store in plastic bags or airtight containers.
Makes 32 crackers. This recipe doubles well.
Use these for appetizers, dips and spreads.

Per serving: 84.7 Calories; 4.9g Fat (50.5% calories from fat); 2.4g Protein; 8.4g Carbohydrate; 0mg Cholesterol; 70mg Sodium

Beverages

Mulled Cranberry-Apple Cider
Serves 10

- 24 ounces apple cider, all natural
- 24 ounces cranberry juice, all natural
- 1/4 cup honey, or beet sugar
- 1/2 teaspoon cloves, ground
- 1 teaspoon cinnamon, ground
- 2 whole cinnamon sticks, optional

Heat apple cider and cranberry juice in large saucepan. Add honey and spices to hot juices. Let simmer for 2 minutes. Serve hot in mugs.

This makes a great holiday punch for guests of all ages. For children, allow the cider to cool to just warm before serving.

Per serving: 104.6 Calories; 0.3g Fat (2.1% calories from fat); 0.2g Protein; 27.1g Carbohydrate; 0mg Cholesterol; 5mg Sodium

Hot Cocoa
Serves 1

- 6 ounces almond milk, or milk of choice
- 1 teaspoon cocoa powder, or carob powder
- 1 1/2 teaspoons beet sugar

Pour almond milk into a small saucepan. Add cocoa powder, and sugar and stir to mix. Warm over low heat until hot and sugar has dissolved. Sugar and cocoa will not mix well until milk warms. Serve hot.

Per serving: 95.0 Calories; 2.1g Fat (19.1% calories from fat); 1.9g Protein; 18.5g Carbohydrate; 0mg Cholesterol; 75mg Sodium

Russian Tea
Serves 10

- 6 single tea bags, of choice
- 2 quarts water
- 1/2 cup beet sugar
- 3 cups orange juice
- 1/3 cup lemon juice
- 1/2 teaspoon cinnamon, or 2 cinnamon stick
- 1/2 teaspoon cloves, or 3 whole cloves

Boil 2 quarts water. Place 6 tea bags, cinnamon, and cloves in water and steep for 10 minutes. Remove tea bags, and stir in sugar to dissolve. Add orange juice and lemon juice. Reheat tea and serve hot in cups.

Per serving: 76.9 Calories; 0.2g Fat (2.0% calories from fat); 0.7g Protein; 19.3g Carbohydrate; 0mg Cholesterol; 8mg Sodium

Almond Tea
Serves 8

  2   quarts water
  6   single tea bags, of choice
1/2 cup beet sugar, or honey
1/3 cup lemon juice
  1   teaspoon almond extract

Bring 2 quarts of water to boil. Remove from heat and add tea bags. Steep for 10 minutes. Strain tea or remove bags. Add sweetener and stir until disssolved. Add lemon juice and flavoring. Serve cold over ice, or reheat and serve hot in cups.

Makes 8 eight ounce servings oe 16 four ounce cups of hot tea.

Per serving: 54.1 Calories; 0.0g Fat (0.2% calories from fat); 0.2g Protein; 14.3g Carbohydrate; 0mg Cholesterol; 9mg Sodium

Lemonade
Serves 4

- 32 ounces water
- 6 medium lemons
- 1 lemon peel
- 4 Tablespoons beet sugar

Place room temperature water in a large pitcher (room temperature water will allow sugar to dissolve easier). Roll lemons on the counter with palm of hand applying firm pressure. This breaks up the lemon pulp so they will be easier to juice. Cut lemons in half and squeeze juice into pitcher of water (to get the most juice from a lemon or lime, insert a large spoon into the lemon half and turn spoon to release all juices). Cut one of the squeezed lemons into rings and place in pitcher with juice and water. Add beet sugar and sitr until dissolved. Serve over ice. Garnish with mint leaves if desired.

Per serving: 79.2 Calories; 0.5g Fat (3.3% calories from fat); 2.0g Protein; 30.0g Carbohydrate; 0mg Cholesterol; 12mg Sodium

Fruit Punch
Serves 30

- 2   10 ounce pkg frozen strawberries, unsweetened
- 3   cups apricot nectar, unsweetened
- 3   cups water
- 1   cup lemon juice, about 6 lemons
- 1   6 ounce can frozen orange juice concentrate, undiluted
- 1   cup beet sugar
- 36 ounces soda water, or seltzer water

Puree strawberries in small batches in the blender.
Heat 3 cups wter just until warm. Add sugar and stir to dissolve. Cool to room temperature.
In a large punch bowl, add strawberries, sugar water, and all ingredients except soda water. Stir well. Chill in pitchers until ready to serve. Add soda water just before serving.

Keep cold with a fruited ice ring.

Per serving: 65.6 Calories; 0.1g Fat (0.8% calories from fat); 0.4g Protein; 17.3g Carbohydrate; 0mg Cholesterol; 2mg Sodium

Fruited Ice Ring For Punch
Serves 30

3 1/2	cups apple juice, or white grape
6	whole strawberries
1	whole kiwi fruit, peeled and sliced
1	whole lemon, cut into rings
20	grapes
1/3	cup berries, of choice
	sprig fresh mint

Using a bundt-type ring pan, freeze 2 cups of the apple juice or white grape juice. After ring is frozen, arrange fruits of choice over ice. Pour remaining juice over fresh fruit and refreeze. When ready to serve, place bundt pan in warm water for 30 seconds and invert into empty punch bowl. Fill punch bowl with punch of choice.

This allows the punch to stay cold and will not dilute the punch with water! The fresh fruit and mint add garnish to individual cups of punch as it melts.

Per serving: 26.7 Calories; 0.2g Fat (5.1% calories from fat); 0.3g Protein; 6.8g Carbohydrate; 0mg Cholesterol; 1mg Sodium

Cranberry Delight C/E
Serves 24

1   can cranberry juice, concentrate
3   cans water
1   can pineapple juice, concentrate
3   cans water
1   liter soda water, or sparkling water
    sprig mint, garnish

Use only unsweetened frozen juice concentrates. Mix all juices and water in pitchers and chill. Pour into a punch bowl and add soda water or mineral water just before serving. Keep chilled with an ice ring.

Makes 24 four ounce servings.

Per serving: 11.8 Calories; 0.0g Fat (1.5% calories from fat); 0.0g Protein;
             3.0g Carbohydrate; 0mg Cholesterol; 3mg Sodium

Banana Shake
Serves 1

- 1 whole banana, peeled
- 4 whole strawberries, stem removed
- 1 cup almond milk, or rice milk
- 1/4 teaspoon vanilla, optional
- 1 Tablespoon honey
- 1 Tablespoon orange juice, frozen concentrate, undiluted
- 4 ice cubes

Place all ingredients in a blender. Replace lid and blend on high for 1 minute. Serve immediately. This makes a wonderful breakfast shake as well as a nutritious afternoon snack.
Try other variations of fruits and juices.

Per serving: 420.0 Calories; 5.0g Fat (9.8% calories from fat); 6.6g Protein; 96.0g Carbohydrate; 0mg Cholesterol; 110mg Sodium

Frostee
Serves 1

2/3   cup Peaches and Cream Rice Milk Ice Cream
2/3   cup soda water, lemon-natural

Mix well and enjoy this frostie Frostee delight. Serve with spoon and straw. Yum. Can use the same amount of rice, almond or soy milk in place of the spritzer with any flavor of sherbert or rice milk ice cream recipes to make a Frostee. A great way to cool a hot summer day!

Per serving: 183.1 Calories; 9.7g Fat (46.0% calories from fat); 1.3g Protein; 24.3g Carbohydrate; 0mg Cholesterol; 34mg Sodium

Pina Colada Shake
Serves 4

1/2   cup pineapple chunks in juice
1/3   cup pineapple juice
1/2   banana, peeled
 1   cup coconut milk, unsweetened
 5   ice cubes

In blender, combine all ingredients and puree for 1-2 minutes until ice has crushed. Makes four 4 ounce servings.

This is a great shake for breakfast with a low fat muffin.

Per serving: 176.9 Calories; 14.4g Fat (68.4% calories from fat); 1.7g Protein; 13.3g Carbohydrate; 0mg Cholesterol; 10mg Sodium

Mango Smooth Day 1
Serves 1

- 1 whole mango, peeled-seeded
- 3/4 cup white grape juice
- 5 ice cubes

Place all ingredients in the blender and blend on high until ice has broken down (about 1 minute). Serve immediately.

Substitution: 3/4 cup mango juice puree
　　　　　　 1/2 cup white grape juice
　　　　　　 5 ice cubes.

Per serving: 208.6 Calories; 0.5g Fat (2.2% calories from fat); 1.8g Protein; 52.7g Carbohydrate; 0mg Cholesterol; 12mg Sodium

Peach Strawberry Freeze Day 2
Serves 1

- 5 whole strawberries, frozen
- 1 cup frozen peach slices
- 3/4 cup almond milk, vanilla flavor

Place all ingredients in a blender and blend on high until ice has broken down (about 1 minute). Serve immediately.

Per serving: 512.6 Calories; 4.8g Fat (7.8% calories from fat); 7.3g Protein; 120.3g Carbohydrate; 0mg Cholesterol; 97mg Sodium

Peach Float Punch
Serves 12

- 16 ounces cranberry juice, unsweetened
- 16 ounces apple juice, unsweetened
- 1 pound pkg. frozen peach slices
- 16 ounces soda water

32 ounces cran-apple juice may be substituted.
In a punch bowl, combine juice and frozen peaches. Add soda water just before serving to retain carbonation.

Per serving: 74.9 Calories; 0.1g Fat (1.5% calories from fat); 0.3g Protein; 18.9g Carbohydrate; 0mg Cholesterol; 5mg Sodium

Raspberry Chill   Day 2   C/E
Serves 1

- 1/2   cup raspberries, fresh or frozen
- 3/4   cup apple juice
- 5   ice cubes

Combine all ingredients in blender and blend on high for 1 minute or until ice is broken down.
Serve for breakfast with muffins, or as a delicious cool summer treat.

Per serving: 116.3 Calories; 0.5g Fat (3.9% calories from fat); 0.7g Protein; 28.6g Carbohydrate; 0mg Cholesterol; 9mg Sodium

Sunny Shake   Day 3
Serves 1

- 1/4   cup frozen orange juice concentrate, unsweetened
- 2   ounces coconut milk-lite, unsweetened
- 5   ice cubes
- 1/2   cup water

Combine all ingredients in a blender and blend on high for 1 minute or until ice is broken down. Serve for breakfast with frozen muffin for a quick breakfast.

Per serving: 166.6 Calories; 5.2g Fat (28.2% calories from fat); 1.7g Protein; 28.1g Carbohydrate; 0mg Cholesterol; 15mg Sodium

Red, White and Blue Freeze   Day 5 C/E
Serves 1

- 1 cup cranberry juice, unsweetened
- 1/2 cup blueberries, frozen
- 5 ice cubes
- 1 Tablespoon rice syrup

Combine all ingredients in a blender and blend on high for 1 minute. Garnish with blueberries.
Serve immediately.

Per serving: 226.5 Calories; 0.5g Fat (2.0% calories from fat); 0.5g Protein; 57.0g Carbohydrate; 0mg Cholesterol; 14mg Sodium

Tropical Delight Shake Day 4
Serves 1

- 1 whole banana, peeled
- 1 cup almond milk, or milk of day
- 2 Tablespoons pineapple juice, frozen concentrate, undiluted
- 4 ice cubes

Place all ingredients in a blender. Replace lid and blend on high for 1 minute. Serve immediately. This Makes a wonderful breakfast shake as well as a nutritious afternoon snack. Try other variations of fruits and juices.

Per serving: 222.6 Calories; 2.9g Fat (11.2% calories from fat); 3.2g Protein; 48.3g Carbohydrate; 0mg Cholesterol; 104mg Sodium

Breads
And
Baked Goods

Food Allergies, What Do I Eat Now?

Introduction to Breads

What!? No pancakes, cookies, cakes or bread? What is buckwheat? What is spelt? What is quinoa? You want me to eat what?

Relax. It is not as catastrophic as you might imagine! We love breads and all those baked goods, too. We knew we could not survive without those comfort foods. So, here they are. They are a little different from what you are accustomed, but they are delicious in their own right. It takes determination on your part to find the acceptable alternatives and satisfy your palate.

We have been brainwashed into thinking that wheat flour is the only source of flour for making bread, when in reality there are many. Granted, wheat flour has been process, bleached, and "enriched" to make it lighter and rise higher. But, with the processing, bleaching, and "enriching", most of the nutritional value has been lost. Here, you will find many alternatives to the scrumptious sandwich bread, hamburger bun, or pizza crust. Bread and baked goods can be one of the biggest challenges to substitute, but work with these recipes (on low humid days) and we are sure you will find alternatives that work for you. There are also many alternative flour breads to be found in health food stores and large grocery stores, but read labels diligently!

Cookies? Yes, we have cookies. Not only cookies, but cakes and pies, too. All those yummy foods you thought you might have to learn to do without are right here in this book waiting for you to discover. We hope we are able to help you through the rough times and give you encouragement. Changes do not have to be difficult to make. It requires that you be determined to make a change so that you feel better and return your life to normal. You can do it!

<u>Alternative flours</u> – The section on wheat in Chapter 5 discusses the variety of flours available and the conversions of ratio to wheat flour.

Food Allergies, What Do I Eat Now?

Can you make your own flours? Sure! Sometimes you may find quinoa, millet or oats, but you cannot, always, find the "flour" for these grains. Do not despair. If you have a blender or food processor, you can make flour. For best results, process no more that 1-cup at a time in as many batches as needed.

Oat flour – Use dry rolled oats. 1 ¼ cup oats yields about 1 cup oat flour.
Depending on your recipe and preference, you can process until you have fine flour or just until the oats are coarsely ground.

Millet flour – Use either finger millet or pearl millet for grinding flour.
1 ¼ cup millet yields about 1 cup flour.
Blend or process until you have fine flour. Millet is good for use in combination with other flours to make a variety of breads, biscuits and muffins.

Amaranth flour – Amaranth seeds (grain) are usually found in health food stores and can be ground into flour that we use in cakes, cookies, and breads.
1 ¼ cup amaranth seed yields 1-cup flour.

Quinoa flour – Quinoa has a wonderful nutty flavor and texture similar to cornmeal. As a matter of fact, we have included a Quinoa Bread that is as close to cornbread as we have tasted. We also have Quinoa Tortillas.
Quinoa seeds have a natural bitter coating that needs to be rinsed before grinding. Rinse the seeds in cold water, drain thoroughly, and place in a single layer on paper towels. An oven that

has been warmed and turned off is a good place to dry the seeds. When they are completely dry, you can process as you would any other grain.

1 ¼ cup quinoa seeds yield about 1-cup flour.

A mail order list in the back of the book is an excellent source for ordering alternative grains.

<u>Leavening-</u> Most commercial leavening (rising agents) contain corn starch, wheat, and/or aluminum. You may be sensitive to the corn or wheat, and aluminum may have health risks that you do not want to take.

    The least reactive rising agent we have found is a homemade variety. For each 2 cups of flour in the batter, use 1-teaspoon cream of tartar and 1 teaspoon baking soda. Cream of tartar and baking soda can be found in the spice/baking section of your grocery store. Cream of tartar is a by-product of the wine making process. It may cause a reaction for those allergic to grapes. This rising agent is the best we have come across.

Rice Potato Bread

Breadmaker or Conventional Oven Recipe

Serves 14

- 1 1/4 cups potato starch flour
- 2 cups white rice flour
- 2 teaspoons guar gum
- 2 teaspoons egg replacer
- 1 1/2 teaspoons salt
- 2 Tablespoons honey, generous
- 1 package yeast
- 4 Tablespoons canola margarine
- 1 2/3 cups rice milk

Breadmaker: Measure dry ingredients in large mixing bowl and mix well. Set aside. Place honey and yeast into breadmaker. Measure milk and canola margarine into microwave measuring cup and heat in the microwave to very warm, but not hot (hot liquids will kill yeast). Use settings for light bread. This recipe is best if second kneading is eliminated. This can be done on newer machines by turning the machine off after the first kneading is complete. Next, allow the bread to rise for 35-40 minutes or until risen 1/2 to double size. Set breadmaker for bake only. Check your breadmaker instruction booklet.

Oven Method: Preheat oven for five minutes only on 150 degrees, no longer. Turn oven off. Follow the above directions mixing honey and yeast into a large mixing bowl. Mix either by hand or by mixer. Very little mixing is required. Place dough in greased baking pan. Place in the warm oven to rise. Make sure the oven is not too hot. You just want the oven warm. Turn oven light on for continuous warmth. Set timer for 30 - 45 minutes rising time. Do not open oven door. When rising time is up, do not open oven door, but set the oven on bake at 350 degrees for 50 minutes. Start checking for doneness with a toothpick after 45 minutes baking time.

Per serving: 279.2 Calories; 3.7g Fat (11.8% calories from fat); 1.8g Protein; 61.1g Carbohydrate; 0mg Cholesterol; 303mg Sodium

Quinoa Bread (Mock Cornbread) C/E
Serves 8

- 1 cup quinoa flour
- 1/2 cup rice flour
- 1/3 cup potato starch flour
- 1 1/3 teaspoons egg replacer, =1 egg
- 3/4 teaspoon cream of tartar
- 3/4 teaspoon baking soda
- 1 1/3 cups rice milk
- 1 teaspoon salt
- 2 Tablespoons oil

Preheat oven to 400 degrees. Heat 6"-8" iron skillet with 2 Tablespoon oil in oven for 4-5 minutes until hot.

In a large bowl, combine quinoa, rice flour, potato starch flour, egg replacer, cream of tartar, baking soda, and salt and mix thoroughly. Stir in rice milk and hot oil from the skillet until no lumps are present. Do not over work batter. Pour into iron skillet and bake at 400 degrees for 30-35 minutes. Edges should be lightly golden. Cut into 8 pieces and serve with a meal as you would cornbread.

We especially like this bread with soups and chili.

Per serving: 275.8 Calories; 5.1g Fat (16.3% calories from fat); 3.6g Protein; 55.8g Carbohydrate; 0mg Cholesterol; 437mg Sodium

Brown Rice Flour Bread

Conventional Oven Recipe
No Yeast

Serves 16

1 1/8	cups brown rice flour
1 1/4	cups potato starch flour
1	cup white rice flour
2	teaspoons guar gum
3	teaspoons egg replacer
1	teaspoon salt
3/4	teaspoon cream of tartar
1 3/4	teaspoons baking soda
1 2/3	cups rice milk
2	tablespoons beet sugar
1/3	cup canola oil

Mix all dry ingredients together. Stir to add air. Set aside. Mix milk, oil, and sugar. Stir until sugar is dissolved. Combine the two mixtures. The dough will be very stiff. Place in a greased bread pan. Bake at 350 degrees for 35 minutes or until done when tested with a toothpick. Cool completely before removing from pan.

Per serving: 288.0 Calories; 5.2g Fat (15.8% calories from fat); 1.5g Protein; 60.7g Carbohydrate; 0mg Cholesterol; 319mg Sodium

Amaranth Bread Day 3
Serves 8

- 2 cups amaranth flour
- 2 Tablespoons tapioca flour
- 2 teaspoons baking soda
- 1 teaspoon cream of tartar
- 1/2 teaspoon salt
- 1 1/3 teaspoons egg replacer, =1 egg
- 1/4 teaspoon pepper
- 1/2 teaspoon dill seed
- 2 Tablespoons dried onions, minced
- 1 1/2 cups nut milk
- 1/3 cup coconut oil

Preheat oven to 375 degrees.
Combine all dry ingredients in a large bowl. Mix well. Add oil and milk and stir well. Spoon batter into an oiled loaf pan. Bake for one hour at 375 degrees until wooden pick inserted in the middle comes out clean. Remove from loaf pan and allow to cool completely before slicing. Nut milk can be replaced with unsweetened- lite coconut milk.

Per serving: 354.9 Calories; 12.7g Fat (31.2% calories from fat); 7.5g Protein; 55.8g Carbohydrate; 0mg Cholesterol; 510mg Sodium

Banana Nut Bread
Serves 10

1 1/2	cups white rice flour
1/2	cup potato starch flour
1	teaspoon baking soda
1	teaspoon cream of tartar
1	teaspoon salt
2 2/3	teaspoons egg replacer, =2 eggs
1/2	cup beet sugar
1/4	cup safflower oil, or oil of choice
1/2	cup almond milk
2	medium bananas, very ripe
1/3	cup pecans, or nut of the day

Preheat oven to 350 degrees.
In a large bowl, combine flours, baking soda, cream of tartar, salt, egg replacer, and pecans. Stir together until well mixed. In another bowl, mash bananas and sugar together. Add oil and milk. Add 1/2 of the flour mixture to banana mix and stir well. Add remaining flour mixture and stir until all dry ingredients are moistened. Spoon into a greased or oiled loaf pan and bake at 350 degrees for 55-60 minutes until knife inserted into the middle comes out clean. Cool for 5 minutes, then turn out onto a carving board. Cool completely before slicing. If you try to slice the loaf while it is still warm, it will fall apart. For the best slicing results, refrigerate overnight wrapped in plastic or foil.

Per serving: 364.1 Calories; 7.3g Fat (17.4% calories from fat); 1.8g Protein; 76.2g Carbohydrate; 0mg Cholesterol; 397mg Sodium

Bean Bread

Conventional Oven Recipe

Serves 32

1	can navy beans, canned, pureed
1/2	cup apple butter, fruit sweetened only
2 1/2	cups rice flour
1/2	cup potato flour
1	teaspoon cinnamon
3/4	teaspoon cream of tartar
1 3/4	teaspoons baking soda
1/2	teaspoon salt
3	teaspoons egg replacer, =2 eggs
2	cups beet sugar
2/3	cup canola oil
2	teaspoons vanilla, alcohol free
2/3	cup raisins, optional
1/2	cup pecans, chopped, optional

Puree beans and apple butter together. Set aside. Mix dry ingredients (except sugar) together. Set aside. In a large bowl mix together oil, sugar, vanilla, and fold in the puree mixture. Gradually add dry ingredients to the oil mixture. Fold in raisins and nuts, if desired. Pour into two greased bread pans. Bake at 375 degrees until done, about an hour.

Variation: This recipe is great for muffins.
  Fruit sweetened apple butter should not contain corn or cane, read label.

Per serving: 215.5 Calories; 5.4g Fat (21.8% calories from fat); 1.7g Protein; 41.9g Carbohydrate; 0mg Cholesterol; 159mg Sodium

Blackeyed Pea Bread

Breadmaker or Conventional Oven Recipe

Serves 24

- 1 cup raisins
- 1 cup boiling water
- 1 cup white rice flour
- 2 cups amaranth flour
- 1 teaspoon cinnamon
- 1 1/2 teaspoons baking soda
- 1/2 teaspoon cream of tartar
- 3 teaspoons egg replacer, =2 eggs
- 1/2 teaspoon salt
- 2/3 cup oil
- 2 cups sugar
- 1 can (lb) blackeyed peas, canned, drained
- 1 teaspoon vanilla, alcohol-free

Pour boiling water over raisins. Allow to set 3-4 hours or over night. Mix dry ingredients (except sugar) together. Set aside. Puree blackeyed peas, place in large mixing bowl. Add sugar, oil, and vanilla to pureed blackeyed peas. Gradually add dry mixture to the blackeyed peas. Mix well. Drain raisins and fold into batter. Add optional ingredients as desired.

Breadmaker: Bake on dark setting on your breadmaker, eliminate second kneading cycle. Check your breadmaker instruction booklet. Turn your machine off, then reset machine for bake only. This is a very moist bread requiring 1 hour or more bake time. Check for doneness. Reset timer if necessary.

Conventional oven: Pour into greased breadpan. Bake at 375 degrees for 55-60 minutes or until toothpick inserted in the middle comes out clean.

Variations: Add 1 cup nuts, or crushed drained pineapple, (squeeze out liquid in a paper towel) as desired.

Per serving: 283.2 Calories; 7.3g Fat (22.4% calories from fat); 3.4g Protein; 53.4g Carbohydrate; 0mg Cholesterol; 182mg Sodium

Pumpkin Bread

Breadmaker or Conventional Oven

Serves 24

- 1 3/4 cups white rice flour
- 2 teaspoons baking soda
- 1 teaspoon cream of tartar
- 1 1/4 teaspoons salt
- 2 teaspoons pumpkin pie spice
- 3 teaspoons egg replacer
- 1 cup beet sugar
- 1/4 cup oil
- 1/2 can (lb) pumpkin, solid pack, plain
- 1/4 cup water

Mix together all dry ingredients and set aside. Place sugar and oil in bottom of bread maker. Set on "dough" let mix a few times and add pumpkin and water. Gradually add the dry ingredients. When mixed, reset breadmaker to bake, light, normal setting. This may require additional baking time. Test for doneness with a toothpick after 50-60 minutes. When toothpick comes out clean, it is done. If not done, reset bake timer and test after 10 to 15 minutes.
This bread has the consistency of a boston brown bread, and a robust pumpkin flavor. To bake in a conventional oven, pour into a greased loaf pan and bake for 1 hour at 350 degrees.

Substitution for pumpkin pie spice: 1/2 teaspoon each of cinnamon, nutmeg, and allspice, plus 1/4 teaspoon cloves.

Per serving: 148.7 Calories; 2.5g Fat (14.3% calories from fat); 0.7g Protein; 32.3g Carbohydrate; 0mg Cholesterol; 241mg Sodium

Pumpkin Quick Bread C/E
Serves 12

- 1 cup beet sugar
- 3 teaspoons egg replacer, =2 eggs
- 1/2 lb. can pumpkin, natural pack
- 1 3/4 cups white rice flour
- 2 teaspoons baking soda
- 1 teaspoon cream of tartar
- 1/2 teaspoon salt
- 2 teaspoons pumpkin pie spice
- 1/3 cup water, if needed

Preheat oven to 350 degrees. Mix all dry ingredients together and set aside. Place pumpkin in a large bowl. Gradually add dry ingrdients to pumpkin until batter is moistened. If needed, add water to batter. Spoon into a greased loaf pan and bake at 350 degrees for 1 hour. Test for doneness by inserting a knife in the middle of the loaf. If it comes out clean, it is done. If the knife has batter adhered to it, let the loaf bake another 10-15 minutes. Remove from pan to cool. Let cool completely before cutting into slices.

Per serving: 257.2 Calories; 0.4g Fat (1.2% calories from fat); 1.4g Protein; 64.7g Carbohydrate; 0mg Cholesterol; 348mg Sodium

Raisin Oat Muffins   Day 1
Serves 10

1	cup oat flour, ground fine
1	cup potato starch flour
1/2	cup raisins, plumped
1/2	cup maple syrup
1	teaspoon baking soda
1	teaspoon cream of tartar
1	teaspoon salt
3/4	cup oat milk, or cashew milk
1/4	cup safflower oil, or sunflower oil
1/4	cup sunflower seeds
1 1/3	teaspoons egg replacer, =1 egg

Preheat oven to 375 degrees.
Spray muffin pan with oil or line with paper cups.
Plump raisins by covering with warm water in a cup. Let sit for 15 minutes, then drain off water.
In a large bowl, combine all dry ingredients. Mix well. Stir in sunflower seeds and plumped raisins. Add milk, syrup and oil. Stir just to incorporate all ingredients. Do not over work batter. Spoon into prepared muffin pan. Makes 10 large or 12 small muffins.
Bake at 375 degrees for 20-25 minutes or until edges of muffins are light golden brown.

This Oat muffin is a favorite for breakfast and dinner.

Per serving: 306.1 Calories;   7.1g Fat (19.9% calories from fat);   2.2g Protein;   61.5g Carbohydrate;   0mg Cholesterol;   466mg Sodium

Oat Muffins With Cashews   Day 1
Serves 10

    1/2   cup potato starch flour
1 1/2   cups oat flour
    1/3   cup maple syrup, or maple sugar
1 1/2   teaspoons baking soda
1 1/2   teaspoons cream of tartar
1 1/3   teaspoons egg replacer, = 1 egg
    1/3   cup safflower oil, or sunflower oil
    1/2   cup oat milk
    1/2   cup cashews, chopped

Preheat oven to 375 degrees.
Spray a 12 count muffin pan with oil or line with baking cups.
Mix dry ingredients well. Stir in nuts to coat with flour mix. In a large measuring cup, mix syrup, oil, and oat milk. Add to dry ingredients and stir just until ingredients are incorporated. Do not overwork batter.
Spoon batter into muffin pan. Makes 10 large muffins or 12 small muffins.
Bake at 375 degrees for 20-25 minutes.
These muffins freeze well, and are also easily thawed for a quick breakfast or snack.

Per serving: 281.4 Calories; 11.2g Fat (34.6% calories from fat); 3.1g Protein; 44.5g Carbohydrate; 0mg Cholesterol; 351mg Sodium

Apple-Almond Buckwheat Muffins Day 2
Serves 12

1 1/2	cups buckwheat flour
1	teaspoon baking soda
1	teaspoon cream of tartar
1/2	teaspoon salt
1 1/3	teaspoons egg replacer, =1 egg
1/2	cup apple, chopped
1/4	cup slivered almonds
1/4	cup almond oil
3/4	cup almond milk
1/4	cup apple juice, frozen concentrate, undiluted

Preheat oven to 425 degrees.
Spray a 12 cup muffin pan with oil of choice or line muffin cups with cupcake liners. In a large bowl, combine all dry ingredients and stir together well. Add slivered almonds and apples and stir to coat with flour mixture. Add oil, milk, and apple juice concentrate and stir until all dry ingredients have been incorporated well. Fill muffin cups 2/3 full with batter. Bake at 425 degrees for 15-18 minutes until golden. Serve with any fruit preserves for day 2.

Per serving: 174.5 Calories; 6.8g Fat (33.1% calories from fat); 2.7g Protein; 28.2g Carbohydrate; 0mg Cholesterol; 225mg Sodium

Granola Muffins with Raisins
Serves 10

3/4	cup potato starch flour
1 1/2	cups amaranth flour
1	teaspoon cream of tartar
1	teaspoon baking soda
1/4	teaspoon salt
1/2	cup beet sugar
1	cup granola, of choice
1/4	cup raisins
1	teaspoon vanilla
1 1/3	teaspoons egg replacer, =1 egg
1 1/4	cups almond milk, vanilla flavor
1/4	cup oil, oil of the day

Preheat oven to 400 degrees.
Spray muffin cups with oil or use paper muffin liners.
In a large bowl, combine flours, salt, soda, cream of tartar, sugar, egg replacer, granola, and raisins. Mix together well. Add almond milk, oil, and vanilla. Stir just until batter is moistened. Spoon into muffin cups and fill muffin cup to 2/3 full. Bake at 400 degrees for 18-20 minutes.

These are great for breakfast with fruit or a breakfast shake. These muffins freeze well for the same rotation day next week.

Per serving: 402.9 Calories; 11.0g Fat (23.6% calories from fat); 6.1g Protein; 73.8g Carbohydrate; 0mg Cholesterol; 227mg Sodium

Carrot Coconut Muffins
Serves 10

1	cup white rice flour
1	cup amaranth flour
1/2	cup potato starch flour
1/4	cup tapioca flour
1	teaspoon baking soda
1	teaspoon cream of tartar
3/4	teaspoon salt
1 1/3	teaspoons egg replacer, =1 egg
1/2	cup beet sugar, or honey
1/4	cup oil, of choice
1	cup carrots, grated
1/2	cup coconut, grated-unsweetened
1/2	cup coconut milk, lite-unsweetened

Preheat oven to 375 degrees.
Spray or oil muffin pan or line muffin cups with paper cupcake liners.
In a large bowl, combine flours, baking soda, cream of tartar, salt, egg replacer, and beet sugar. Stir well to incorporate all the dry ingredients. Add carrots and coconut and stir well. (Coating the carrots and coconut with the flour mix will prevent them from sinking to the bottom of the batter.) Make a "well" in the center of the flour mix. Pour in coconut milk and oil and stir until all dry ingredients are moistened. (If honey was used as the sweetener instead of sugar, then decrease the coconut milk to 1/4 cup) Spoon the batter into each muffin cup, filling 2/3 full. Makes 10 large or 12 small muffins. Bake at 375 degrees for 20-25 minutes, until golden around the edges. Do not over cook.

These muffins are great for lunches and breakfast. They freeze well after cooking. Place in individual wraps for quick lunch or breakfast preparation.

Per serving: 360.6 Calories; 10.5g Fat (25.4% calories from fat); 4.2g Protein; 65.3g Carbohydrate; 0mg Cholesterol; 322mg Sodium

Almond Poppyseed Muffins
Serves 10

- 1 1/2 cups rice flour
- 1/2 cup tapioca flour
- 1 teaspoon baking soda
- 1 teaspoon cream of tartar
- 3/4 teaspoon salt
- 1 1/3 teaspoons egg replacer, =1 egg
- 1/2 cup beet sugar
- 1/3 cup canola oil
- 1 Tablespoon lemon zest
- 1 Tablespoon poppy seeds
- 1/2 cup rice milk
- 2 Tablespoons lemon juice
- 1 teaspoon almond extract, alcohol-free

Preheat oven to 375 degrees.
Spray or oil muffin pan or line pan with paper cupcakes liners.
In a large bowl, combine flours, baking soda, cream of tartar, salt, egg replacer, sugar, poppy seeds, and lemon zest. Stir well to incorporate all ingredients. Add rice milk, lemon juice, and almond extract. Stir until all dry ingredients are moistened. Fill muffin cups 2/3 full with batter. Makes 10 large or 12 small muffins. Bake at 375 degrees for 20-25 minutes or until golden.

Per serving: 262.2 Calories; 8.1g Fat (27.0% calories from fat); 1.7g Protein; 47.5g Carbohydrate; 0mg Cholesterol; 317mg Sodium

Food Allergies, What Do I Eat Now?

Cranberry Rice Muffins   Day 5   C/E
Serves 10

- 1 1/2   cups rice flour
- 1   teaspoon baking soda
- 1   teaspoon cream of tartar
- 3/4   teaspoon salt
- 1 1/3   teaspoons egg replacer, =1 egg
- 1/2   cup rice syrup
- 3/4   cup cranberries, fresh or frozen
- 1/3   cup canola oil
- 1/4   teaspoon cloves, optional
- 1/2   cup rice milk
- 1   teaspoon vanilla, alcohol-free

Preheat oven to 375 degrees.
Spray or oil muffin pan or use paper liners.
In a large bowl, combine all dry ingredients and mix well. Add cranberries and toss to coat with flour mix. This prevents berries from sinking to the bottom of the muffin. Add rice syrup, oil, rice milk, and vanilla and stir gently until ingredients are incorporated. Over mixing will cause berries to break into batter.
Makes 10 large or 12 small muffins.
Bake at 375 degrees for 20-25 minutes or until golden around edges.

Per serving: 253.2 Calories; 7.7g Fat (27.1% calories from fat); 1.5g Protein; 45.2g Carbohydrate; 0mg Cholesterol; 318mg Sodium

Blueberry Rice Muffins   Day 5 C/E
Serves 10

1 1/2	cups rice flour
1	teaspoon baking soda
1	teaspoon cream of tartar
3/4	teaspoon salt
1 1/3	teaspoons egg replacer, =1 egg
1/2	cup rice syrup
3/4	cup blueberries, fresh or frozen
1/3	cup canola oil
1/4	teaspoon cloves
1/2	cup rice milk
1	teaspoon vanilla, alcohol-free

Preheat oven to 375 degrees.
Spray or oil muffin pan or use paper liners.
In a large bowl, combine all dry ingredients and mix well. Add blueberries and toss to coat with flour mix. This prevents berries from sinking to the bottom of the muffin. Add rice syrup, oil, rice milk, and vanilla and stir gently just until ingredients are incorporated. Over mixing will cause berries to turn the batter blue.
Makes 10 large or 12 small muffins.
Bake at 375 degrees for 20-25 minutes or until golden around edges.

Per serving: 255.9 Calories; 7.8g Fat (26.9% calories from fat); 1.5g Protein; 45.9g Carbohydrate; 0mg Cholesterol; 318mg Sodium

Burger Bun
Serves 2

- 1/2 cup rice flour
- 1/4 cup potato starch flour
- 1/4 teaspoon xanthan gum
- 3/4 teaspoon baking soda
- 1/4 teaspoon cream of tartar
- 3/4 cup rice milk
- 1 Tablespoon safflower oil
- 1 teaspoon sesame seeds

Mix all dry ingredients together except sesame seeds. Add milk and oil. Mix until smooth with wire wisk. Spray individual (4") baking dishes with cooking oil. Pour batter into dishes and top with sesame seeds. Bake at 350 degrees for 10 to 15 minutes or until done. Remove from baking dish immediately. Allow to cool completely before slicing with a sharp serrated knife for use as burger bun.
Yield: 2 Large Buns

Serving suggestion: Serve with favorite sandwich goodies, as breakfast sandwich, or with burgers. Try this with our Aloha Burger.

Per serving: 372.5 Calories; 9.0g Fat (21.6% calories from fat); 3.1g Protein; 70.3g Carbohydrate; 0mg Cholesterol; 508mg Sodium

Crumble Biscuits
Serves 12

- 1 cup rice flour
- 1/2 teaspoon baking soda
- 1/2 teaspoon cream of tartar
- 1 teaspoon guar gum
- 3 Tablespoons margarine, softened
- 1/2 cup rice milk
- 1 Tablespoon rice milk

Preheat oven to 450 degrees. Measure flour, baking soda, cream of tartar, and guar gum into a bowl. Add margarine to bowl and rub butter into flour with your fingers or a fork. Add milk to make a thick batter, stirring only until dough sticks together. Drop by spoonfuls on an ungreased baking sheet. Bake 7-8 minutes in preheated oven.

Variation: For a hot appetizer, roll each piece of dough in soft butter, then grated rice parmesan cheese and parika. Bake in a hot oven (450 degrees) 7-8 minutes, until brown.
Variation: Make biscuit in 2 layers. Sandwich cheese and meat in middle, see Sombrero Bundles.

Per serving: 79.5 Calories; 3.1g Fat (35.5% calories from fat); 0.9g Protein; 11.8g Carbohydrate; 0mg Cholesterol; 90mg Sodium

Dumplings
Serves 4

- 3/4 cup rice flour
- 1/4 cup tapioca flour
- 1 1/2 teaspoons baking powder
- 1/2 teaspoon salt
- 1 teaspoon oil
- 1/3 cup rice milk
- 2 Tablespoons rice milk, if needed

Mix all dry ingredients together. Mix 1/3 cup rice milk and oil together. Combine liquid mixture into the dry mixture. Mix only until all ingredients are moistened. Add up to 2 Tablespoons more rice milk if needed. Drop by teaspoonfuls into boiling broth or stew. Cover tightly. Reduce to medium heat. Cook over medium heat for 6-8 minutes without lifting lid. If you cook too long or lift the lid during cooking time the result will be heavy dumplings. They will be edible, just heavy rather than fluffy.

Serving suggestions: Use in chicken broth with chicken pieces for Chicken and Dumplings.

Use with any beef stew recipe.

Per serving: 137.4 Calories; 1.8g Fat (11.7% calories from fat); 1.9g Protein; 28.4g Carbohydrate; 0mg Cholesterol; 413mg Sodium

Flatbread Medallions

Unleavened Bread

Serves 8

- 1 cup rice flour
- 1/4 cup buckwheat flour
- 2 teaspoons egg replacer
- 1 teaspoon xanthan gum
- 1 1/2 cups rice milk

Mix all dry ingredients together. Add milk. Mix until smooth. Pour out like pancakes, in 4" rounds, onto oil sprayed non-stick cookie sheet. Bake in oven at 375 degrees for 10 - 14 minutes or until done. Turn over about half done, when won't fall apart. Serve: Use in place of breads for sandwiches. Will not fall apart. These medallions are great for burgers.

Per serving: 215.2 Calories; 0.8g Fat (3.1% calories from fat); 1.8g Protein; 52.1g Carbohydrate; 0mg Cholesterol; 67mg Sodium

Focaccia
Serves 8

1	pizza crust, recipe
2	Tablespoons olive oil, or oil of the day
10	basil leaves, julienned
1	medium tomato, sliced
1	medium onion, sliced
1/2	teaspoon oregano, dried
1/2	teaspoon garlic salt
1/4	teaspoon salt and pepper

Prepare recipe for pizza crust according to recipe. Top with basil, tomato slices, onion rings, and spices. Drizzle with olive oil. Bake in 400 degrees oven for 20-25 minutes or until crust is golden. Cut into squares and serve with a large antipasto salad or as an appetizer.

Nutritional analysis includes pizza crust and toppings.

Per serving: 126.8 Calories; 4.5g Fat (32.6% calories from fat); 3.3g Protein; 17.5g Carbohydrate; 0mg Cholesterol; 286mg Sodium

Individual Pizza Crusts
Serves 6

- 1 package dry yeast, rapid rise variety
- 1/4 cup warm water, not hot
- 1 Tablespoon beet sugar, or sweetener of day
- 3 Tablespoons oil, oil of the day
- 1 1/2 teaspoons salt
- 1 1/2 cups buckwheat flour, light
- 1 1/2 cups rice flour
- 1 1/2 cups warm water
- 1/2 cup buckwheat flour, for kneading dough

In cup, combine yeast, 1/4 cup warm water, and honey. Let set about 5 minutes or until mixture is foamy and yeast has totally dissolved. Add oil.
In large mixing bowl, combine salt, and flours. Add yeast mix and gradually add 1-1/2 warm water to flour. All of the water may not be required. Dough should be the consistency of biscuit dough. Spread 1/2 cup rice flour on clean counter. Turn out dough onto floured counter and knead dough for about 3 minutes. If dough is too sticky to work with, continue to incorporate more flour until desired consistency. Divide dough into 6 small portions. Place dough on well-greased baking sheet and spread to make small pizza rounds. Place cookie sheets in a warm oven to rise for about 30 minutes. To warm oven for rising, place a pan of boiling water in the bottom of the oven before placing dough in the oven. At the end of 30 minutes, gently remove water and pizza doughs from oven. Preheat oven to 400 degrees. Top pizza dough with your favorite toppings.
Bake at 400 degrees for 20-25 minutes until crust is browned on the edges and toppings are bubbly.

Nutritional analysis does not include topping.
Serving size is 2 slices.

Per serving: 352.5 Calories; 8.7g Fat (21.6% calories from fat); 8.2g Protein; 62.7g Carbohydrate; 0mg Cholesterol; 540mg Sodium

Pizza Crust
Serves 6

- 1 package dry yeast, rapid rise variety
- 1 Tablespoon beet sugar, or honey
- 1/4 cup warm water, not hot
- 3 Tablespoons oil
- 1 1/2 teaspoons salt
- 1 1/2 cups buckwheat flour, light
- 1 1/2 cups rice flour
- 1 1/2 cups warm water
- 1/2 cup buckwheat flour, for kneading dough

In a cup, combine yeast, 1/4 cup warm water, and honey. Let set about 5 minutes or until mixture is foamy and yeast has totally dissolved. Add oil.
In a large mixing bowl, combine salt, and flours. Add yeast mix and gradually add 1-1/2 warm water to flour. All of the water may not be required. Dough should be the consistency of biscuit dough. Spread 1/2 cup buckwheat flour on clean counter. Turn out dough onto floured counter and knead dough for about 3 minutes. If dough is too sticky to work with, continue to incorporate more flour until desired consistency. Place dough on well-seasoned baking stone and spread to cover stone. Using oil on your hands will make spreading of dough easier. Place stone in a warm oven to rise for about 30 minutes. To warm oven for rising, place a pan of boiling water in the bottom of the oven before placing dough in the oven. At the end of the 30 minutes, remove the pan of water and the dough from the oven and top with your favorite pizza toppings. Turn the oven on to 400 degrees and replace topped pizza in the oven. Bake for 20-25 minutes until crust is browned on the edge and topping is bubbly.

Per serving: 352.5 Calories; 8.7g Fat (21.6% calories from fat); 8.2g Protein; 62.7g Carbohydrate; 0mg Cholesterol; 540mg Sodium

Quinoa Tortillas C/E
Serves 12

- 2 cups quinoa flour
- 2 cups rice milk, or milk of the day
- 1 teaspoon salt
- 1 1/3 teaspoons egg replacer, =1 egg
- 3/4 teaspoon baking soda
- 3/4 teaspoon cream of tartar
- 2 Tablespoons oil, oil of the day

Mix all dry ingredients (include egg replacer in this mix if you are sensitive to eggs). Add milk, egg (if egg is being used instead of egg replacer) and oil and mix well. Heat a pancake griddle or large nonstick skillet. Prepare tortillas as you would pancakes. Batter should be thin enough to roll around in pan to make tortilla as thin as possible. No oil should be used in the pan. When tortilla is lightly browned on one side, turn to cook other side. Do not over cook. This will make tortillas break when they are rolled. Use as you would a soft taco shell or a burrito shell.

Per serving: 194.4 Calories; 4.3g Fat (19.1% calories from fat); 3.9g Protein; 36.7g Carbohydrate; 0mg Cholesterol; 299mg Sodium

Soft Shell Taco Roll-up

Unleavened Bread

Serves 4

- 1/2 cup rice flour
- 1/4 cup potato flour
- 1/4 teaspoon xanthan gum
- 1 Tablespoon safflower oil
- 2/3 cup rice milk

Mix all dry ingredients together. Add milk and oil. Mix until smooth. Spread 1/8 inch thick into an eight inch spray coated pie or cake pan, or onto a cookie sheet to the desired size. They will look like pale colored pancakes.

Bake: 400 degrees for 10-14 minutes or til done. The roll-up will not brown. Turn the roll-up over when done enough to not fall apart. When baking is complete remove from oven and drape each roll-up over a coffee mug laying on its side, to cool. You could use doubled heavy duty aluminum foil made into U-shaped tents instead of coffee mugs. Use immediately, or store in plastic, resealable bags or freeze.

Variation:

Make roll-ups silver dollar size to use for party snacks topped with your favorite finger food topping or make into mini sandwiches.

Place on cookie sheet in a rectangle shape 4" x 5" to bake, use in place of hot dog bun.

Use with Breakfast Taco Recipe, or as medallions for sandwiches or mini pizzas

----

Per serving: 161.7 Calories; 4.1g Fat (22.9% calories from fat); 2.3g Protein; 28.9g Carbohydrate; 0mg Cholesterol; 19mg Sodium

Breakfast

Mango Syrup Day 1
Serves 4

  2   large mango
  1   cup grape juice, concentrate-unsweet
  1   teaspoon potato starch flour

Remove the seed from mangoes and then peel. To remove the seed, cut mango with a knife down to the seed from top to bottom of fruit. Run a large spoon into mango and around the seed. Do this to both halves of the mango. When the seed is removed, peel the fruit by scooping out the pulp with the spoon. Place the pulp in the blender with the grape juice concentrate and potato starch flour. Blend on high for 1 minute. Place the puree into a small saucepan and bring to a slow boil until the puree is the thickness of gravy. Serve hot over pancakes or cold over icecream.

Per serving: 89.7 Calories; 0.3g Fat (2.3% calories from fat); 0.7g Protein;
              22.8g Carbohydrate; 0mg Cholesterol; 3mg Sodium

Maple-Raisin Syrup   Day 1
Serves 4

  3/4   cup maple syrup
  1/4   cup raisins, plumped

In a small sauce pan, combine raisins and maple syrup. Heat just until warm and serve over pancakes and waffles.
Microwave: In a small microwavable bowl, warm syrup and raisins. Warm 1 minute at a time until warm.

Per serving: 181.9 Calories; 0.2g Fat (0.8% calories from fat); 0.3g Protein;
              46.9g Carbohydrate; 0mg Cholesterol; 6mg Sodium

Blackberry Syrup   Day 2 C/E
Serves 4

- 1 cup blackberries, fresh or frozen
- 1/3 cup apple juice, frozen concentrate
- 1 teaspoon tapioca flour
- 1/4 cup water

Place apple juice concentrate and blackberries in a sauce pan and cook over medium heat until blackberries begin to burst. In a small measuring cup, wisk together water and tapioca flour until combined. Add to berries and apple juice. Stir constantly until syrup begins to thicken. Remove from heat.   Serve over pancakes, waffles, and over desserts.

Per serving: 57.3 Calories; 0.2g Fat (3.4% calories from fat); 0.4g Protein; 14.1g Carbohydrate; 0mg Cholesterol; 6mg Sodium

Raspberry Syrup   Day 2
Serves 4

- 1 cup raspberries, fresh or frozen
- 1/3 cup apple juice, from frozen concentrate
- 1 teaspoon tapioca flour

Combine apple juice concentrate and tapioca flour. Stir until flour and apple juice are completely incorporated. Place raspberries, apple juice and tapioca flour in a small sauce pan and cook over medium heat until syrup begins to thicken. Serve over pancakes, waffles, and desserts.

Per serving: 24.2 Calories; 0.2g Fat (6.2% calories from fat); 0.3g Protein; 5.8g Carbohydrate; 0mg Cholesterol; 1mg Sodium

Citrus Sauce   Day 3
Serves 4

  1   cup frozen orange juice concentrate
1/2   cup honey
1/3   cup coconut, unsweetened-flaked
  1   teaspoon potato starch flour

In a small sauce pan, combine orange juice concentrate, honey, coconut, and potato starch flour. Stir well until potato starch flour is completely incorporated. Place over low heat and warm until potato starch flour begins to thicken sauce, stirring constantly.

Serve warm over pancakes and waffles.

Per serving: 258.7 Calories; 1.3g Fat (4.3% calories from fat); 2.0g Protein; 63.8g Carbohydrate; 0mg Cholesterol; 5mg Sodium

Tropical Syrup   Day 4
Serves 4

14   ounces pineapple chunks in juice, canned or fresh
 1   teaspoon potato starch flour

Drain pineapple and reserve juice. Place juice in a medium sauce pan and stir in potato starch flour until completely incorporated. Add pineapple pieces and place over medium heat. Stir until liquid begins to thicken. Serve warm over pancakes, waffles, and desserts.

Per serving: 64.2 Calories; 0.1g Fat (1.0% calories from fat); 0.4g Protein; 16.8g Carbohydrate; 0mg Cholesterol; 1mg Sodium

Blueberry Syrup   Day 5   C/E
Serves 4

  1   cup blueberries, fresh or frozen
1/4 cup water
1/2 cup Rice syrup

Combine blueberries and water in a small sauce pan. Cook over medium heat until berries start to break. Add rice syrup and heat until just warm. Serve over pancakes, waffles, and desserts.

Per serving: 104.9 Calories; 0.1g Fat (1.2% calories from fat); 0.2g Protein; 26.0g Carbohydrate; 0mg Cholesterol; 5mg Sodium

Cranberry Syrup   Day 5   C/E
Serves 4

  1   cup cranberries, fresh or frozen
1/4 cup water
1/2 cup rice syrup
  1   teaspoon lemon zest

In a medium sauce pan, combine water, cranberries and lemon zest. Cook over medium heat until berries begin to break. Remove from heat and add rice syrup. Stir just until heated through. Serve warm over pancakes, waffles, and desserts.

This syrup is fat free, low in calories, but high in flavor.

Per serving: 96.1 Calories; 0.0g Fat (0.4% calories from fat); 0.1g Protein; 23.9g Carbohydrate; 0mg Cholesterol; 3mg Sodium

Pancakes C/E
Serves 4

- 1 cup oat flour
- 1/2 cup rice flour, or buckwheat flour
- 1 teaspoon baking soda
- 1 teaspoon cream of tartar
- dash salt
- 1 cup almond milk, or milk of day
- 1/4 cup oil, not olive oil
- 1 teaspoon vanilla, alcohol-free
- 1 1/3 teaspoons egg replacer, = 1 egg

Combine flours, baking soda, cream of tartar, and salt. Add milk, oil, egg replacer, and vanilla. Stir well. You may need to make the batter thinner, if so add more almond milk until desired consistency. Drop about 1/4 cup batter onto heated griddle or skillet. Roll batter around in pan by tilting skillet or gridlle in a circular motion. Turn pancakes over when bubbles begin to form and pop on surface. Serve with fresh fruit, maple syrup, rice syrup, honey or preserves of the day.
Nutritional values do not include toppings.

Per serving: 436.8 Calories; 15.7g Fat (31.6% calories from fat); 4.8g Protein; 71.7g Carbohydrate; 0mg Cholesterol; 610mg Sodium

Oat Pancakes With Maple Syrup   Day 1 C/E
Serves 4

1	cup oat flour
1/2	cup potato starch flour
1	teaspoon baking soda
1	teaspoon cream of tartar
	dash salt
1	cup oat milk
1/4	cup safflower oil
1	teaspoon vanilla, optional
1 1/3	teaspoons egg replacer, =1 egg

Mix together all dry ingredients in a medium bowl. Add oat milk, oil, and vanilla. Stir until smooth. Heat non-stick skillet or griddle until a drop of water sizzles on it. Do not use oil on the cooking surface. Pour about 1/4 cup of batter onto cooking surface. Bubbles will begin to form on the top of the pancake. When bubbles are uniform on top, turn pancake and cook on other side. The first pancake always turns out wrong. The rest of the pancakes should cook perfectly.

Serve warm with maple syrup. Read labels and make sure your maple syrup has no sugar added.
Nutritional values are for pancakes only.

Per serving: 473.3 Calories; 15.1g Fat (27.9% calories from fat); 3.9g Protein; 84.0g Carbohydrate; 0mg Cholesterol; 638mg Sodium

Hazelnut Pancakes with Citrus Sauce Day 3 C/E
Serves 4

- 1 cup hazelnuts, ground into meal
- 1 teaspoon orange zest
- 2/3 cup amaranth flour
- 1/3 cup tapioca flour
- 1/4 cup honey
- 1 cup water
- 3 teaspoons egg replacer, or 1 egg
- 1/2 teaspoon baking soda
- 1/2 teaspoon cream of tartar
- 3/4 cup orange juice

Grind hazelnuts (or nuts of choice) in blender.
Combine nuts meal, orange zest, flours, soda, cream of tartar, and egg replacer in a large bowl. Mix well. Add honey, orange juice, and water. Stir until smooth and there are no lumps. You may need to add more water to be able to pour batter into skillet.
Heat a nonstick skillet or griddle until a drop of water "dances" on the surface. Pour 1/4 cup batter into skillet. When bubbles begin to form and pop on surface, turn and cook on the other side.

Serve with Citrus Sauce

Per serving: 620.6 Calories; 10.5g Fat (14.3% calories from fat); 6.8g Protein; 134.9g Carbohydrate; 0mg Cholesterol; 316mg Sodium

Buckwheat Pancake
Serves 4

- 1 cup buckwheat flour
- 3/4 teaspoon cream of tartar
- 3/4 teaspoon baking soda
- 1/2 teaspoon salt
- 1 teaspoon egg replacer
- 1 cup rice milk
- 2 Tablespoons canola margarine, melted

Mix all dry ingredients together thoroughly. Mix milk and margarine together in separate container.
Gradually combine the two mixtures together. Stir with fork or wire wisk until smooth. Pour batter onto greased griddle or skillet in desired pancake size.
Cook for 1-2 minutes until bubbles form and edges begin to look done. Flip pancake over to cook on other side.

Per serving: 289.8 Calories; 6.9g Fat (20.4% calories from fat); 4.0g Protein; 56.7g Carbohydrate; 0mg Cholesterol; 638mg Sodium

Pecan Pancakes
Serves 4

- 1 cup rice flour
- 1 cup pecan flour
- 1 teaspoon baking soda
- 1 teaspoon cream of tartar
- dash salt
- 2 Tablespoons beet sugar
- 1/4 cup canola oil, or oil of the day
- 1 teaspoon vanilla, alcohol-free
- 1 1/3 teaspoons egg replacer, =1 egg
- 1 1/4 cups almond milk, or rice milk

Combine flours, baking soda, cream of tartar, salt, sugar, and egg replacer. Mix together well. Add milk, oil, and vanilla. You may need to add more milk to make batter thin enough to pour. Pour about 1/4 cup of batter onto hot griddle or non-stick skillet. "Roll" batter in pan by tilting in a circular motion. This prevents panckes from becoming too thick. Turn pancake when batter begins to form bubbles and pop on surface. Cook on second side until golden. Serve with rice syrup, honey, maple syrup, or fresh fruit. This is especially good when the topping is heated and chopped pecans are added to the syrup. You can heat syrup in a glass measuring cup in the microwave.
Nutritional values do not include topping.
Serving size: 4 medium pancakes.

Per serving: 566.3 Calories; 15.4g Fat (23.9% calories from fat); 12.9g Protein; 97.6g Carbohydrate; 0mg Cholesterol; 412mg Sodium

Banana Nut Pancakes
Serves 8

1	cup rice flour
3/4	cup tapioca flour
1/2	cup buckwheat flour
1	teaspoon egg replacer
1	teaspoon cream of tartar
1	teaspoon baking soda
2	Tablespoons beet sugar
1	dash salt
1/4	cup pecans, optional, chopped
2	medium banana, ripe, mashed
1 1/2	cups rice milk
6	Tablespoons safflower oil

Mix all dry ingredients except nuts together well. Mash 2 bananas thoroughly. Add milk and 4 tablespoons of the oil to the bananas. Mix well. Remainder of the oil is to be used for electric fry pan or griddle surface for cooking pancakes. Combine banana and milk mixture with the dry ingredients. Mix well. Fold in nuts if desired. Bananas may be omitted by increasing the milk.

Note: Buckwheat, being related to dock and rhubarb, does not contain gluten. Plan ahead for those busy mornings. Freeze leftover pancakes layered between wax paper, place in resealable plastic bag. Freeze. When you are too busy to cook, pop one in the toaster or microwave.

Per serving: 312.3 Calories; 12.4g Fat (34.5% calories from fat); 2.7g Protein; 50.4g Carbohydrate; 0mg Cholesterol; 233mg Sodium

Company Waffles C/E
Serves 8

- 3/4 cup rice flour, white
- 3/4 cup amaranth flour
- 1/2 cup potato starch flour
- 1/2 cup tapioca flour
- 3 teaspoons egg replacer, =2 eggs
- 1 teaspoon vanilla, alcohol-free
- 1 1/4 cups almond milk, vanilla flavor
- 1/2 teaspoon salt
- 1 teaspoon baking soda
- 1 teaspoon cream of tartar
- 1/3 cup canola oil, or oil of the day

Preheat waffle iron.
Combine all dry ingredients and mix well. Stir in eggs (if used), vanilla, and milk. Mix well. Spoon onto hot waffle surface (about 1/4 cup per waffle section) and close lid. Do not lift lid prematurely, or waffle will seperate. Generally, when steam stops coming out of the waffle iron, the waffle will be done. If batter is too thick to "flow" into squares, add a little more almond milk.
Variation: omit 1/2 cup flour and add 1 cup pecan meal to batter.

Any combination of flours can be used. Experiment!

Top with fresh fruit for a low calorie breakfast. Or, top with maple syrup, rice syrup, honey, or jams.

Per serving: 440.8 Calories; 10.9g Fat (21.4% calories from fat); 3.8g Protein; 85.9g Carbohydrate; 0mg Cholesterol; 385mg Sodium

Breakfast Granola
Serves 8

- 2 cups rolled oats, toasted
- 2 cups crispy rice cereal
- 1 cup nuts, chopped
- 3/4 cup rice syrup
- 1 teaspoon vanilla, alcohol-free
- 1/2 teaspoon salt, optional
- 1 cup raisins

Preheat oven to 400 degrees.
Spray nonstick cookie sheet with oil, or use foil to line cookie sheet.
Mix all ingredients well and toss well to coat with syrup evenly. Spread on cookie sheet and bake at 400 degrees for 10 minutes, stirring occassionally. Remove from oven and cool completely.

Store in airtight container in refrigerator.
Serve for breakfast with rice milk or milk of the day, or serve for snack-time.

Per serving: 333.7 Calories; 11.4g Fat (29.6% calories from fat); 7.3g Protein; 53.7g Carbohydrate; 0mg Cholesterol; 191mg Sodium

Oat Granola With Raisins and Sunflower Seeds Day 1 C/E

Serves 4

- 2 cups oats, toasted
- 1/2 cup sunflower seeds
- 1/3 cup maple syrup
- 1/2 teaspoon vanilla, alcohol-free
- 1/2 cup raisins
- 1 Tablespoon sunflower oil, or safflower oil

Preheat oven to 400 degrees.
To toast oats:
Place 2-4 cups oats on a non-stick cookie sheet. Place in a 400 degree oven for 5-10 minutes, stirring occassionally, until lightly golden. Cool and store in an air tight container until needed.
In a measuring cup, combine maple syrup and vanilla. Set aside.
Place 2 cups toasted oats in a large bowl. Add sunflower seeds and raisins and mix well. Add syrup and vanilla and mix well. Rub oil on the non-stick cookie sheet. Spread granola mix evenly on the cookie sheet and bake at 400 degrees for 8-10 minutes, stirring occasionally. Cool and store in an air tight container. Serve with milk of the day, or alone as a snack. This also makes a great topping for a fruit cobbler on Day 1.

Per serving: 512.7 Calories; 13.7g Fat (23.3% calories from fat); 16.0g Protein; 85.6g Carbohydrate; 0mg Cholesterol; 6mg Sodium

Breakfast Rice Day 5 C/E
Serves 2

- 2 cups brown rice, cooked-leftover
- 2 Tablespoons rice syrup
- 2 Tablespoons chopped dates
- dash cloves, or allspice
- 1 cup rice milk

In a medium sauce pan, warm rice milk, rice syrup and spice. When warm, add rice and dates. Continue to warm over low heat until thick and most of liquid is absorbed.
This is a nice change from oatmeal in the morning, and reminds me of rice pudding for breakfast.

Per serving: 820.9 Calories; 6.1g Fat (6.7% calories from fat); 15.0g Protein; 175.9g Carbohydrate; 0mg Cholesterol; 54mg Sodium

Drop Biscuits C/E
Serves 8

- 1 cup rice flour, white
- 1/2 teaspoon salt
- dash red pepper, optional
- 1/2 teaspoon baking soda
- 1/2 teaspoon cream of tartar
- 1/3 cup canola margarine, or safflower
- 1/2 cup rice milk, or milk of the day

Preheat oven to 425 degrees.
In a medium mixing bowl, combine flour, salt, pepper, baking soda, and cream of tartar and stir to mix well. Cut in margarine with fork until crumbs are about pea size. Add milk and stir gently. Drop by heaping tablespoonfuls onto lightly oiled pan with 1-2" sides. (Raised sides will help prevent over browning). A baking stone works well for biscuits. Bake at 425 degrees 10-12 minutes. If the rest of the meal is not ready, cover with foil to prevent drying.
Makes 8 biscuits.

If served on a rotation day that allows almond cheese or rice cheese, add 1 cup of cheese to biscuit dough for an added treat.

Per serving: 146.9 Calories; 7.7g Fat (48.1% calories from fat); 1.2g Protein; 17.5g Carbohydrate; 0mg Cholesterol; 298mg Sodium

Stir Fry Breakfast Medley
Serves 6

8	ounces ground turkey
1/4	cup onion, chopped
1	cup zucchini, sliced
1/2	cup mushroom, sliced
1	cup brown rice, cooked
1/8	teaspoon garlic powder
1/4	cup rice vinegar
1	teaspoon beet sugar
	salt and pepper, to taste
1	teaspoon hot pepper sauce, optional

Brown turkey in a large skillet or frying pan which has been sprayed with cooking oil. When about half done, add onion and garlic powder and continue cooking. When meat is cooked add vegetables, sugar, and vinegar. Cover and cook over low heat for 2-3 minutes. Season with salt & pepper to taste. Hot sauce may be served with this dish if desired.

This recipe is great served Taco Style with a roll up or quinoa tortilla.

Per serving: 180.7 Calories; 4.0g Fat (20.1% calories from fat); 9.4g Protein; 26.6g Carbohydrate; 30mg Cholesterol; 62mg Sodium

Prudy's Turkey Breakfast Sausage
Serves 8

1 1/2	pounds turkey, ground
2	teaspoons sage, ground or rubbed
1/4	teaspoon nutmeg
1	teaspoon marjoram
1	teaspoon garlic powder
1/4	teaspoon black pepper
1/4	teaspoon cumin
1/4	teaspoon salt

Mix all ingredients well. Divide into family servings. Form into desired shape: patties, links, or sausage balls. Cook one, and freeze the rest for a later date.

Note: Best if allowed to refrigerate over night to blend the flavors before cooking or freezing. Pork can be used instead of turkey if desired, but will nearly double calories.

Per serving: 110.3 Calories; 5.5g Fat (46.1% calories from fat); 13.8g Protein; 0.5g Carbohydrate; 46mg Cholesterol; 111mg Sodium

Campfire Cooking

Best Trail Mix C/E
Serves 28

	cup raisins, or currants
1/2	cup nuts
1/2	cup coconut shreds, unsweetened
1/2	cup sunflower seeds
4	cups crispy rice cereal, natural
1/2	cup dried apples
1/2	cup blueberries, dried
1/2	cup cranberries, dried

Serving size is 1/4 cup.
If you are sensitive to sugars and sulfites, use only fruits you have dried by the slow oven method or in a dehydrator.
Mix all ingredients and store in airtight containers or in resealable plastic bags.

Per serving: 53.6 Calories; 2.8g Fat (44.3% calories from fat); 1.1g Protein; 6.7g Carbohydrate; 0mg Cholesterol; 36mg Sodium

Dry Fruit and Nut Mix Day 1 C/E

Serves 2

- 1/2   cup raisins, light or dark
- 1/2   cup mango, dried
- 1   Tablespoon sunflower seeds
- 2   Tablespoons cashews, pieces

Mix all fruits, nuts and seeds and place in two plastic sandwich bags. Pack for lunch or snacks.

Per serving: 188.0 Calories; 5.4g Fat; 3.2g Protein; 36.3g Carbohydrate; 0mg Cholesterol; 6mg Sodium

Variations - Dry Fruit and Nut Mix Day 2 C/E (serves 1)
- 1/4 cup dried apples, unsweetened
- 1/4 cup strawberries, dried
- 1/4 cup slivered almonds

Perserving: 137.4 Calories; 9.6g Fat; 3.9g Protein; 11.6g Carbohydrate; 0mg Cholesterol; 11mg Sodium

Variation - Alternate Fruit and Nut Mix Day 2 C/E (serves 2)
- 1/2 cup dried pears, pieces or sticks
- 1/2 cup dried peaches, pieces
- 1/2 cup dried prunes, quartered
- 1/4 cup almonds or macadamia nuts

Per serving: 337.7 Calories; 4.5g Fat; 4.6g Protein; 78.9g Carbohydrate; 0mg Cholesterol; 8mg Sodium

----

Per serving: 188.0 Calories; 5.4g Fat (23.4% calories from fat); 3.2g Protein; 36.3g Carbohydrate; 0mg Cholesterol; 6mg Sodium

Food Allergies, What Do I Eat Now?

Dry Fruit and Nut Mix   Day 3 C/E
Serves 2

- 1/2   cup Dried Honey Carrots
- 1/4   cup coconut, pieces
- 1/4   cup filberts
- 1   Tablespoon Candied Citrus Peel

Mix all ingredients and place in 2 plastic sandwich bags.
Pack for lunch or snacks.

Per serving: 125.5 Calories; 6.0g Fat; 1.6g Protein; 18.4g Carbohydrate;
   0mg Cholesterol; 26mg Sodium

Variation - Dry Fruit and Nut Mix Day 4 C/E (serves 2)
- 1/2 cup Honey Banana Chips, dried
- 1/2 cup dried pineapple pieces
- 2 Tbs. pecan pieces

Per serving: 206.4 Calories; 3.8g Fat; 1.7g Protein; 47.2g Carbohydrate;
   0mg Cholesterol; 4mg Sodium

Variation - Dry Fruit and Nut Mix Day 5 C/E (serves 2)
- 1/4 cup Brazil nuts
- 1/2 cup dried sweet potatoe pieces
- 1/2 cup dried cranberries unsweetened

Per serving: 146.5 Calories; 5.8g Fat; 1.9g Protein; 23.5g Carbohydrate;
   0mg Cholesterol; 5mg Sodium

Per serving: 125.5 Calories; 6.0g Fat (40.2% calories from fat); 1.6g Protein;
   18.4g Carbohydrate; 0mg Cholesterol; 26mg Sodium

Honey Banana Chips
Serves 8

- 4 whole banana, peeled
- 1 Tablespoon lemon juice
- 2 cups water
- 1/3 cup honey

In a medium bowl, combine lemon juice and water. Slice bananas and place immediately in lemon water bath. Scoop out and drain on paper towel. Gently pat dry with towels to remove excess water. With soft paint brush, coat banana slices with honey on one side. Place on dehydrator trays, honey side down, and brush other side with remaining honey. Dehydrate until dry and crisp.

Slow oven method: Heat oven to 175-200 degrees. Place coated banana chips on foil lined cookie sheet. Bake until dry and crisp. Check every hour.

Per serving: 77.5 Calories; 0.2g Fat (1.9% calories from fat); 0.4g Protein; 20.5g Carbohydrate; 0mg Cholesterol; 3mg Sodium

Dried Cranberries C/E
Serves 8

1   pound fresh cranberries

Wash and slice cranberries in half. Line dehydrator trays with foil (berries will fall through otherwise). Place berries in a single layer on the foil and dry just until leathery. Check often.
Slow oven method: Place on foil lined cookie sheet and bake at 175-200 degrees until leathery about 1 1/2-2 hours. Will not take these long, so check frequently.
Store in an air tight container.

Per serving: 26.4 Calories; 0.1g Fat (3.4% calories from fat); 0.2g Protein;
      6.8g Carbohydrate; 0mg Cholesterol; 1mg Sodium

Dried Sweet Potatoes C/E
Serves 8

2   large sweet potatoes
1/3   cup rice syrup

Peel sweet potatoes and slice into 1/4" slices. Brush each slice with rice syrup, then, quarter each slice to make bite size pieces.
Slow oven method works great for this. Place slices on a foil lined cookie sheet and bake at 175-200 degrees until dry but pliable (about 2-4 hours). Cool and place in air tight containers.

Per serving: 52.9 Calories; 0.1g Fat (1.2% calories from fat); 0.4g Protein;
      12.7g Carbohydrate; 0mg Cholesterol; 4mg Sodium

Dried Mushrooms
Serves 8

1   pound mushrooms, of choice

Wash mushrooms and pat dry with paper towel. Slice into thin slices and arrange on dehydrator trays or on cookie sheet for slow oven method. Plug in dehydrator and place trays in dehydrator. use drying times suggested by instruction booklet. For slow oven method: place cookie sheet with mushrooms in 175 degree oven for about 2 hours. Check at the end of 2 hours. Mushrooms should be completely dry and break when bent. Store in resealable plastic bags or airtight containers.

Per serving: 13.8 Calories; 0.2g Fat (11.9% calories from fat); 1.1g Protein; 2.6g Carbohydrate; 0mg Cholesterol; 2mg Sodium

Dried Honey Carrots
Serves 8

1 pound carrots, peeled-sliced 1/4"
3 Tablespoons honey

Bring 2 quarts water to the boil. Place sliced carrots in boiling water for 3 minutes. Remove from heat and drain off water. Place carrots in cold water to stop cooking process. Drain when cool and pat dry with towel. Place in a bowl and add honey. Toss gently to coat with honey. Place in a single layer on dehydrator trays. For slow oven method, place on a foil lined cookie sheet.

Dehydrator: plug in and let dehydrate for 12-16 hours. You will need to rotate trays about every 4 hours. When dry, cool and store in plastic containers.

Slow oven: Turn oven on to 175- 200 degrees and slow bake until dry. Takes only a few hours. Check every hour. It is more efficient to dry many items at a time. So, plan a drying day for the slow oven method and dry many types of fruits and vegetables.

Per serving: 45.9 Calories; 0.1g Fat (1.6% calories from fat); 0.5g Protein; 11.7g Carbohydrate; 0mg Cholesterol; 18mg Sodium

Dried Cinnamon Apples
Serves 8

- 4 medium apples, cored and sliced
- 2 teaspoons lemon juice
- 2 cups water
- 4 Tablespoons beet sugar
- 4 teaspoons cinnamon

Preheat dehydrator or oven to 175 degrees.
Place 2 teaspoons lemon juice in a bowl with 2 cups water (this citric acid water bath will prevent the apples from turning brown before dehydrating). Soak apple slices in lemon water bath for 2 minutes. Drain off water; then, pat the apple slices dry with paper towels. Combine sugar and cinnamon in a small bowl and stir well. Sprinkle apples with sugar and cinnamon mixture. Place slices of apples on the dehydrator racks and arrange in the dehydrator. Allow to dry overnight and check in 12 hours. Drying times will vary depending on the thickness of the slices. Trays may need to be rotated during drying process. When dry, but still pliable, remove from the dehydrator and allow to cool. For slow oven method: place apples on a cookie sheet and dry in a 175 degree oven for about 2-4 hours (depends on the thickness of the apple slices). Check after 2 hours for pliablility. (Apple should be dry, but pliable) Place in plastic resealable bags or airtight containers. These can be used in dried fruit mixes, pies or baked goods.

Per serving: 64.2 Calories; 0.3g Fat (3.4% calories from fat); 0.2g Protein; 17.0g Carbohydrate; 0mg Cholesterol; 2mg Sodium

Cajun Jerky
Serves 24

  2   pounds beef, turkey or chicken
  2   teaspoons cajun seasoning, all natural
1/4   cup balsamic vinegar, all natural

Select meats that have little or no fat throughout the meat. The fat will leave moisture in the jerky.
Freeze meat, then thaw slightly, just until you can slice it easily. Cut off all pieces of fat. Slice into 1/4" slices.
In a large resealable storage bag, pour balsamic vinegar and spices. Mix thoroughly. Place meat slices into bag and release excess air. Kneed gently to distribute the marinade. Place in refrigerator for at least 1 hour.

Plug in dehydrator and allow it to warm. Drain off marinade and blot meat strips gently with towel to remove excess marinade. Place on dehydrator racks, with space between each piece of meat, and open bottom and top ports by 1/2. Dehydrate overnight(usually 12-14 hours for most 1/4" meat), and check in the morning for desired doneness. If signs of moisture remain on meat, continue to dehydrate, checking every few hours. Racks may need to be rotated to allow for even dehydrating. Meat should be dry but pliable. Store in plastic bags.

You may use this as a high protein snack, or break up and use as a meat in soups and stews. These strips are great for camping and hiking.

SLOW OVEN METHOD: Place meat strips on a foil lined cookie sheet and place in a 175-200 degree oven for 1 1/2-2 hours. Jerky should be dry but pliable. You may need to increase or decrease slow oven times.

Per serving: 85.6 Calories; 6.5g Fat (69.3% calories from fat); 6.2g Protein; 0.3g Carbohydrate; 23mg Cholesterol; 37mg Sodium

Dried Mushroom Soup
Serves 4

- 2 cups dried mushrooms
- 1 Tablespoon dried onions
- 1/2 teaspoon salt
- 1/4 teaspoon pepper
- 1 Tablespoon parsley, dried
- 3 cups hot water
- 3 cups chicken broth, or water

Place mushrooms and onion in a bowl with 3 cups hot water. Make sure all of the mushrooms are under water. You may have to weight them down with a saucer. Soak for 30 minutes. Save the liquid. Place mushrooms, onion, and liquid into a 2 quart sauce pan and add salt, pepper, parsley, and chicken broth (water works as well). Bring to a boil, and cook for 10 minutes, covered, at a low simmer. Serve hot. For trail cooking, place all dry ingredients in individual servings in plastic bags. Use all water as the liquid in the soup (to cut down on what you will need to carry), and prepare recipe for one or four. This soup is packed with flavor.

Variation: Add jerky pieces to soup. If you need more calories for energy, add rice pasta when soaking the mushrooms. They will be done by the time the soup cooking time is complete.

Per serving: 414.2 Calories; 3.3g Fat (6.2% calories from fat); 19.8g Protein; 91.8g Carbohydrate; 2mg Cholesterol; 1,465mg Sodium

Dried Trail Soup Mix
Serves 4

1/2	cup Cajun Jerky
1/2	cup carrots, dried
1/2	cup celery, dried
1/2	cup dried mushrooms
1/2	cup peas, dried
1/2	cup dried tomatoes, pieces
1/2	teaspoon salt
1/4	teaspoon pepper
1/4	teaspoon garlic salt
1/2	teaspoon oregano
4	cups hot water
4	cups chicken broth, or water

In a large sauce pan, place jerky, carrots, celery, mushrooms, peas, dried tomato pieces, and 4 cups hot water. You may need to weight the vegetables down with a saucer. Soak for 30 minutes. Add spices and chicken broth or additional water. Bring to a boil and simmer on low heat for 10 minutes. For added calories for hiking, add 1 cup rice noodles (macaroni shaped) while soaking the vegetables. This soup can be prepared for an individual if scaled down. To pack in individual servings, place 1/4 of each ingredient in a resealable plastic bag (4). Prepare as directed using only 2 cups liquid called for.

Per serving: 268.0 Calories; 8.0g Fat (25.3% calories from fat); 20.5g Protein; 32.7g Carbohydrate; 19mg Cholesterol; 2,029mg Sodium

Jerky and Rice Soup
Serves 4

- 1/2 cup Cajun Jerky
- 1/2 cup celery, dried
- 1 cup instant rice, all natural
- 1/2 teaspoon salt
- 3 cups hot water
- 4 cups vegetable broth

Place jerky, celery, and rice in 3 cups hot water. Soak for 20 minutes. Pour in vegetable broth or broth of choice (may use water). Add salt and bring to a boil. Let simmer on low for 10 minutes and serve hot. For trail packing, you can pack soup in individual servings in plastice resealable bags. At the campfire, add 2 cups water or broth.

Per serving: 319.7 Calories; 8.7g Fat (24.7% calories from fat); 12.5g Protein; 47.3g Carbohydrate; 19mg Cholesterol; 1,964mg Sodium

Grill Top Potato Medley
Serves 4

    2   medium potato, washed, sliced
    1   medium onion, small
    1   medium green pepper, cleaned and sliced
    1   medium apple, chopped small
    2   Tablespoons canola margarine
1 1/2   teaspoons nutmeg

Melt margarine in pan or foil on grill top. Place sliced potatoes on top of margarine. Layer onion and green pepper over potatoes. Top with apple, sprinkle on nutmeg. Turn the potatoes occasionally. Cook 20 - 30 minutes, until potatoes are tender. If cooking on the grill, cooking times may vary. This dish is a delightful flavor to tantilize the taste buds.

Per serving: 117.6 Calories; 6.0g Fat (44.8% calories from fat); 1.4g Protein; 15.3g Carbohydrate; 0mg Cholesterol; 200mg Sodium

Sombrero Bundles
Serves 4

- 1 cup rice flour
- 1/2 teaspoon baking soda
- 1/2 teaspoon cream of tartar
- 1 teaspoon guar gum
- 3 Tablespoons canola margarine, softened
- 1/2 cup rice milk
- 1 Tablespoon rice milk
- 4 ounces Rubbed Pork Tenderloin, sliced thin
- 2 ounces almond cheese

Measure flour, baking soda, cream of tartar, and guar gum into a bowl. Mix well set aside. Add margarine to dry ingredients, cut margarine into flour mixture with your fingers or a fork. Add all of the milk to make a thick batter, stirring only until dough sticks together. Tear off a large enough piece of aluminum foil to make a square. Place center of foil piece over the bottom of an upside down glass or cup. Press foil to the glass to make a 1 - 1 1/2 inch deep impression in the foil. Form should look like a square brimmed hat. Spray the inside of the hat with cooking oil. Drop a spoonful of dough inside of hat. Gently smooth out dough slightly flattening it. Place about one ounce of meat on top of dough, then a small slice of cheese. Place scant spoonfuls of dough on top of meat and cheese. Gently smooth out dough. Place a flat piece of foil on top, This actually will make the bottom of the hat. Roll the edges of the foil together rounding it off to form the brim of the sombrero. Place on the grill sombrero upside down first. Bake for 6-7 minutes over a medium to low heat. Turn the sombrero over and bake a few more minutes.

Substitution: May substitute rice cheese, or soy cheese for the rice cheese, read the labels.
This is a fun one to have the kids help make.

Per serving: 308.7 Calories; 11.9g Fat (35.2% calories from fat); 11.5g Protein; 37.5g Carbohydrate; 18mg Cholesterol; 420mg Sodium

Fresh Fish Pouch
Serves 4

- 4   6 ounce fish fillet, fresh
- 1   large onion, sliced 1/2" thick
- 4   cloves garlic, sliced
- 4   large carrots, shredded
- 4   teaspoons margarine, or oil of choice
      salt and pepper, to taste
- 2   Tablespoons lemon juice

Any vegetable combination will do.
Use one piece of 12" heavy duty aluminum foil for each pouch. Place one fish fillet in the center of each piece of foil. Season with salt, pepper, lemon, and other spices if desired. Top with onion and garlic slices. Next, top with shredded carrots and pull up sides of foil to completely seal the pouch. Place on the grill for 20-25 minutes or until fish flakes. If cooking over a fire, place on the edge of the hot coals and rotate to other side after 10 minutes. Cook another 10-15 minutes. Check after 15 minutes total cooking time. To bake in the oven: preheat oven to 375 degrees and bake for 20 minutes.

This recipe calls for little or no clean-up.

Per serving: 263.6 Calories; 5.5g Fat (19.2% calories from fat); 42.4g Protein;
      9.5g Carbohydrate; 99mg Cholesterol; 329mg Sodium

Burger Pouch
Serves 6

- 1 pound ground round, patties
- 1 medium onion, sliced
- 2 large carrots, grated
- 3 medium turnips, chopped
- 6 teaspoons canola margarine
- 1/2 teaspoon salt and pepper, to taste
- 1/2 teaspoon garlic salt

Preheat grill or oven to 375 degrees.
Form ground beef into 6 thin patties. Use a 12"x12" piece of aluminum foil to form a pouch for patties and vegetables. Place one patty on each piece of foil. Sprinkle with salt, pepper, and garlic. Place slices of onion, grated carrots, and turnips on top of patty. Top with 1 teaspoon of margarine. Fold foil over the beef and vegetable medley and fold edges over to form an envelope or pouch. Repeat this sequence with each patty. Place in a 375 degree oven for 35 minutes, or place on a preheated grill away from the direct flame. Check patty for doneness after 25 minutes. Continue to cook until done.

Perserving: 238.6 Calories; 16.7g Fat; 15.1g Protein; 6.5g Carbohydrate;
    52mg Cholesterol; 344mg Sodium

Variation - CHICKEN POUCH (serves 4)
- 4 6 ounce chicken breast halves, boneless-skinless
- 1 Medium onion thinly sliced
- 1 Medium tomato thinly sliced
- 1 3 ounce can black olives sliced
- 1 teaspoon oregano, dried
- 1/4 teaspoon garlic salt
  - dash salt and pepper to taste

Per serving: 264.4 Calories; 13.7g Fat; 30.8g Protein; 3.1g Carbohydrate;
    93mg Cholesterol; 242mg Sodium

Per serving: 238.6 Calories; 16.7g Fat (63.6% calories from fat); 15.1g Protein;
    6.5g Carbohydrate; 52mg Cholesterol; 344mg Sodium

Breakfast Taco
Serves 4

- 3 whole eggs, optional
- 1 small onion, minced
- 1/4 cup green pepper, chopped
- 1/2 recipe Turkey Breakfast Sausage
- 1 Tablespoon hot pepper sauce, optional
- 1 recipe Soft Shell Taco Roll-up, prepared

Eggs are optional. Brown sausage in skillet. Add onion and green pepper. Cook until onion is almost transparent. Lightly beat eggs (if used). Pour beaten eggs into skillet with sausage, onion and pepper. Stir, scrambling egg with meat mixture. Season with salt and pepper if desired. Scoop into soft shell taco roll-up and top off with hot sauce or the hot sauce can be mixed into meat and egg mixutre before serving. Enjoy.
Note: Use our Turkey Breakfast Sausage and Soft Shell Taco Roll-up or Quinoa Tortilla recipes made in advance.
Serving Suggestion: Add your favorite soy (if permitted), rice, or almond cheese. Omit hot pepper sauce and use salsa as a topping. Add a teaspoon of rice sour cream. You will be delighted.
This recipe contains egg. Egg can be omitted and only the meat mixture used. When omitting the egg, add vegetables as you would for an omelette, then add bits of cheese (soy, rice, or almond). Heat through and serve taco style. We do not miss the eggs!

Per serving: 114.9 Calories; 5.2g Fat (41.0% calories from fat); 7.2g Protein; 9.6g Carbohydrate; 143mg Cholesterol; 207mg Sodium

Desserts

Bread Pudding
Serves 6

10	slices rice bread, or bread of the day
2	Tablespoons canola margarine, margarine of choice
1/4	cup raisins
1/4	cup pecans
4	teaspoons egg replacer, = 3 eggs
1	teaspoon cinnamon
1 1/4	cups almond milk
1	teaspoon vanilla, alcohol-free
1/4	cup date sugar, beet sugar or honey

Preheat oven to 350 degrees.

Spread each slice of bread with a little margarine and sprinkle with cinnamon. Cut each slice of bread into small pieces about 1 1/2". Arrange bread pieces in an oiled deep dish pie plate. Sprinkle raisins and nuts over bread. In a medium bowl, combine milk, egg substitute (or eggs), and vanilla. Wisk together until all is blended. Pour over bread. Sprinkle date sugar, beet sugar or honey evenly over all ingredients in the pie plate. Bake in a 350 degree oven for 40-45 minutes or until a knife inserted in the middle comes out clean. Serve warm alone or with one our "Icecream" recipes.

This is a great way to use the stale bread in your rotation plan!
Do not use rye bread for this recipe. Its flavor is not what you would want in a bread pudding.

Per serving: 597.4 Calories; 10.0g Fat (14.5% calories from fat); 4.1g Protein; 128.6g Carbohydrate; 0mg Cholesterol; 201mg Sodium

Rice Pudding Day 5
Serves 8

- 2 cups cooked rice
- 2 cups almond milk, or milk of day
- 1 teaspoon vanilla, alcohol-free
- 1/2 cup raisins
- 3 teaspoons egg replacer, =2 eggs
- 2/3 cup beet sugar, or sweetener of day
- 1 Tablespoon potato starch flour
- 1 teaspoon cinnamon

Cook enough rice to make 2 cups. Place raisins on top of hot rice; this will moisten and plump raisins. Place milk and potato starch flour in a small bowl and wisk to mix well. Add egg replacer, sugar, cinnamon and vanilla to milk. Stir well, then pour into sauce pan. Heat mixture on medium-low setting. When mixture begins to steam, time for 2-3 minutes. Do not allow milk mixture to boil. Stir rapidly until it begins to thicken. Remove from heat and add rice and raisins. Stir well. Transfer to large serving bowl or individual cups. Refrigerate at least 2 hours or until ready to serve.

Per serving: 348.4 Calories; 0.8g Fat (2.0% calories from fat); 2.2g Protein; 87.4g Carbohydrate; 0mg Cholesterol; 101mg Sodium

Basic Tapioca C/E
Serves 6

- 3 cups almond milk, or milk of choice
- 1/4 cup beet sugar, or honey
- 1 1/3 teaspoons egg replacer, =1 egg
- 3 Tablespoons tapioca, quick cooking
- 1 teaspoon vanilla, alcohol-free

In a medium saucepan, combine milk, beet sugar, egg replacer, and tapioca. Let set for 5-10 minutes. Cook over medium heat, stirring frequently until pudding mix begins to boil. Remove from heat and add vanilla. Stir well, then let set for 20 minutes or until cool enough to place in serving dishes. Place in the refrigerator until ready to serve, or serve warm.

Variations: Add any fresh fruit after cooking tapioca. Simply puree or chop fruit and stir into tapioca.

Add lemon, lime or orange zest before cooking tapioca.

For a Key Lime treat, add 1/4 cup Key Lime juice and decrease milk to 2 3/4 cup. Add 1 teaspoon lime zest.

1/4 cup cocoa powder can be wisked into the tapioca mix before boiling for a rich chocolate pudding treat.

Per serving: 189.1 Calories; 1.3g Fat (5.7% calories from fat); 1.0g Protein; 45.9g Carbohydrate; 0mg Cholesterol; 94mg Sodium

Orange Filled Crepes
Serves 10

- 1 recipe Hazelnut Pancakes with Citrus Sauce Day 3
- 1 recipe Citrus Sauce   Day 3
- 2 large orange, peeled-sectioned
- 1/4 cup honey
- 1 Tablespoon orange rind
- 1 teaspoon tapioca flour
- 1/2 cup orange juice

Prepare Hazelnut Pancakes according to recipe. Cover and set aside.
Prepare Citrus Sauce recipe. Set aside.
Orange Filling: Place orange sections in a medium sauce pan with honey and orange rind and bring to a boil. In a measuring cup, combine orange juice and tapioca flour. Stir to mix well. Add tapioca and orange juice mix to oranges. Cook on low until it thickens. Remove from heat.
Place a pancake on a serving plate. Fill with orange filling (about 2 Tablespoons). Fold pancake and top with Citrus Sauce. Garnish with mint leaves. For an added treat, serve with rice ice cream or orange ice.

Per serving: 128.4 Calories; 1.2g Fat (8.0% calories from fat); 1.2g Protein; 30.6g Carbohydrate; 0mg Cholesterol; 33mg Sodium

Homemade Chocolate Chips
Serves 16

- 3 Tablespoons cocoa powder, pure
- 1 Tablespoon canola margarine
- 2 cups beet sugar
- 2 Tablespoons bees wax, 3" x 4" approx.
- 1 Tablespoon almond milk

Melt sugar, cocoa, and margarine. Boil for 2 minutes, stirring constantly. Add bee's wax while hot, and stir until melted. Line a large cookie sheet with foil and spread chocolate mix on sheet in a thin layer. Cool, then place in the freezer, covered until needed (at least overnight). When frozen hard, cut into small 1/4 " squares with a knife or pizza cutter. Will store well in an airtight container or plastic bag. Use for cookies, baking cakes, cake topping, or "rice cream" topping.

Per serving: 102.7 Calories; 0.8g Fat (6.8% calories from fat); 0.2g Protein; 25.6g Carbohydrate; 0mg Cholesterol; 8mg Sodium

Basic Sugar Cookies
Serves 24

3/4	cup rice flour, white
1	cup amaranth flour
1/2	cup tapioca flour
1	cup sugar
1/2	cup canola margarine
1	teaspoon baking soda
1	teaspoon cream of tartar
1/2	teaspoon salt
1 1/3	teaspoons egg replacer, =1 egg
1	teaspoon vanilla
1/2	recipe Homemade Chocolate Chips, optional

Prheat oven to 425 degrees.
Combine all dry ingredients and mix well. Cut in margarine. Add egg or egg replacer and vanilla. Mix well. Cookie dough will be crumbly. Gently fold in chocolate chips. Make 1" balls with dough and place on cookie sheet or baking stone. Bake 8-12 minutes until golden. Remove from cookie sheet immediately and place on cooling rack.
One half of the dough can be made into a roll, wraped in plastic, and frozen for later use. Remove from freezer for 10 minutes and slice in 1/4" slices. Place on cookie sheet and bake as directed.

Serving size: 2 cookies.

Per serving: 142.1 Calories; 4.3g Fat (26.6% calories from fat); 1.5g Protein; 25.2g Carbohydrate; 0mg Cholesterol; 150mg Sodium

Boiled Cookies
Serves 36

  2   cups beet sugar, or maple sugar
1/3 cup cocoa, unsweetened
1/4 cup canola margarine
1/2 cup vanilla almond milk, or milk of day
  3   cups oats, dry, uncooked
1/2 cup peanut butter, optional
  2   teaspoons vanilla

In medium sauce pan, bring sugar, cocoa, butter, and milk to boil. Boil for 2 full minutes stirring constantly. Add vanilla and stir. Add oats and stir well. Allow to set about 1 minute. Drop by spoonfuls onto waxpaper. Allow to cool. Store in airtight container. If you are sensitive to peanuts, omit peanut butter. It will be like a crunchy fudge. I have made these cookies since I was a little girl and was delighted that I could adapt this favorite recipe for you.

Per serving: 127.8 Calories; 4.1g Fat (27.2% calories from fat); 3.3g Protein; 21.1g Carbohydrate; 0mg Cholesterol; 32mg Sodium

Southern Pecan Cookies
Serves 36

- 1 cup rice flour
- 1/4 cup potato starch flour
- 1/2 cup beet sugar
- 1 1/3 teaspoons egg replacer, =1 egg
- 3/4 teaspoon baking soda
- 3/4 teaspoon cream of tartar
- 1/4 teaspoon salt
- 1/3 cup canola margarine
- 1 cup pecans
- 1 Tablespoon coconut milk, or milk of choice

Preheat oven to 400 degrees.

Combine flours, sugar, egg replacer, baking soda, cream of tartar, salt, and mix well. Cut in canola margarine until flour mixture has crumbs smaller than peasize. Add pecans and stir well. Add milk and stir briefly until moist but still crumbly. Press crumb batter into a heaping teaspoon. Using finger or another spoon, remove from the teaspoon onto an ungreased cookie sheet. Place 2 1/2" apart on cookie sheet. (Use foil to line the cookie sheet to minimize clean up. Use the same foil on each consecutive batch.) Bake for 8-10 minutes at 400 degrees. Edges should be golden, but not brown. Remove from the cookie sheet to a cooling rack immediately. These cookies are very crunchy and delicious.

Makes about 3 1/2 dozen.
These cookies freeze well.

Per serving: 75.2 Calories; 2.9g Fat (33.3% calories from fat); 0.4g Protein; 12.5g Carbohydrate; 0mg Cholesterol; 66mg Sodium

Rice Pecan Cookies
Serves 48

- 1/4 cup canola margarine, softened
- 1/4 cup beet sugar
- 1 teaspoon vanilla, alcohol-free
- 3/4 cup white rice flour
- 1/2 cup pecans, chopped
- 1/4 teaspoon guar gum
- 2 Tablespoons beet sugar, optional
- 1/2 teaspoon cinnamon, optional

Mix flour and guar gum together thoroughly. Set aside. Place margarine in bowl, add sugar, and mix well. Add vanilla. Gradually add flour mixture. Fold in pecans. Form balls by rolling a spoonful of dough in your hands. Roll in optional coating discribed below if desired. Place on cookie sheet. Use a fork and lightly depress the centers.
Bake 7-10 minutes at 375 degrees. Allow to cool for one minute and gently remove from cookie sheet. Cookie is very soft when hot. Place on wax paper to cool.
Cookie does not expand when baked. Makes 48 small cookies.
Variation: Combine the optional ingredients: sugar and cinnamon, and roll the balls in the mixture before baking.

Per serving: 27.4 Calories; 1.4g Fat (44.1% calories from fat); 0.2g Protein; 3.7g Carbohydrate; 0mg Cholesterol; 10mg Sodium

Pumpkin Cookies
Serves 36

- 1 cup rice flour
- 1/2 cup beet sugar
- 3/4 teaspoon baking soda
- 3/4 teaspoon cream of tartar
- 1/4 teaspoon salt
- 1/3 cup canola margarine
- 1/4 teaspoon cinnamon
- 1/4 teaspoon nutmeg
- 1/4 teaspoon cloves
- 1/2 cup pumpkin, natural pack
- 1/3 cup coconut, shredded-unsweetened

Preheat oven to 400 degrees. Line a cookie sheet with foil to minimize clean up. In a medium bowl, combine all dry ingredients and mix well. Cut in margarine with fork until crumbs are smaller than pea size. Add pumpkin puree from the can and coconut. Stir until dough is uniform in color. Drop onto ungreased cookie sheet by teaspoonfuls. Bake at 400 degrees for 10 minutes. Do not allow to brown. Remove immediately from cookie sheet to cooling racks.

These freeze well in individual portions for lunches.

Per serving: 43.3 Calories; 1.8g Fat (37.8% calories from fat); 0.3g Protein; 6.5g Carbohydrate; 0mg Cholesterol; 59mg Sodium

Granola Oat Cookies
Serves 24

- 3 cups oats, toasted
- 1 cup oat flour
- 1 cup cashews, chopped
- 1/2 cup sunflower seeds
- 3/4 cup maple syrup
- 1 teaspoon vanilla
- 1/2 teaspoon salt
- 1 cup white raisins
- 1 1/3 teaspoons egg replacer, = 1 egg
- 1 teaspoon baking soda
- 1 teaspoon cream of tartar
- 1 cup almond milk, or cashew milk

Preheat oven to 400 degrees.
Mix vanilla and maple syrup. Set aside. Mix salt, oat flour, baking soda, cream of tartar, oats, nuts, raisins, and sunflower seeds. Combine maple syrup mix and dry ingredients. Stir to coat with syrup. Add almond milk and egg replacer (or egg) Stir until well mixed. Place teaspoonsful on baking stone or greased cookie sheet (you may spray cookie sheet with oil). Bake at 400 degrees for 8-10 minutes. Remove from cookie sheet or baking stone immediately. Store in an airtight container. Great for lunches and snacks.
Serving size is 2 cookies.

Per serving: 200.9 Calories; 5.1g Fat (21.9% calories from fat); 5.3g Protein; 35.5g Carbohydrate; 0mg Cholesterol; 149mg Sodium

Ginger Cookies Day 3
Serves 36

- 1 cup amaranth flour
- 1/4 cup tapioca flour
- 1/2 cup honey
- 1 teaspoon ginger, ground
- 1 teaspoon orange zest, grated fine
- 1/3 cup canola margarine
- 3/4 teaspoon baking soda
- 3/4 teaspoon cream of tartar
- 1/4 teaspoon salt
- 1 Tablespoon milk, if needed

Preheat oven to 400 degrees.
Line a cookie sheet with foil.
In a medium bowl, combine flours, ginger, orange zest, soda, cream of tartar, and salt. Mix well. Add canola margarine and cut into flour mix with a fork until crumbs resemble small peas. Add honey and mix well. Dough will still be crumbly, but should hold together when pressed into a ball. Press dough into a heaping teaspoon and drop onto cookie sheet. Press down a little with fingers.
Bake at 400 degrees for 8-10 minutes. Remove from cookie sheet immediately to cooling rack. For a crisper cookie, cook a minute or two longer, but do not allow to brown completely.

These cookies pack well in lunches and freeze well for quick snacks.

Per serving: 50.5 Calories; 2.0g Fat (34.4% calories from fat); 0.8g Protein; 7.7g Carbohydrate; 0mg Cholesterol; 60mg Sodium

Coconut Snowballs
Serves 48

- 1 cup white rice flour
- 1/4 cup potato starch flour
- 1/2 cup beet sugar
- 1 1/3 teaspoons egg replacer, =1 egg
- 3/4 teaspoon baking soda
- 3/4 teaspoon cream of tartar
- 1/4 teaspoon salt
- 1/3 cup canola margarine, margarine of choice
- 1 cup coconut, unsweetened
- 1/4 cup coconut milk
- 1 teaspoon coconut flavoring, optional

Note: Most flavorings contain alcohol (corn?). Some are available at health food stores that are made with natural oils and glycerine. If in doubt, leave it out.

Preheat oven to 400 degrees.
In a medium bowl, combine all dry ingredients except coconut. Cut in margarine with a fork and work until dough crumbs are smaller than pea size. Stir in coconut. Add coconut milk and flavoring. Batter will still be crumbly. Press dough into a heaping teaspoon. Remove from teaspoon with you finger or another spoon. Cookies should be rounded on top to resemble snowballs. Bake at 400 degrees for 8-10 minutes. Do not let cookies brown. Brown Snowballs are not attractive!! Remove from cookie sheet immediately to a cooling rack.
These store in the freezer well when placed in airtight plastic containers or bags.
Pack these Snowballs for lunch.
Nutritional analysis is per cookie.

Per serving: 53.8 Calories; 1.9g Fat (30.3% calories from fat); 0.3g Protein; 9.4g Carbohydrate; 0mg Cholesterol; 50mg Sodium

Peanut Butter Cookies
Serves 24

1	cup beet sugar
1/2	cup amaranth flour
1/2	cup rice flour
1/2	cup tapioca flour
1/2	cup potato starch flour
1/2	cup peanut butter, crunchy
1/3	cup margarine
1 1/3	teaspoons egg replacer, = 1 egg
1	teaspoon vanilla
1/3	cup vanilla almond milk, or milk of day
1 1/2	teaspoons baking soda
1 1/2	teaspoons cream of tartar

Preheat oven to 350 degrees. Mix all dry ingredients. Cream margarine and peanut butter. Add vanilla, egg replacer (or egg), and milk. Fold into dry ingredients. Mix with hands if desired. Form small 1" balls and place on ungreased cookie sheet or baking stone. Flatten balls with bottom of cup. Make marks on top of cookie if desired with fork dipped in beet sugar.   Bake for 8-12 minutes. Remove immediately to cooling rack. These freeze well in plastic freezer bags. When only baking half of the cookie dough, form roll with remaining dough and wrap in plastic wrap. Place in freezer. When ready to bake, slice into thin pieces and bake as directed. Makes 4 dozen cookies.
Serving size: 2 cookies.

Per serving: 158.7 Calories; 5.6g Fat (30.1% calories from fat); 2.2g Protein; 26.9g Carbohydrate; 0mg Cholesterol; 147mg Sodium

Raisin Peanut Butter Bars or Cookies
Serves 32

- 1/2 cup peanut butter, all natural
- 1/2 cup canola margarine, or choice
- 1 cup beet sugar
- 3 teaspoons egg replacer, =2 eggs
- 1 teaspoon vanilla, alcohol-free
- 1 cup rice flour
- 1 teaspoon baking soda
- 1 teaspoon cream of tartar
- 1 1/2 cups raisins
- 2 ounces Homemade Chocolate Chips, optional

For bars: Preheat oven to 350 degrees.
In a small sauce pan, heat peanut butter and margarine until melted and smooth. Remove from heat.
In a large bowl, combine all dry ingredients and mix well. Stir in raisins until coated with flour mixture. Add melted peanut butter, margarine and vanilla and stir until mixed together to form a ball of dough. Line a 13x9 inch baking pan with foil. Spread dough into pan evenly. Bake at 350 degrees for 25 minutes. Remove foil liner with baked dough from pan to a cooling rack. Top with homemade chocolate chips (or carob chips) if desired and let cool on rack before cutting into 32 bars.

For cookies: Preheat oven to 375 degrees. On a cookie sheet, drop by teaspoonsful onto ungreased cookie sheet, and bake for 8-10 minutes until golden. Do not let cookies brown around edges. Makes about 6 dozen cookies.

Per serving: 157.6 Calories; 4.9g Fat (26.7% calories from fat); 1.5g Protein; 28.9g Carbohydrate; 0mg Cholesterol; 108mg Sodium

Chocolate Nut Bars
Serves 24

- 3/4 cup canola margarine
- 3/4 cup beet sugar
- 1 1/4 cups white rice flour
- 2 Tablespoons coconut milk-lite, unsweetened
- 1 1/2 cups pecans, chopped
- 1 cup coconut, unsweetened-flaked
- 4 ounces semisweet chocolate, chips

Preheat oven to 350 degrees.
With hand mixer, beat 1/4 cup sugar and 1/2 cup margarine until smooth and creamy. Add flour and mix with fork until incorporated well. Press into the bottom of an ungreased 9"x9"x2" pan. Bake at 350 degrees for 18 minutes or until edges are lightly brown.
 Heat 1/2 cup sugar, 1/4 cup margarine, and coconut milk in saucepan until margarine melts and ingredients are blended. Set aside. Sprinkle coconut, pecans, and chocolate over crust. Pour melted margarine mixture over all and bake for 20 more minutes or until golden. Cool completely and cut into 24 squares.

These treats are not your everyday snacks, but are wonderful when prepared for holidays or celebrations.

Per serving: 157.2 Calories; 10.1g Fat (56.1% calories from fat); 1.0g Protein; 16.8g Carbohydrate; 0mg Cholesterol; 61mg Sodium

Rice Fruit Bars Day 5
Serves 24

  1   cup rice flour
  2   cups crispy rice cereal, natural only
1/4 teaspoon salt
1/2 teaspoon baking soda
1/2 teaspoon cream of tartar
  1   teaspoon cinnamon
1/2 cup nuts, chopped
3/4 cup canola margarine, or 1/2 cup oil
1/2 cup rice syrup
3/4 cup blueberry preserves

Preheat oven to 325 degrees.
Combine rice flour and margarine. Add crispy rice cereal, salt, baking soda, cream of tartar, cinnamon, nuts, margarine, and rice syrup and mix thoroughly. Press 3/4 of mixture into a 9x13 pan. Spread preserves on top of crust layer. Sprinkle remaining crust mixture over preserves.
Bake at 325 degrees for 15-20 minutes. Cool completely and cut into 24 squares. You may want to line the pan with foil and spray with cooking oil to make clean up easier. These go well in lunches and for snacks.

Per serving: 140.4 Calories; 7.3g Fat (46.1% calories from fat); 1.1g Protein; 18.0g Carbohydrate; 0mg Cholesterol; 130mg Sodium

Rice Granola Bars   Day 5
Serves 24

- 4 cups crispy rice cereal, natural
- 1 1/2 cups brazil nuts, chopped
- 3/4 cup rice syrup
- 1 cup cranberries, dried blueberries, or dates chopped

Preheat oven to 400 degrees.
Mix rice cereal, nuts, and fruits. Add rice syrup and mix well. Press into foil lined 9x13" pan treated with cooking oil. Press firmly with back of spoon to compress mixture. Bake at 400 degrees 8-10 minutes.
Cool completely. Cut into 24 squares and carefully remove from pan. Some of the squares may crumble, but the majority will stay together and will taste delicious.

Per serving: 69.1 Calories; 2.8g Fat (35.8% calories from fat); 0.9g Protein; 10.4g Carbohydrate; 0mg Cholesterol; 35mg Sodium

Oat Squares
Serves 24

- 2 3/4 cups oats, uncooked
- 1 cup oat flour
- 3/4 teaspoon salt
- 2 teaspoons baking soda
- 2 teaspoons cream of tartar
- 1 teaspoon cinnamon
- 1/2 cup nuts, chopped
- 3/4 cup canola margarine, or
- 1/2 cup oil of the day (not olive oil)
- 1/2 cup Maple sugar
- 3/4 cup grape preserves-unsweetened

Preheat oven to 350 degrees.
Mix all ingredients except preserves. Mix with hands until crumbly and all ingredients are incorporated well. Reserve about 1 cup of mixture for topping. Press remaining oat mixture into lighted greased or oiled 9x13" pan. Spread preserves evenly over batter. Sprinkle remaining oat mixture over preserves. Bake for 20 minutes. Cool completely. Cut into 24 squares.
Great for lunches and snacks.

Per serving: 166.6 Calories; 8.6g Fat (45.9% calories from fat); 4.1g Protein; 18.8g Carbohydrate; 0mg Cholesterol; 267mg Sodium

Applesauce Cake
Serves 16

- 1 cup buckwheat flour, light
- 1 cup white rice flour
- 3/4 cup beet sugar
- 1 teaspoon salt
- 2 teaspoons cinnamon
- 1 teaspoon cloves
- 1 teaspoon nutmeg
- 1 cup raisins, optional
- 1/4 cup safflower oil
- 3 teaspoons egg replacer, =2 eggs
- 2 cups applesauce, unsweetened
- 1 1/2 teaspoons baking soda
- 1 1/2 teaspoons cream of tartar

Preheat oven to 350 degrees.
Lightly oil two 8" round cake pans.
In a large bowl, combine flours, sugar, salt, cinnamon, cloves, nutmeg, egg replacer, baking soda, cream of tartar, and raisins. Stir together until mixed well. Add applesauce and oil and stir until all dry ingredients are moistened. Spoon into two cake pans. Bake at 350 degrees for 30-35 minutes. Cool in the pan for 5 minutes then remove by inverting onto a serving plate.

This is a fairly heavy cake and works best when left in 2 single layers. If the layers are stacked, the top layer will flatten the lower cake. Cut each layer seperately and top with fruit topping or "rice"cream.

Per serving: 261.5 Calories; 4.0g Fat (12.9% calories from fat); 1.9g Protein; 58.4g Carbohydrate; 0mg Cholesterol; 292mg Sodium

Fresh Apple Cake
Serves 10

1	cup	beet sugar, or sweetener of day
1	cup	rice flour
2/3	cup	amaranth flour
1/3	cup	potato starch flour
4 1/2	teaspoons	egg replacer, = 3 eggs
1	teaspoon	baking soda
1	teaspoon	cream of tartar
1	teaspoon	cinnamon
1	teaspoon	salt
2	cups	apples, chopped
1/2	cup	pecans, chopped
1/4	cup	oil, of the day
1/2	cup	almond milk, or milk of choice

Preheat oven to 375 degrees.
Lightly grease and flour a large loaf pan.
Mix all dry ingredients in a large bowl. Add apples and pecans and stir until all apples are coated with flour mixture. Add oil and milk and stir until all dry ingredients are moistened well. Spoon into loaf pan and spread evenly in the pan. Place on middle rack in oven and bake for 45 minutes.

This makes a good cake to pack for lunches.

Per serving: 490.6 Calories; 8.7g Fat (15.2% calories from fat); 3.2g Protein; 105.8g Carbohydrate; 0mg Cholesterol; 436mg Sodium

Brown Honey Cake
Serves 8

- 3/4 cup buckwheat flour, light
- 1/2 cup potato starch flour
- 1/2 cup rice flour
- 1 teaspoon baking soda
- 1 teaspoon cream of tartar
- 2 Tablespoons cocoa powder
- 1/8 teaspoon salt
- 1 1/3 teaspoons egg replacer, =1 egg
- 1/3 cup canola oil
- 1/3 cup rice syrup
- 1/3 cup honey

Preheat oven to 350 degrees.
Combine all dry ingredients and mix thoroughly. Combine oil, rice syrup, and honey in a small bowl and stir well. Combine dry and wet ingredients and stir with spoon until smooth. Grease or spray an 8" cake pan with oil. May put a round of parchment paper on bottom if desired. Bake at 350 degrees for 25-30 minutes. Top with fresh fruit or serve plain.

Per serving: 357.6 Calories; 9.8g Fat (23.5% calories from fat); 2.3g Protein; 69.2g Carbohydrate; 0mg Cholesterol; 227mg Sodium

German Chocolate Cake

Serves 8

- 1/2 cup beet sugar
- 1/2 cup amaranth flour
- 3/4 cup white rice flour
- 1/4 cup potato starch flour
- 1/2 teaspoon salt
- 1 teaspoon baking soda
- 1 teaspoon cream of tartar
- 1/4 cup oil, (not olive oil)
- 1 1/3 teaspoons egg replacer, =1 egg
- 1 teaspoon vanilla, alcohol-free
- 3/4 cup almond milk, or milk of choice
- 1/4 cup cocoa powder

Preheat oven to 325 degrees.
Lightly oil two round cake pan.

In a large mixing bowl, combine all dry ingredients: flours, sugar, salt, baking soda, cream of tartar, egg replacer, and cocoa powder. Stir until incorporated well. Add oil, vanilla, and milk. Stir well. Pour into oiled cake pans and bake on center rack for 30-35 minutes or until tooth pick inserted in the center comes out clean. Cool for 5 minutes, then turn out of pan onto cooling rack. Place on cake plate when cool.
Frost with Coconut Frosting.
Nutritional data is for cake only.

Per serving: 323.0 Calories; 8.4g Fat (22.4% calories from fat); 3.4g Protein; 62.1g Carbohydrate; 0mg Cholesterol; 336mg Sodium

Coconut Frosting
Serves 8

- 1/4 cup canola margarine, or oil of choice
- 1/3 cup beet sugar
- 1/3 cup pecan milk, or almond milk
- 1 teaspoon potato starch flour
- 1/2 cup pecans, chopped
- 1/2 cup coconut, unsweetened-shredded

Melt margarine and sugar in a medium saucepan. Combine milk and potato starch flour with a wisk. Add to the melted margarine and sugar in the saucepan. When mix begins to thicken, add pecans and shredded coconut. Stir constantly over medium-low heat until mixture is the consistency to spread over the cake. Frost the cake while the frosting is still very warm. It will be easier to spread warm and will be less likely to tear the cake. This recipe will frost the one layer German Chocolate Cake.

Per serving: 120.4 Calories; 8.9g Fat (64.4% calories from fat); 0.5g Protein; 10.6g Carbohydrate; 0mg Cholesterol; 65mg Sodium

Heavenly Chocolate Fudge Brownie Cake
Serves 20

2	cups beet sugar, maple or date sugar
1	cup rice flour
3/4	cup amaranth flour
3/4	cup Hershey's® cocoa, or carob powder
1 1/2	teaspoons baking soda
1 1/2	teaspoons cream of tartar
1	teaspoon salt
3	teaspoons egg replacer, (=2 eggs)
1	cup almond milk, or milk of choice
1/2	cup oil, (not olive oil)
2	teaspoons vanilla
3/4	cup boiling water

Preheat oven to 350 degrees. Grease or oil two non-stick 8" round cake pans. Combine dry ingredients in a large bowl and mix until uniform color. Add milk, oil, and vanilla (and 2 eggs if eggs are being used). Beat for 1 minute on medium speed. Stir in boiling water (batter will be very thin-this is what gives it the fudge brownie consistency. Pour batter in the two non-stick cake pans. Bake at 350 degrees for 30-35 minutes. Do not over bake. Cool for ten minutes and remove from pans. Tapping the bottom of the cake pan will usually pop it out. Cool on cake rack. Place on cake plate and frost with Fudge Frosting. Works best when the cake is left in two seperate layers and frosted as two cakes.

This cake can stand alone without the frosting. It does not turn out properly if you bake it in a sheet cake. It is too moist to hold that large a piece together. You can also make the batter into all cupcakes for lunches and desserts in a flash. Makes 30 cupcakes. Reduce baking time to 25-30 minutes for cupcakes. If chocolate is a problem, try carob powder and reduce the sugar to 1 1/2 cups.

Surprisingly, the fat grams are only 6.6gms.

Per serving: 256.5 Calories; 6.6g Fat (21.7% calories from fat); 2.2g Protein; 51.1g Carbohydrate; 0mg Cholesterol; 238mg Sodium

Heavenly Chocolate Frosting
Serves 20

- 1/4 cup canola margarine, margarine of choice
- 1/2 cup Hershey's® cocoa, powder
- 2 cups beet sugar
- 1/4 cup coconut milk, unsweetened
  or almond milk, milk of the day
- 1/2 teaspoon vanilla

If you or your children are sensitive to chocolate, do not prepare this recipe.
The sugar for this recipe has to be made into 4X confectioner's sugar before using. To do this: In a food processor with the blade in place, start motor and slowly pour the sugar (1 cup a time) into the feeding tube. Process that cup of sugar for 3 minutes, holding your hand flat over the feeding tube top, or replace the feeding tube cover to prevent the sugar dust from escaping.. Then, process other cup of sugar in the same manner. This will break up the sugar crystals and produce a finer (4X) size granule. Do not process any more sugar than is needed for one recipe, because it will cake together.

In a microwavable bowl, melt margarine. Stir in cocoa completely. Add sugar and stir until combined evenly (will be crumbly). Add milk and vanilla. Stir until smooth. Place bowl in microwave and cook on high for 2 minutes. Remove and stir well with wooden or plastic spoon. Place back in microwave and cook on high for 2 more minutes. Mixture should be bubbling. Remove and stir well. Replace in microwave and cook on high for 3 final minutes. Stir well and set aside to cool for about 10 minutes. Spoon generously over cake, allowing it to run down the sides of the cakes. For cupcakes, spoon over top to fill to top of cup or in a thin layer. Freeze for lunches and later snacks.

If you have leftover frosting, spread it on a foil lined cookie sheet and freeze. When completely frozen, cut into small chunks to use for chocolate chips in cookies and cakes.

This recipe is very low in fat, but high in flavor and satisfies the urge for an acceptable chocolate dessert.

Per serving: 106.6 Calories; 3.2g Fat (24.9% calories from fat); 0.5g Protein; 21.3g Carbohydrate; 0mg Cholesterol; 25mg Sodium

Golden Pound Cake

Serves 16

1 1/4	cups potato starch flour
2	cups white rice flour
2	teaspoons guar gum
3	teaspoons egg replacer
1 1/2	teaspoons salt
3/4	teaspoon cream of tartar
1 3/4	teaspoons baking soda
1 2/3	cups rice milk
1 1/2	cups beet sugar
2/3	cup canola oil

Combine all dry ingredients except sugar. Mix well to fluff and add air. Set aside. Mix milk, sugar, and oil together. Stir until sugar dissolves. Combine dry ingredients and liquid mix. Stir well. This is a thin batter. Pour into a greased bread pan. Bake at 350 degrees for 1 hour 15 minutes or until done when tested with a toothpick. Allow to cool before slicing.

Serving Suggestion: Serve with our Hawaiian Fruit Salad recipe, placing fruit on top of pound cake slice and drizzle with sauces from the fruit. Serve in place of commercial bread in Strawberry Dessert recipe. This also makes a great base for Trifle with pudding and fresh fruit.

Per serving: 386.9 Calories; 9.6g Fat (21.6% calories from fat); 1.3g Protein; 77.0g Carbohydrate; 0mg Cholesterol; 385mg Sodium

Orange Cake
Serves 8

- 1/2 cup canola margarine
- 2 Tablespoons orange zest, grated
- 1 Tablespoon lemon zest, grated
- 1 cup beet sugar
- 2 Tablespoons lemon juice
- 3/4 cup orange juice
- 1 1/3 teaspoons egg replacer, =1 egg
- 1/2 teaspoon salt
- 1 teaspoon baking soda
- 1 teaspoon cream of tartar
- 1 cup amaranth flour
- 1 cup white rice flour
- 1/2 cup potato starch flour

Preheat oven to 350 degrees.
Lightly oil one 9" round cake pan.
In a large bowl, cream together margarine, sugar, orange and lemon zest. Add lemon and orange juice and stir just until combined. Add flours, salt, baking soda, cream of tartar, and egg replacer. Stir until all dry ingredients are moistened. Spoon into oiled cake pan immediately. Place on the middle rack in the center of the oven. Bake at 350 degrees for 25-30 minutes, until golden around the edges and a toothpick inserted in the middle comes out clean.

This cake is delicious served with the "Citrus Sauce-Day 3".
Nutritional data is for cake only.

Per serving: 497.7 Calories; 12.9g Fat (22.7% calories from fat); 4.9g Protein; 94.2g Carbohydrate; 0mg Cholesterol; 450mg Sodium

Pecan Cake
Serves 12

- 1 cup amaranth flour
- 1 cup rice flour
- 1 cup pecan flour, pureed pecans
- 2 teaspoons baking soda
- 2 teaspoons cream of tartar
- 3 teaspoons egg replacer, =2 eggs
- 1/2 cup beet sugar
- 1/3 cup almond oil, or oil of the day
- 2 teaspoons vanilla
- 1/4 teaspoon salt
- 2 1/4 cups almond milk, or milk of day

Preheat oven to 350 degrees.
Spray two 8" round cake pans with oil of the day (not olive oil). Combine all dry ingredients and mix well. Add milk, vanilla, and oil. Mix by hand with spoon until smooth. Pour into cake pans and bake on top rack of oven for 35-40 minutes until cakes are golden brown. Let cool for 5-10 minutes. Turn out of cake pans and place on cooling rack. You may serve warm with fresh sliced strawberries on top, or place a layer of your favorite juice sweetened preserves on top.
Another great topping is our Sinful Pecan Sauce. Serve over warm slices of cake.

Nutritional analysis is for cake without topping.

Per serving: 354.8 Calories; 7.9g Fat (19.4% calories from fat); 6.8g Protein; 67.1g Carbohydrate; 0mg Cholesterol; 326mg Sodium

Hazelnut Cake
Serves 8

1	cup amaranth flour
1	cup rice flour
1	cup hazelnuts, ground into meal
2	teaspoons baking soda
2	teaspoons cream of tartar
3	teaspoons egg replacer, =2 eggs
1/2	cup beet sugar
1/3	cup canola oil
2	teaspoons almond extract, alcohol-free
1/4	teaspoon salt
2 1/4	cups almond milk, or milk of day

Preheat oven to 350 degrees.
In a large mixing bowl, combine all dry ingredients: amaranth flour, rice flour, hazelnut meal, baking soda, cream of tartar, egg replacer, sugar, and salt. Stir in oil, almond extract, and milk. Stir just until smooth. Pour into greased round cake pan and bake at 350 degrees for 35-40 minutes. Top with fresh strawberries sweetened with honey or beet sugar. This is also good with Cranberry Sauce on top. Delicious combination. Another excellent topping is 1 cup chopped hazelnuts mixed with 1/4 cup honey. Heat and pour over individual slices.

Nutritional analysis is for cake without topping.

Per serving: 522.7 Calories; 15.8g Fat (26.3% calories from fat); 6.1g Protein; 93.6g Carbohydrate; 0mg Cholesterol; 489mg Sodium

Raspberry Cake with Sauce
Serves 8

2	12 ounce raspberries, frozen, no sugar added
1/4	cup beet sugar
1/2	cup beet sugar
1/2	cup amaranth flour
3/4	cup rice flour
1/4	cup potato starch flour
1/2	teaspoon salt
1	teaspoon baking soda
1	teaspoon cream of tartar
1/4	cup oil, (not olive oil)
1 1/3	teaspoons egg replacer, =1 egg
1	teaspoon vanilla, alcohol-free
3/4	cup raspberry juice, (from drained rasp.)

Sauce: Thaw raspberries in a bowl. Drain off 3/4 cup liquid and save for use in cake recipe. Place raspberries and 1/4 cup sugar in sauce pan. Heat until sugar is melted, stirring constantly. Set aside.
Preheat oven to 325 degrees.
Cake: Mix all dry ingredients. Add egg replacer, oil, and vanilla. Stir to moisten. Begin stirring quickly and add juice. Incorporate juice into batter quickly and thoroughly. Pour into round cake pan prepared with a cooking spray or light oil. Bake on top rack at 325* for 30-35 minutes or until tooth pick inserted in the center comes out clean.
Serve warm with raspberry sauce.

Per serving: 405.6 Calories; 7.9g Fat (16.9% calories from fat); 3.1g Protein; 84.3g Carbohydrate; 0mg Cholesterol; 327mg Sodium

Pineapple Upside-Down Cake
Serves 8

- 1 can crushed pineapple, packed in juice
- 2 Tablespoons beet sugar
- 2 Tablespoons canola margarine, melted
- 1/2 cup beet sugar
- 1/4 cup canola oil, not olive oil
- 1 teaspoon vanilla
- 1/2 cup pineapple juice, (saved from can)
- 1/4 cup potato starch flour
- 3/4 cup rice flour
- 1/2 cup amaranth flour
- 1 teaspoon salt
- 1 teaspoon baking soda
- 1 teaspoon cream of tartar
- 1 1/3 teaspoons egg replacer, = 1 egg

Preheat oven to 325 degrees.

Drain crushed pineapple and reserve juice. Place drained pineapple in an 8" square baking dish or cake pan. Sprinkle with 2 Tablespoons beet sugar. Drizzle with the melted margarine. Set aside.

Cake: Combine 1/2 cup beet sugar, flours, baking soda, salt, cream of tartar, egg replacer and stir with fork. Add 1/2 cup pineapple juice, vanilla, and 1/4 cup oil. Mix well and carefully spoon batter over pineapple in baking dish.

Bake at 325 degrees for 30-35 minutes.

Per serving: 372.7 Calories; 10.6g Fat (24.8% calories from fat); 2.8g Protein; 69.4g Carbohydrate; 0mg Cholesterol; 490mg Sodium

Strawberry Dessert
Serves 4

1   package strawberries, fresh or frozen
1   cup beet sugar
4   slices rice almond bread, lightly toasted
2   teaspoons canola margarine, optional

Fresh strawberries: Slice and add sugar. Mix well and let set.
Frozen strawberries: Place in bowl and add sugar. Mix well. Cover and let set for couple of hours or until thawed. Mix occasionally. The rice almond bread is a commercially prepared bread.
When sugar is dissolved and strawberries thawed, you are ready. Lightly toast the bread. Spread canola or safflower margarine on toast. Place in microwave for 15 seconds on high. Cover with strawberry mixture and serve.

Per serving: 334.7 Calories; 4.5g Fat (11.6% calories from fat); 2.2g Protein; 74.5g Carbohydrate; 0mg Cholesterol; 25mg Sodium

Baked Apples
Serves 4

```
  4    large apples
1/2    cup raisins, or dried cranberries
  4    teaspoons date sugar, or sweetener of day
       dash cinnamon
3/4    cup apple juice
1/4    cup honey
```

Preheat oven to 350 degrees.

Core apples with a corer or sharp knife. Set cored apples upright in a glass baking dish. Sprinkle apple's core area with cinnamon and date sugar. Stuff raisins or dried cranberries into core hole. Pour apple juice around apples and drizzle honey over apple. Cover dish with lid or foil. Bake for 40 minutes or until apples are tender. Serve warm as a dessert.

Per serving: 226.6 Calories; 0.6g Fat (2.1% calories from fat); 0.9g Protein; 59.6g Carbohydrate; 0mg Cholesterol; 4mg Sodium

Banana Boats
Serves 4

- 2 banana, unpeeled
- 1/4 cup pecans, pieces
- 4 teaspoons honey
- dash cinnamon, optional

Line a cookie sheet with foil.
Cut unpeeled bananas in half lengthwise and place, cut side up, on cookie sheet.
Place pecan pieces on top of bananas and lightly press into banana flesh. Sprinkle with cinnamon.
Drizzle each banana with honey and place under broiler or in toaster oven for 1-2 minutes until golden and bubbly.
Serve warm for dessert or as a different breakfast food.

Per serving: 79.4 Calories; 2.6g Fat (27.0% calories from fat); 0.7g Protein; 15.1g Carbohydrate; 0mg Cholesterol; 1mg Sodium

Baked Pears C/E
Serves 6

  6   medium pears
  4   Tablespoons honey
  1   whole lemon, juice and zest
3/4 cup raspberry juice

Preheat oven to 350 degrees.
Peel pears. Slice in half and core. Place pears, flat side down, in a glass baking dish. Remove zest from lemon and sprinkle zest over pears. Cut lemon in half and squeeze juice over pears. Pour raspberry juice around pears. Drizzle pears with honey. Place lid or foil on top of baking dish and bake, covered for 20 minutes. Remove from oven and serve warm.

A sweet white wine may be used instead of the raspberry juice if tolerated. This dish is simple and easy enough for any day dining, but is also elegant enough to serve to guests.

Serving size: 2 pear halves.

Per serving: 149.1 Calories; 0.7g Fat (3.5% calories from fat); 0.9g Protein; 39.9g Carbohydrate; 0mg Cholesterol; 1mg Sodium

Plain Pastry
Serves 8

- 3/4 cup rice flour, white
- 1/2 cup tapioca flour
- 1/2 cup potato starch flour
- 1/2 teaspoon salt
- 1/2 cup canola margarine, or oil of the day
- 4 Tablespoons cold water

Flour can consist of any one or combination of flour.
Peheat oven to 400 degrees and lightly grease a pie plate.
Cut margarine or oil into dry ingredients. Add cold water until dough will form a ball. Press pastry dough into an 8" or 9" pie plate or individual muffin tins. For cold fillings, prebake for 10-12 minutes. For pie fillings that need to be cooked, fill the pie shell with uncooked pastry and bake according to pie filling instructions.

Nutritional analysis is for pie shell only.

Per serving: 214.8 Calories; 11.2g Fat (46.9% calories from fat); 0.9g Protein; 27.7g Carbohydrate; 0mg Cholesterol; 254mg Sodium

Oat Pie Crust
Serves 8

- 1 cup oats, uncooked
- 1/3 cup nuts, chopped (nut of day)
- 1/4 cup beet sugar, or sweetener of day
- 4 Tablespoons canola margarine, or oil of the day
- 1/2 teaspoon cinnamon, optional
- 1/4 teaspoon salt

Preheat oven to 375 degrees. Melt margarine, or use oil of the day (not olive oil). Mix all ingredients until crumbly. Pat into a 9" pie plate.
For a cold pudding type filling: pre-bake pie shell at 375 degrees 8-10 minutes. Cool, then fill with prepared filling.
For baked fillings: bake at 375 degrees for 4 minutes, then, fill with favorite filling and bake according to filling recipe directions.
Cool before slicing into 8 pieces.

Per serving: 186.2 Calories; 10.2g Fat (47.9% calories from fat); 4.3g Protein; 20.5g Carbohydrate; 0mg Cholesterol; 128mg Sodium

Rice Coconut Pie Crust
Serves 8

- 1 1/2 cups white rice flour
- 1/2 cup beet sugar
- 1/2 cup coconut, unsweetened
- 1/2 cup canola margarine

Mix all ingredients in a mixing bowl. Place 2/3 of mixture into pie baking dish. Press out evenly on bottom and sides of dish using a fork. Fill the crust with your favorite filling and sprinkle the remainder of the crust mixture on top. Bake according to filling recipe directions. This recipe is good with fruit, nut or pumpkin fillings. The topping is crunchy. If pie is to be filled with a cold custard type filling, bake pie crust before filling. Bake at 350 degrees for 10-15 minutes or until coconut begins to turn golden. If you have an allergy to cane sugar, you will want to use fresh coconut or unsweetened coconut from a health food store.

Per serving: 264.5 Calories; 12.3g Fat (41.8% calories from fat); 1.9g Protein; 36.6g Carbohydrate; 0mg Cholesterol; 121mg Sodium

Coconut Pie Crust Day 3
Serves 10

- 3 1/2 cups coconut, unsweetened
- 3 Tablespoons canola margarine, melted
- 3 Tablespoons coconut milk-lite, unsweetened
- 4 Tablespoons tapioca flour
- 2 Tablespoons beet sugar

Place coconut, tapioca flour, and beet sugar in a bowl and mix well with spoon. Drizzle melted butter and coconut milk over coconut mix and toss well to coat. Press into an 8 or 9" pie plate. Bake at 325 degrees for 15 minutes or until lightly golden brown. Fill with any cold filling, fruit filling, or pudding.

For a quick dessert, I bake these in individual baking cups and fill with IMAGINE rice pudding in chocolate, lemon, butterscotch, or banana.

Nutritional analysis is for pie crust only.

Per serving: 96.6 Calories; 8.6g Fat (76.7% calories from fat); 0.5g Protein;
5.4g Carbohydrate; 0mg Cholesterol; 39mg Sodium

Coconut Cream Pie Filling
Serves 36

1	cup rice flour
1/2	cup beet sugar
3/4	teaspoon baking soda
3/4	teaspoon cream of tartar
1/4	teaspoon salt
1/3	cup canola margarine
1/4	teaspoon cinnamon
1/4	teaspoon nutmeg
1/4	teaspoon cloves
1/2	cup pumpkin, natural pack
1/3	cup coconut, shredded-unsweetened

Preheat oven to 400 degrees. Line a cookie sheet with foil to minimize clean up. In a medium bowl, combine all dry ingredients and mix well. Cut in margarine with fork until crumbs are smaller than pea size. Add pumpkin puree from the can and coconut. Stir until dough is uniform in color. Drop onto ungreased cookie sheet by teaspoonfuls. Bake at 400 degrees for 10 minutes. Do not allow to brown. Remove immediately from cookie sheet to cooling racks.

These freeze well in individual portions for lunches.

Per serving: 43.3 Calories; 1.8g Fat (37.8% calories from fat); 0.3g Protein; 6.5g Carbohydrate; 0mg Cholesterol; 59mg Sodium

Dutch Pear Pie Filling
Serves 8

- 5 cups pears, peeled and sliced
- 1/2 cup beet sugar
- 1/4 teaspoon salt
- 3 Tablespoons potato starch flour
- 1 teaspoon cinnamon
- 1 teaspoon grated lemon rind
- 1 Tablespoon lemon juice
- 1/2 cup date sugar
- 1/2 cup canola margarine, margarine of choice
- 1/4 teaspoon cinnamon
- 1/4 teaspoon nutmeg
- 1 cup rice flour
- 1/2 cup chopped pecans

This recipe may be used with any pie crust. Mix filling ingredients together well. Put filling into pie shell. Mix topping ingredients together. Stir until crumbly. Add nuts and mix well. Sprinkle over pie filling. Bake at 450 degrees for 10 munutes, then reduce oven temperature to 350 degrees. Bake for an additional 35-40 minutes until pears are tender.

Per serving: 355.2 Calories; 14.1g Fat (34.5% calories from fat); 1.9g Protein; 58.3g Carbohydrate; 0mg Cholesterol; 187mg Sodium

Old Fashion Apple Pie
Serves 8

- 5 cups apples, peeled-cored-sliced
- 1/2 cup beet sugar
- 2 teaspoons cinnamon, ground
- 1 recipe oat pie Crust, or one of choice

Preheat oven to 400 degrees.
Peel, core, and thinly slice apples. Place in a large bowl and sprinkle with sugar and cinnamon. Toss to coat apples.
Do not pre-cook pie crust. Make pie crust according to recipe directions. Arrange apple slices in pie crust. Place pie on the middle rack in preheated oven. Bake for 40 minutes at 400 degrees. Remove from oven and allow to cool before serving. Serve with one of our "ice cream" recipes.

Per serving: 109.1 Calories; 1.5g Fat (11.7% calories from fat); 0.7g Protein; 25.2g Carbohydrate; 0mg Cholesterol; 16mg Sodium

Deep Dish Blueberry Pie
Serves 10

- 1 1/2 cups amaranth flour
- 3/4 cup rice flour
- 1/3 cup potato starch flour
- 1/3 cup tapioca flour
- 1 Tablespoon beet sugar, or sweetener of day
- 1 cup oil, or oil of the day
- 4 1/2 Tablespoons almond milk, or milk of day
- 5 cups blueberries, or any fruit
- 1 1/3 cups beet sugar, or sweetener of day
- 5 Tablespoons tapioca flour
- 2 Tablespoons lemon juice
- dash salt

Preheat oven to 450 degrees.
Crust:
Mix first 7 ingredient in large bowl. Pat 2/3 of the mixture on the bottom and about 1-1/2" up the side of an ungreased 9x13" baking pan.
Filling:
In large bowl toss blueberries, sugar, flour, lemon juice, and salt together. Sprinkle evenly onto crust in baking dish. Sprinkle remaining 1/3 crust mixture over top of filling. Bake at 450* degreesfor 10 minutes. Reduce heat to 350 degrees and bake for 40 more minutes. Serve warm or cold.

Per serving: 527.7 Calories; 24.2g Fat (39.9% calories from fat); 5.5g Protein; 76.6g Carbohydrate; 0mg Cholesterol; 14mg Sodium

Pecan Pie Filling
Serves 12

- 1 1/8 Tablespoons egg replacer
- 2 Tablespoons water
- 1 cup beet sugar
- 1/2 teaspoon salt
- 2 Tablespoons canola margarine, melted
- 1/2 cup rice syrup
- 1/2 cup rice milk
- 1 Tablespoon xanthan gum
- 1 1/2 teaspoons vanilla, alcohol-free
- 1/4 cup orange marmalade, Sorrell Ridge
- 1 teaspoon orange zest
- 2 cups pecan halves

Make one unbaked rice coconut pie shell. Set aside. Lightly beat water and egg replacer together. Add sugar, salt, margarine, and syrup. Set aside. Beat together milk and xanthan gum at high speed for a minute or so; it will thicken. Pour milk mixture into sugar mixture. Stir in marmalade, vanilla, and pecans. Pour mixture into pie shell and bake at 375 degrees for 50 to 60 minutes or until filling is set and pastry golden brown. Cool before serving, store covered in the refrigerator.

Per serving: 314.4 Calories; 8.4g Fat (22.6% calories from fat); 0.8g Protein; 63.5g Carbohydrate; 0mg Cholesterol; 173mg Sodium

Pumpkin Pie Filling Day 2   C/E
Serves 8

1 1/2	cups mashed pumpkin, fresh or canned
3/4	cup beet sugar, or sweetener of day
1/2	teaspoon salt
1	teaspoon ground cinnamon
1	teaspoon ground ginger
1/2	teaspoon ground nutmeg
1/2	teaspoon ground cloves
5	teaspoons egg replacer, = 3 eggs
1 1/4	cups almond milk, or milk of day

Preheat oven to 400 degrees.
You may use any part of an egg that you are not sensitive to, or you can use Egg Replacer from Ener-g.
Mix all ingredients with a hand mixer and pour into pie shell. Bake 50 minutes in a 400 degree oven.
Nutritional values do not include pie shell.

Per serving: 372.3 Calories; 0.6g Fat (1.4% calories from fat); 0.9g Protein; 97.7g Carbohydrate; 0mg Cholesterol; 275mg Sodium

Any Berry Cobbler
Serves 8

- 2 cups blueberries, rinsed
- 1/2 cup beet sugar
- 1 Tablespoon potato starch flour, or tapioca flour
- 1/8 teaspoon salt
- 3/4 cup water
- 1/4 teaspoon guar gum
- 1 teaspoon cinnamon
- 3/4 cup rice flour
- 1/4 cup potato starch flour
- 1 teaspoon cream of tartar
- 1 teaspoon baking soda
- 1/4 teaspoon salt
- 1/2 teaspoon guar gum
- 2 Tablespoons date sugar
- 1/2 cup beet sugar
- 3 Tablespoons canola margarine
- 1/3 cup rice milk

Fruit Mixture: Combine all ingredients for fruit mixture, except the berries, in a medium sauce pan. Cook over medium to low heat until begins to thicken. Add berries to the heated sauce and continue to cook over lowest heat for another 2-3 minutes. Remove from heat. Pour into greased bread pan.

Batter Topping: This makes a medium to thin batter. In a medium bowl, combine 3/4 cup of rice flour, 1/4 cup potato starch flour, cream of tartar, baking soda, salt, and guar gum. In a separate bowl, mix together remaining ingredients for batter: sugar, canola margarine, and rice milk. Combine the two mixtures. Stir well. Pour batter over berry mixture. Bake at 375 degrees for 35-40 minutes or until topping tests done with a toothpick.

To change this cobbler to another flavor, reduce or omit the cinnamon when using a lighter, more delicate flavored fruit.

Per serving: 255.5 Calories; 4.6g Fat (15.5% calories from fat); 1.2g Protein; 54.7g Carbohydrate; 0mg Cholesterol; 309mg Sodium

Blueberry Cobbler Day 5 C/E
Serves 8

- 5 cups fresh blueberries, frozen unsweetened
- 1 Tablespoon tapioca flour, or rice flour
- 1/2 cup honey, of choice
- 1 1/2 cups white rice flour
- 1/2 cup canola margarine
- 1 cup crispy rice cereal
- 2 teaspoons cinnamon
- 1/2 teaspoon salt

Preheat oven to 375 degrees.
In a large bowl, combine white rice flour, salt, cinnamon, and canola margarine. Cut in margarine with a fork until crumbs are the size of peas. Stir in crispy rice cereal. Press 2/3 of the mixture into a 7 x 10 baking dish (or one approximately that size).
Place blueberries in a large bowl and sprinkle with tapioca flour. Toss to coat berries with flour. Spoon blueberries into baking dish with the crust on the bottom. Drizzle berries with the honey. Sprinkle the remaining crumbs on top. Bake for 35-40 minutes at 375 degrees. Serve warm or cold.

Per serving: 338.5 Calories; 11.8g Fat (30.6% calories from fat); 2.7g Protein; 57.5g Carbohydrate; 0mg Cholesterol; 285mg Sodium

Crunchy Cobbler Topping   Day 1
Serves 8

- 1 cup oats, toasted
- 1/2 cup nuts, of choice
- 1/2 cup oat flour
- 3 Tablespoons maple syrup, or sugar
- 3 Tablespoons oil, not olive oil
- 1/4 teaspoon salt
- 1/2 teaspoon cinnamon, optional

Mix all dry ingredients. Add oil and maple syrup. Mix well and sprinkle over fruit filling of choice in baking dish.
Bake at 350 degrees for 20-25 minutes, until topping starts to brown.

Nutritional analysis is for topping only.

Per serving: 214.2 Calories; 11.8g Fat (48.0% calories from fat); 5.6g Protein; 23.1g Carbohydrate; 0mg Cholesterol; 120mg Sodium

Crunchy Amaranth Cobbler Topping Day 3
Serves 10

- 1 1/2 cups amaranth flour
- 1/2 cup tapioca flour
- 4 Tablespoons honey
- 1/2 cup coconut oil
- 1/2 cup hazelnuts, chopped
- 1/2 cup coconut, unsweetened flaked
- 1/4 cup coconut milk
- 1/4 teaspoon salt

Mix all ingrdients until crumbly and sprinkle on top of fruit filling of choice in a 9x13" baking pan. Bake at 350 degrees for 30-35 minutes or until fruit is bubbling and topping is golden.

Nutritional analysis is for topping only.

Per serving: 270.4 Calories; 16.6g Fat (52.8% calories from fat); 4.8g Protein; 28.5g Carbohydrate; 0mg Cholesterol; 61mg Sodium

Crunchy Topping for Cobblers   Day 5 C/E
Serves 10

   2   cups crispy rice cereal, natural
   3   Tablespoons rice syrup
1/4 cup Brazil nuts, chopped fine
1/4 teaspoon cloves

Combine crispy rice cereal, sunflower seeds, and cinnamon in a bowl. Mix well, then sprinkle over fruit in baking dish. Drizzle with rice syrup, and bake according to cobbler directions.

Nutritional values are for topping only.

Per serving: 46.1 Calories; 1.1g Fat (22.3% calories from fat); 0.6g Protein; 8.4g Carbohydrate; 0mg Cholesterol; 42mg Sodium

Strawberry Rhubarb Cobbler
Serves 8

- 2 cups rhubarb, cut in 1/2" pieces
- 3/4 cup beet sugar
- 1/2 cup water
- 1 cup strawberries, washed, sliced
- 1/2 cup beet sugar
- 2 Tablespoons date sugar
- 3 Tablespoons canola margarine
- 1/3 cup rice milk
- 1/4 cup potato starch flour
- 3/4 cup rice flour
- 1 teaspoon cream of tartar
- 1 teaspoon baking soda
- 1/4 teaspoon salt
- 1/2 teaspoon guar gum

Cook rhubarb completely before adding strawberries. Rhubard is completely cooked when chunks of rhubard have turned into a sauce and no chunks remain. Remove from heat and stir in the strawberries. This will prevent over cooking of strawberries and undercooking of rhubarb. Pour cooked fruit into a greased baking dish. Prepare batter. Pour batter over top of fruit.
Bake at 375 degrees for 35-40 minutes or until topping tests done with a toothpick.
Variation: See our Any Berry Cobbler recipe for other flavors.

Per serving: 261.3 Calories; 4.5g Fat (15.1% calories from fat); 1.2g Protein; 56.1g Carbohydrate; 0mg Cholesterol; 275mg Sodium

Peach Crisp C/E
Serves 8

- 6 cups sliced peaches, fresh or frozen
- 3 Tablespoons tapioca flour
- 5 Tablespoons beet sugar

Spray 8x8" deep dish baking pan with cooking oil. Preheat oven to 350 degrees. In large bowl, toss peaches with flour and sugar. Mix well. Spread in even layer in baking pan and top with favorite topping or one of our topping recipes.
Bake at 350 degrees for 20-25 minutes.

Per serving: 85.7 Calories; 0.1g Fat (1.0% calories from fat); 0.9g Protein; 22.5g Carbohydrate; 0mg Cholesterol; 0mg Sodium

Strawberry Banana Sherbert
Serves 12

  1   pint strawberries, pureed
  2   large bananas, pureed
32   ounces rice milk, vanilla flavored
  2   cups beet sugar

Wash and top strawberries and place in a blender. Add bananas and puree. (4 cups of fruit puree works well.) Mix ingredients thoroughly. Combine fruit puree, sugar, and milk. Place mixture in ice cream maker. Follow freezing directions for your ice cream maker.
Note: In some grocers health foods section or produce departments you can find pureed friut drinks without perservatives. It is a nice convenience for this recipe if ingredients are safe for your diet. Read the label.

Variation: BLACK CHERRY SHERBERT
              Substitute one pound of pitted, pureed, black cherries in the recipe
              above. Omit strawberries and bananas, and follow above directions.

Per Serving: 270.3 Calories; 1.2g Fat (3.8% calories from fat); 1.0g Protein;
           68.1g Carbohydrates; 0mg Cholesterol; 43mg Sodium

Variation: ORANGE SHERBERT
              12 ounces frozen orange juice concentrate, unsweetened
              1 2/3 cups beet sugar
              32 ounces rice milk, vanilla flavor

Per serving: 224.4 Calories; 0.8 g Fat (3.2% calories from fat); 1.2g Protein;
           55.8g Carbohydrate; 0mg Cholesterol; 35mg Sodium

Per serving: 181.2 Calories; 0.8g Fat (3.6% calories from fat); 0.6g Protein;
           45.7g Carbohydrate; 0mg Cholesterol; 29mg Sodium

Peaches and Cream Rice Milk Ice Cream
Serves 6

1 3/4	cups rice milk, vanilla
1/2	cup Mystic Lake Fruit Concentrate Sweetener, or rice milk
5/8	teaspoon xanthan gum
1 1/4	teaspoons vanilla
1	cup coconut milk
3/4	cup peaches, pureed

Mix xanthan gum into rice milk using wire wisk or mixer. Add all other ingredients and blend thoroughly. Place mixture into ice cream maker. Follow ice cream maker directions.

Per serving: 191.6 Calories; 10.1g Fat (46.0% calories from fat); 1.3g Protein; 25.4g Carbohydrate; 0mg Cholesterol; 34mg Sodium

Chocolate Rice Milk Ice Cream
Serves 24

1	Tablespoon vanilla, alcohol-free
1	can coconut milk-lite
2	teaspoons egg replacer
2	teaspoons xanthan gum
3	Tablespoons cocoa powder
1 2/3	cups beet sugar
1/2	gallon rice milk, carob flavor

Mix cocoa, sugar and 1 cup of rice milk in saucepan. Heat to dissolve cocoa and sugar into milk. Remove from heat, add remaining rice milk to make 1/2 gallon. Mix thoroughly, then set aside. Mix vanilla, coconut milk, egg replacer, and xanthan gum together and beat with mixer for 2-3 minutes. Combine two mixes together and beat on low speed until smooth. Follow ice cream maker directions for operation of machine. May be served immediately as soft serve ice cream or placed in freezer for firm, frozen delight.

Per serving: 132.4 Calories; 1.0g Fat (6.2% calories from fat); 0.5g Protein; 32.3g Carbohydrate; 0mg Cholesterol; 47mg Sodium

Pumpkin Rice Milk Ice Cream
Serves 12

- 4 cups rice milk
- 1/2 cup pumpkin, solid pack, plain
- 1 teaspoon pumpkin pie spice
- 1/2 cup rice syrup
- 1/2 teaspoon nutmeg
- 1 Tablespoon vanilla, alcohol-free
- 1 teaspoon xanthan gum

Mix all ingredients in large bowl, using wire wisk. Pour mixture into ice cream maker. Follow ice cream maker's directions for operation of machine. This recipe sets up quickly, 10 to 20 minutes depending on temperature of ingredients. May be served immediately like soft serve ice cream, or placed in freezer for firm frozen delight.
Variation:
    Almond milk can be used in place of rice milk.
    Fruit, preserves or nuts may be added before freezing.
    One cup of pumpkin may be used for vibrant pumpkin flavor.

Per serving: 71.4 Calories; 0.7g Fat (9.2% calories from fat); 0.4g Protein; 15.8g Carbohydrate; 0mg Cholesterol; 31mg Sodium

Mocha Rice Milk Ice Cream
Serves 10

- 4 cups rice milk, vanilla flavor
- 1/2 cup Mystic Lake Fruit Concentrate Sweetener, or rice syrup
- 1 Tablespoon vanilla, alcohol-free
- 1 Tablespoon instant coffee
- 1 can coconut milk
- 1 teaspoon xanthan gum

Dissolve coffee in 1/2 cup of milk warmed in microwave. Mix all ingredients in large bowl, using wire wisk. Pour mixture into ice cream maker. Follow directions on ice cream maker for operation of machine. This recipe sets up quickly (10 to 20 minutes depending on temperature of ingredients). May be served immediately like soft serve ice cream, or placed in freezer for firm frozen delight.

Variation: Pero or Roma could be used if coffee is not desired.
        To make vanilla flavor, omit coffee, and use vanilla flavor rice milk.
        Almond milk can be used in place of rice milk.
        Fruit, preserves or nuts may be added before freezing.

Per serving: 138.6 Calories; 6.5g Fat (41.3% calories from fat); 1.0g Protein; 19.9g Carbohydrate; 0mg Cholesterol; 41mg Sodium

Lemon Ice   Day 3
Serves 1

1   Recipe Lemonade

Freeze Lemonade in a 9 x 13" pan until solid. After frozen, remove from freezer and break up by dragging a fork along the length of the pan. An easier method is to use The Pampered Chef-Ice Shaver. The lemonade can be frozen in the tubs provided and shaved in less than a minute.
My children have always loved this treat with other flavors, too.

Per serving: 103.0 Calories; 0.0g Fat (0.0% calories from fat); 0.0g Protein;
26.9g Carbohydrate; 0mg Cholesterol; 13mg Sodium

Lemon Lime Sherbert
Serves 10

- 6   ounces lemon juice
- 1 2/3   cups beet sugar
- 1   teaspoon lemon zest
- 1   teaspoon lime zest
- 2   ounces lime juice
- 32   ounces rice milk

Mix all ingredients well (sugar should be dissolved). Pour into cylinder of ice cream maker. Follow directions for your ice cream maker.
Note: You may use fresh squeezed lemon juice, or bottled.

Per serving: 176.1 Calories; 0.8g Fat (3.7% calories from fat); 0.5g Protein;
44.8g Carbohydrate; 0mg Cholesterol; 34mg Sodium

Fruits, Salads And Dressings

Chicken Cashew Salad   Day 1
Serves 6

- 2 cups chicken, cooked and cubed
- 1/2 cup cashews, halved
- 1/4 cup safflower oil mayonnaise
- 1/2 cup raisins
- 1/4 cup grape juice, white
- 2 teaspoons maple syrup

Place chicken, cashews, and raisins in a bowl. Set aside.
Dressing:
In a small bowl, mix mayonnaise, white grape juice, and maple syrup. Pour over chicken, raisins, and cashews and toss well. Serve over bed of mixed greens, or on oat bread for sandwiches.
When serving sandwiches, this recipe can serve 8.

Per seving: 284.3 Calories; 17.5g Fat; 16.2g Protein; 16.5 Carbohydrate;
   46mg Cholesterol; 112mg Sodium

ALTERNATE CHICKEN SALAD DAY 1:
- 2 chicken breast halves, cooked and diced
- 2 Tbs. sweet pepper, diced
- 3 Tbs. safflower mayonnaise
- dash salt and pepper

Combine all ingredients and mix well. Serve on oat bread for sandwiches. For appetizer, serve on toasted bread triangles or crackers.

Per serving: 138.5 Calories; 10.5g Fat; 10.1g Protein; 0.1g Carbohydrate;
   33mg Cholesterol; 80mg Sodium

Per serving: 284.3 Calories; 17.5g Fat (54.6% calories from fat); 16.2g Protein;
   16.5g Carbohydrate; 46mg Cholesterol; 112mg Sodium

Prudy's Chicken Salad
Serves 10

1 1/2	pounds chicken, cook, cut, sm pieces
1	can pineapple chunks in juice, drained
1	cup apple, diced
1/2	cup pecans, chopped
1/2	cup raisins, seedless
1/2	cup celery, chopped
1/2	cup dates, chopped
1/4	teaspoon garlic salt
1/2	cup canola mayonnaise
1	head shredded lettuce

Combine chopped ingredients (except lettuce) in large mixing bowl. Stir in mayonnaise. Season with salt and pepper as desired, cover tightly, and refrigerate over night. Serve scoop of chicken salad on top of shredded lettuce.

Substitution: You may substitute eggless mayonnaise, but check ingredients thoroughly.

Per serving: 260.1 Calories; 15.3g Fat (52.1% calories from fat); 12.9g Protein; 18.7g Carbohydrate; 41mg Cholesterol; 123mg Sodium

Company Chicken Salad
Serves 10

4	cups cooked chicken breast, cubed
1/4	cup canola mayonnaise
1	can mandarin oranges, sectioned-drained
2	medium apples, diced large
3/4	pound seedless grapes, sliced in half
1/3	cup walnuts, chopped
1/2	cup celery, chopped
1	teaspoon curry powder, mild
1/4	cup apple cider vinegar
4	Tablespoons honey
1	teaspoon ginger, powder
2	teaspoons lemon juice
2	cups water

Place water and lemon juice in bowl. Soak apple pieces in lemon water for one minute. This will prevent apples from turning dark after being cut. Drain the apples and place in a large salad bowl with chicken, oranges, grapes, celery, and nuts. Set aside.

Dressing: Mix canola mayonnaise, ginger, honey, vinegar, and curry powder. Mix well. Pour over fruit and chicken and toss gently to coat with dressing. Serve on a bed of crisp lettuce or on rolls for sandwiches. Make ahead and store in airtight container in refrigerator.

Per serving: 261.4 Calories; 11.5g Fat (39.6% calories from fat); 23.5g Protein; 16.0g Carbohydrate; 66mg Cholesterol; 103mg Sodium

Turkey Taco Salad
Serves 4

- 1/2 recipe Taco Meat
- 4 medium green onions, sliced thin
- 2 ounces black olives, sliced
- 1/4 cup Cactus Salsa (Tomatoless)
- 1/2 medium red bell pepper, chopped
- 4 ounces refried beans
- 2 Tablespoons water
- 1 head lettuce, shredded
- 2 ounces almond cheese, grated

Prepare veggies and grate cheese in advance. Make one half Taco Meat recipe with ground chicken, turkey or beef. Arrange beds of shredded lettuce in large serving bowls. Thin refried beans with two Tablespoons of water and heat in microwave. Place one large spoonful of refried beans in the center of each lettuce bed. Top with drained scoop of taco meat. Top off with sprinkle of cheese, red bell pepper, green onions, and black olives. Place a Tablespoon of our Cactus Salsa recipe in the center. Serve with Quinoa Chips, or a Tablespoon of fresh cooked hot brown rice. Brown rice makes a wonderful accompaniment to this dish. Humus may be served in place of refried beans. Soy or rice cheese may be substituted for almond cheese if desired. Surprise, you can enjoy the flavors of a taco salad without tomatoes!

Per serving: 168.1 Calories; 5.4g Fat (26.8% calories from fat); 10.2g Protein; 23.0g Carbohydrate; 5mg Cholesterol; 685mg Sodium

Turkey-Rice-Cranberry Salad Day 5
Serves 4

- 2 cups brown rice, cooked-leftover
- 1 cup turkey, cooked-diced
- 2/3 cup cranberries, dried
- 1/2 cup celery, diced
- 1 Tablespoon lemon zest, grated
- salt and pepper, to taste
- 1/4 cup oil, of the day
- 1/4 cup rice vinegar
- 1 teaspoon ginger, powdered
- 1 Tablespoon lemon juice

If you do not have dried cranberries on hand, or cannot find them without sugar or preservatives, you may substitute 1 cup fresh cranberries, cut in half.

Combine oil, rice vinegar, ginger, lemon juice, salt, and pepper and mix well.

In a large bowl, combine rice, turkey, cranberries, celery, and lemon zest. Toss lightly to mix. Pour dressing over turkey and rice mix and toss to coat with dressing. Serve over lettuce or in containers for lunch packing.

Per serving: 553.2 Calories; 20.0g Fat (32.5% calories from fat); 16.9g Protein; 76.5g Carbohydrate; 32mg Cholesterol; 46mg Sodium

Rice-Broccoli-Turkey Salad Day 5
Serves 4

- 2 cups brown rice, cooked-leftover
- 1 cup turkey, cooked-diced
- 1 cup broccoli florets, blanched
- 1/4 cup brazil nuts, chopped
- 1/2 teaspoon garlic powder
- 1 Tablespoon parsley, fresh chopped
- 1 teaspoon oregano, dried
- 1/4 cup canola oil
- 1/4 cup rice vinegar

Dressing: combine oil, vinegar, oregano, garlic powder, and parsley. Mix well and set aside.

Mix together rice, turkey, broccoli florets, and nuts. Toss to combine. Pour dressing over turkey and rice mix and toss lightly to coat with dressing.

Serve on bed of lettuce or in containers for lunch packing.

Per serving: 584.9 Calories; 22.9g Fat (35.0% calories from fat); 18.8g Protein; 76.8g Carbohydrate; 32mg Cholesterol; 45mg Sodium

Salmon Salad C/E
Serves 6

- 2   cups salmon, leftover-chunked
- 3   Tablespoons onion, chopped fine
- 1   Tablespoon pimiento, chopped fine
- 2   teaspoons olive oil, or oil of the day
- 1   teaspoon dill, dried or
- 2   Tablespoons dill, fresh
- 1/2 cup cucumber, peeled and chopped
- 1   head iceberg lettuce, washed

If using canned salmon, buy only natural with no preservatives or additives. Remove skin and bones. For leftover salmon, break-up into small bite size pieces, and remove skin and bones. In a large bowl, combine all ingredients and toss gently to combine well. Serve over a bed of lettuce or use for sandwiches on bread of the day.

Per serving: 120.8 Calories; 4.5g Fat (33.6% calories from fat); 16.9g Protein; 2.9g Carbohydrate; 41mg Cholesterol; 82mg Sodium

Shrimp Salad With Dill C/E
Serves 6

- 1 1/4 pounds shrimp, peeled and deveined
- 2 Tablespoons olive oil, or oil of the day
- 1 clove garlic, minced
- 1 Tablespoon dill, fresh chopped
- 6 cups mixed salad greens, or lettuce of choice

Wash salad greens, place in individual bowls and set aside.
Heat oil in nonstick skillet. Add garlic and warm for 30 seconds, being careful not to let garlic brown. Add shrimp and toss for 5-6 minutes until pink. Do not over cook shrimp. Remove from heat and add dill. Toss lightly to coat with dill. Let sit 2 minutes to allow dill to release its flavor. Serve warm over a bed of mixed salad greens.

Serving size about 8-10 shrimp per person for small-medium size shrimp.

For appetizers, omit greens and serve on a platter with other shrimp dishes. Offer picks to guests for serving.

Per serving: 151.6 Calories; 6.2g Fat (37.7% calories from fat); 20.2g Protein; 3.0g Carbohydrate; 144mg Cholesterol; 155mg Sodium

Tuna Salad   C/E
Serves 4

1   can tuna in water, natural
2   Tablespoons canola mayonnaise, or safflower mayo
1   teaspoon onion, chopped
1   teaspoon bell pepper, chopped
1   Tablespoon pickle relish, homemade
4   leaves lettuce

Drain liquid off tuna. Discard liquid.
In medium bowl, combine tuna, mayonnaise, onion, bell pepper, and relish. Stir gently to combine ingredients. Serve on lettuce leaves, or make 4 sandwiches on bread of the day.

Per serving: 169.8 Calories; 7.4g Fat (36.9% calories from fat); 14.9g Protein; 13.5g Carbohydrate; 15mg Cholesterol; 253mg Sodium

Savory Croutons
Serves 16

- 16 slices rice bread, thawed
- 3 Tablespoons canola margarine
- 1 teaspoon oregano, dried
- 1 teaspoon thyme, dried
- 1/2 teaspoon garlic salt

Preheat oven to 400 degrees.
Spread canola margarine in thin layer on bread slices. Place on foil lined cookie sheet in single layer. Sprinkle with spices listed or ones that you like. Bake for 8-10 minutes, checking frequently to prevent over browning. Turn off oven and allow to dry in oven until completely dry. Store in air tight container or thick plastic freezer bag.

These are great to use on salads or as savory toppings on casseroles. This recipe works great with stale bread.

Per serving: 139.3 Calories; 4.6g Fat (29.9% calories from fat); 2.0g Protein; 22.1g Carbohydrate; 0mg Cholesterol; 28mg Sodium

Mandarin Orange Salad C/E
Serves 6

- 6 cups mixed greens, of choice
- 2 cans mandarin oranges, or 2 fresh oranges
- 1/3 cup slivered almonds
- Raspberry Dressing, recipe

Place washed and torn mixed greens on individual salad plates. Arrange orange sections on top of greens. Sprinkle almonds on top of salad. Drizzle with dressing as desired.

Per serving: 69.6 Calories; 4.4g Fat (50.9% calories from fat); 3.2g Protein; 6.3g Carbohydrate; 0mg Cholesterol; 14mg Sodium

Raspberry Dressing C/E
Serves 6

- 1 cup raspberry jam, sweetened with juice
- 1/4 cup apple cider vinegar, or choice
- 1/4 cup apple juice

Combine jam, apple juice, and vinegar and mix well.
Serve over salads or as a dip for meatballs and chicken strips.

Per serving: 135.3 Calories; 0.1g Fat (0.7% calories from fat); 0.4g Protein; 36.2g Carbohydrate; 0mg Cholesterol; 22mg Sodium

Chinese Salad Dressing
Serves 6

- 3 Tablespoons rice vinegar
- 2 teaspoons sesame oil
- 3 teaspoons soy sauce, optional
- 1/2 teaspoon salt
- 1 Tablespoon beet sugar

Mix together in shaker container and serve. Can be used over green salads or cooked, drained bean thread. May be served chilled with julienne vegetables and cold cuts. Suggested veggies for oriental salad: green onions, water chestnuts, tomatoes, red pepper, bamboo shoots, and rice crisp rounds. I sometimes double or triple this recipe, and place it in a decanter to be served in amounts to suit individual preference. Omit the soy sauce if you are sensitive to soy.

Per serving: 23.5 Calories; 1.5g Fat (54.4% calories from fat); 0.1g Protein; 2.7g Carbohydrate; 0mg Cholesterol; 316mg Sodium

Italian Dressing
Serves 8

- 1/2 cup water
- 1/4 cup olive oil
- 1/4 cup apple cider vinegar
- 1 teaspoon oregano, dried
- 1 teaspoon basil, dried
- 1 Tablespoon parsley, flakes
- 1 teaspoon minced garlic, or garlic salt
- dash red pepper, optional
- 1/4 teaspoon salt
- 1/4 teaspoon pepper
- 1 teaspoon prepared mustard

Combine all ingredients in a medium bowl and wisk with fork or wire wisk. Or you can mix all ingredients in a salad dressing bottle. Shake well. Place in the refrigerator for at least 2 hours so that flavors can blend. Store leftover in the refrigerator for later use.

Per serving: 64.2 Calories; 6.8g Fat (92.1% calories from fat); 0.2g Protein; 1.1g Carbohydrate; 0mg Cholesterol; 77mg Sodium

Honey Mustard Dressing
Serves 8

- 1/3 cup honey
- 1/3 cup prepared mustard, of choice
- 3 Tablespoons apple cider vinegar

Combine all ingredients and stir well with a fork. Pour into dressing bottle. Serve with any green salad or as a dip for chicken strips.

This dressing may be simple and easy to make, but it is packed with flavor.

Check the label on all prepared mustards-some are made with white or distilled vinegars- a source of wheat or corn. Find one that uses apple cider vinegar.

Per serving: 51.2 Calories; 0.4g Fat (7.0% calories from fat); 0.5g Protein; 12.6g Carbohydrate; 0mg Cholesterol; 126mg Sodium

Herbed Vinegars
Serves 20

1 liter vinegar, any nonallergic type
1 sprig basil, or herb of choice
1 clove garlic, optional

Choose a good quality vinegar-apple cider vinegar, rice vinegar, rice wine vinegar, white vinegar, red wine vinegar, or choose a vinegar from a vineyard that will sell theirs. Most distilled vinegars use a grain in the distillation process. Use one that is safe for you. Apple cider vinegar is usually safe.

Sterilize decorative glass containers. You may use new ones purchased for this purpose, or you may recycle wine bottles. Purchase new corks at any department store that has a kitchen department.

Choose herbs that are fresh and unblemished. Wash the herbs and pat dry. Stuff them gently into the bottle along with the garlic if desired. A clean new pencil works well for stuffing herbs into bottle.

Heat vinegar just to boil. Allow it to cool completely. Slowly fill the bottle with the cool vinegar. Leave plenty of room at the top for the cork. Place in the refrigerator and allow the flavors to mingle for about 2 weeks before using. These make wonderful additions to salad dressings and marinades. They also make wonderful gifts.

Per serving: 7.9 Calories; 0.0g Fat (0.7% calories from fat); 0.0g Protein; 3.2g Carbohydrate; 0mg Cholesterol; 1mg Sodium

Fruited Vinegars
Serves 20

  1   liter vinegar, of choice
1/3 cup berries, of choice

Choose good quality vinegar.

Sterilize decorative glass containers. You may use new ones or recycle wine bottles. Purchase new corks.

Choose berries that are fresh, firm, ripe (but not over ripe), and unblemished. Wash and dry berries.
You may use raspberries, cranberries, blueberries, loganberries, boysenberries, etc.

Carefully, and without damaging berries, stuff berries into bottle. You may need to choose small berries to accommodate the neck of the bottle.

Heat vinegar to boiling and allow to cool thoroughly. Pour into bottle with berries. Leave plenty of room at the top for the cork. Cork and place in the refrigerator for 2 weeks to let berries completely flavor the vinegar. Use in salad dressings and marinades. These make an especially good addition to poultry marinades.

Per serving: 7.8 Calories; 0.0g Fat (0.7% calories from fat); 0.0g Protein; 3.2g Carbohydrate; 0mg Cholesterol; 1mg Sodium

Flavored Oils
Serves 32

   1   cup oil, of choice
         choose from the following:
   1   whole red pepper, dried
   1   sprig fresh basil, or herb of choice
   1   clove garlic
 1/4 teaspoon dried oregano, or herb of choice

Select good quality oils: olive, canola, safflower, peanut, walnut, etc.

Sterilze decorative bottles and purchase new corks.

Use only fresh unblemished garlic, peppers, herbs and spices.

Pour oil into sterilzed glass containers. Add desired flavorings, cork top, and label. You may want to remove herb sprigs after two weeks. Herbs will have given up their flavors to the oil, and they may look wilted and unattractive in the bottle. Store in the refrigerator between uses.

Garlic oil adds new flavors to sauted vegetables and marinades.

Whole red pepper oil adds fire to Chinese and Mexican dishes.

Herbed oils infuse new life into vegetables and meat dishes.

These oils make great gifts along with flavored vinegars. I gave these one year as Christmas gifts in beautiful colored bottles.

Per serving: 61.0 Calories; 6.8g Fat (98.6% calories from fat); 0.0g Protein;
        0.2g Carbohydrate; 0mg Cholesterol; 0mg Sodium

Spinach Salad With Chickpeas Day 4   C/E
Serves 4

- 1 bunch spinach leaves, washed
- 1 cup chickpeas, canned-natural
- salt and pepper, to taste
- 1 Tablespoon peanut oil
- 2 Tablespoons lemon juice

Wash spinach and remove stems. Dry with paper towels. Arrange in individual salad plates. Place 1/4 of the chickpeas on each bed of spinach.

Dressing: Combine oil, lemon juice, salt, and pepper in a bowl. Wisk with a fork and drizzle over individual salads.
This salad is packed with flavor.

Per serving: 216.0 Calories; 6.4g Fat (26.0% calories from fat); 10.0g Protein; 31.3g Carbohydrate; 0mg Cholesterol; 20mg Sodium

Seven Layer Salad
Serves 8

5	cups lettuce leaves, washed and torn
1 1/2	cups green peas, blanched
1 1/2	cups carrots, grated
3/4	cup green onion, sliced
3/4	cup bell pepper, chopped
3/4	cup celery, chopped
1 1/2	cups almond cheese, herbed flavor-grated
1	cup canola mayonnaise

In large glass bowl, layer lettuce, peas, carrots, onion, bell pepper, and celery. In small bowl, combine almond cheese and mayonnaise and mix well. Spread dressing layer on top of layered vegetables. Do not toss together. Cover and refrigerate for at least 2 hours before serving. Toss just before serving if desired.
This makes a delightful dish to carry to a pot luck dinner.

Per serving: 331.1 Calories; 27.2g Fat (73.5% calories from fat); 8.5g Protein; 13.6g Carbohydrate; 10mg Cholesterol; 436mg Sodium

Mustard Potato Salad
Serves 6

- 1 1/2   cups brown rice, or rice of choice
- 3 1/2   cups chicken broth, or vegetable broth
- 2   teaspoons olive oil, or oil of choice
- 1/2   cup onion, diced
- 1/2   cup celery, diced
- 1/2   cup carrots, diced
- 1/4   cup bell pepper, diced
- 1   cup mushrooms, chopped
- 1   teaspoon minced garlic

In a large sauce pan with lid, heat oil. Saute vegetables in oil for 5 minutes. Add rice and stir to coat rice with vegetables and oil. Add chicken broth and stir well. Bring to boil, then reduce heat to slow simmer. Cover with lid and cook for about 55 minutes or according to package directions. Check frequently and stir occassionally to prevent rice from sticking to the bottom of the pan. Serve as a side dish to any meat, fish or seafood dish.

Per serving: 243.5 Calories; 4.4g Fat (16.3% calories from fat); 10.6g Protein; 40.1g Carbohydrate; 1mg Cholesterol; 975mg Sodium

Hot German Potato Salad
Serves 6

- 3 Tablespoons canola oil
- 4 whole green onions, chopped
- 1 Tablespoon potato flour
- 1 Tablespoon beet sugar
- 1 Tablespoon parsley
- 2 Tablespoons mustard
- 1/2 teaspoon salt
- 1/4 teaspoon pepper
- 1/4 cup apple cider vinegar
- 2 ounces Rubbed Pork Tenderloin, chopped
- 3 medium potatoes, cooked, sliced.
- 1 cup chicken broth

Saute' onions in oil until tender. Stir in flour, sugar, parsley, mustard, salt, and pepper. Gradually add chicken broth and vinegar. Cook, stirring constantly, until sauce thickens and boils. Stir in potatoes and pork tenderloin bits and heat through. Serve hot. Use our Rubbed Pork Tenderloin. It takes the place of bacon used in other german potato salads.

Per serving: 170.7 Calories; 8.1g Fat (40.2% calories from fat); 7.0g Protein; 20.0g Carbohydrate; 6mg Cholesterol; 529mg Sodium

Dirty Potato Salad
Serves 10

1	pound potatoes, chopped and cooked
1/2	cup onion, chopped
1/2	cup celery, chopped
1/2	cup zucchini relish
4	whole eggs, hard-boiled, optional
3/4	cup canola mayonnaise, eggless, if desired
2	teaspoons mustard
2	Tablespoons vinegar
2	Tablespoons beet sugar
	salt and pepper, to taste
1/4	teaspoon garlic
2	dashes paprika
1	Tablespoon parsley, chopped

Mix mayonnaise, mustard, sugar, and vinegar together. Set aside giving time for the sugar to dissolve and the flavors to blend. Drain cooked potatoes and allow to cool. Mix in chopped onion, celery, relish and three of the sliced eggs. Stir dressing into the potato mixture. Add salt, pepper, garlic, parsley, and paprika. Mix well. Transfer to serving dish. Arrange remaining egg slices (optional) on top and sprinkle with paprika.
Our Zuchinni Relish is made with beet sugar. It is better to use white potatoes, wash and cube, then cook. White potatoes have thinner skins. For an eggless dish, omit eggs and use eggless mayonnaise.

Per serving: 208.7 Calories; 16.3g Fat (70.5% calories from fat); 3.2g Protein; 12.2g Carbohydrate; 78mg Cholesterol; 264mg Sodium

Honey Carrot Raisin Salad
Serves 12

- 1 cup canola mayonnaise, eggless, if desired
- 2 Tablespoons lemon juice
- 1 Tablespoon lemon zest
- 1/2 teaspoon salt
- 1/4 teaspoon ground ginger
- 1/3 cup honey
- 1 pound carrots, grated
- 3/4 cup raisins

Peel and grate carrots into large mixing bowl, add raisins. In blender, combine mayonnaise, lemon juice, zest, salt, ginger, and honey. Blend well. Pour over carrots and raisins. Toss to mix well. Best if refrigerated to blend flavors before serving. The lemon juice in the dressing is flavorful and will maintain freshness of carrots for several days. This has always been a favorite at our house. A great make ahead salad. May be made with canola mayonnaise, or an eggless mayonnaise.

Per serving: 217.7 Calories; 16.1g Fat (65.2% calories from fat); 0.7g Protein; 18.7g Carbohydrate; 7mg Cholesterol; 235mg Sodium

Donna's Cole Slaw
Serves 6

- 1/2 head cabbage, core removed
- 1/3 cup canola mayonnaise
- 1/3 cup apple cider vinegar, herb flavored
- 1/2 teaspoon salt and pepper, to taste
- 1/2 cup onion, diced fine
- 1/2 cup fresh parsley, chopped
- 1/4 teaspoon garlic salt

Finely shred cabbage with a knife or food processor. Place in a large bowl with diced onion and parsley.

In a small bowl, combine mayonnaise, vinegar, salt, pepper, and garlic salt. Wisk together with a fork and pour over cabbage. Toss together until mixed well.

Per serving: 118.7 Calories; 10.8g Fat (80.4% calories from fat); 1.0g Protein; 4.9g Carbohydrate; 4mg Cholesterol; 271mg Sodium

Cool Cucumber Salad
Serves 6

- 2 medium cucumber, peeled, sliced
- 1 medium onion, sliced into rings
- 1/2 cup apple cider vinegar
- 1/4 cup canola oil
- 1/4 cup beet sugar
- salt and pepper, to taste

Place cucumber and onion in plastic sealable container. Add remaining ingredients. Salt and pepper to taste. Put lid on tightly. Gently shake to mix. Drain to serve. Best if marinated over night. Sugar may be adjusted to your individual taste, 1/4 cup is the usual amount.

Per serving: 131.7 Calories; 9.2g Fat (59.6% calories from fat); 0.9g Protein; 13.2g Carbohydrate; 0mg Cholesterol; 94mg Sodium

Carrot-Raisin Salad
Serves 6

 1 pound carrots, peeled and grated
1/2 cup raisins, or currants
1/2 cup pecans, or nut of the day
3/4 cup pineapple rings in juice, crushed or tidbits
1/4 cup canola mayonnaise

Place grated carrots, nuts, raisins, and drained pineapple into bowl. Mix mayonnaise with 1/2 cup of the pineapple juice. Pour over carrot mixture and toss well. Refrigerate in airtight container.

Per serving: 189.1 Calories; 11.4g Fat (52.0% calories from fat); 1.6g Protein; 22.2g Carbohydrate; 3mg Cholesterol; 92mg Sodium

Black Bean Quinoa Salad
Serves 8

2	cups quinoa, cooked and cubed
1 1/2	cups black beans, cooked and drained
4	green onion, diced
1/2	cup parsley, fresh diced
1/2	cup green bell pepper, diced
1	clove garlic, minced
1/4	teaspoon chili powder
1	large tomato, diced
1/4	cup rice vinegar
1/4	cup olive oil
1/8	teaspoon cumin

Dressing:
Mix vinegar, oil, chili powder, and garlic. Set aside.
In a large bowl, combine quinoa, black beans, onion, parsley, bell pepper, and tomatoes.
Pour dressing over salad and toss lightly to coat with dressing.
Serve on bed of lettuce or in containers for lunch packing.

Per serving: 382.5 Calories; 10.1g Fat (22.9% calories from fat); 15.8g Protein; 60.8g Carbohydrate; 0mg Cholesterol; 42mg Sodium

Rice-Black Bean Salad
Serves 8

- 2 cups brown rice, cooked
- 1 1/2 cups black beans, cooked-drained
- 8 ounces salsa, all natural
- 2 Tablespoons olive oil, or oil of the day
- 1/4 cup black olives, sliced

Combine all ingredients in a large bowl and mix well. Serve on a bed of shredded lettuce or in a tortilla "bowl".
This dish is also great packed for lunch.
Canned black beans may be used if all natural.

Cactus salsa can be substituted for tomato salsa.

Per serving: 368.9 Calories; 9.0g Fat (21.8% calories from fat); 11.8g Protein; 61.0g Carbohydrate; 1mg Cholesterol; 109mg Sodium

Rice Salad
Serves 10

- 3 cups brown rice, cooked
- 3 ounces slivered almonds
- 1/2 cup green onion, sliced
- 1/2 cup red bell pepper, finely chopped
- 1/2 cup raisins
- 1 cup orange sections
- 1 Tablespoon apple cider vinegar
- 1/4 cup frozen orange juice concentrate
- 2 Tablespoons olive oil
- salt and pepper, to taste

Dressing: Combine orange juice concentrate, vinegar, oil, and salt and pepper. Wisk together and set aside.

In large bowl, combine rice, almonds, onion, red bell pepper, raisins, orange sections, and orange zest. Pour dressing over rice and vegetables and toss lightly to coat with dressing. Chill for at least one hour before serving.

Variations: Add 1-1/2 cups diced chicken or turkey to salad.

Per serving: 322.4 Calories; 8.8g Fat (24.1% calories from fat); 6.7g Protein; 55.8g Carbohydrate; 0mg Cholesterol; 5mg Sodium

Pasta Salad
Serves 6

10	ounces rice pasta, penne or twists
1/2	cup carrots, chopped fine
1/4	cup onions, chopped fine
1/4	cup bell pepper, chopped fine
3	ounces black olives, sliced
1/4	cup olive oil, or oil of the day
1/4	cup vinegar
1/2	teaspoon oregano, dried
1/4	teaspoon black pepper
1/2	teaspoon salt

Cook pasta according to package directions. Combine oil, vinegar, spices and salt to make dressing. Mix well. Add vegetables and coat with dressing. Toss pasta into vegetables and dressing. Cover and refrigerate 1-2 hours until ready to serve.

This recipe is delicious served with grilled chicken or chicken sausages.

Per serving: 223.8 Calories; 11.1g Fat (43.6% calories from fat); 3.7g Protein; 28.5g Carbohydrate; 0mg Cholesterol; 329mg Sodium

Zucchini Relish
Serves 60

    10   cups zucchini, washed and chopped
     1   cup carrots, chopped
     4   cups onion, chopped
     3   Tablespoons salt
 1 1/2 cups green bell pepper, chopped
 1 1/2 cups red bell pepper, chopped
 2 1/4 cups apple cider vinegar
     3   cups beet sugar
     1   teaspoon mustard seed
     1   teaspoon celery seed
     1   teaspoon turmeric
   1/2 teaspoon black pepper

Place first four ingredients in container with lid weighted down overnight. Next day, drain and rinse well in cold water. Place in large cooking pot and add rest of ingredients. Cook 30 minutes, pour into washed hot jars and seal.

Per serving: 46.2 Calories; 0.1g Fat (1.2% calories from fat); 0.4g Protein; 12.1g Carbohydrate; 0mg Cholesterol; 361mg Sodium

Waldorf Salad
Serves 6

- 2 medium apples, cored and diced
- 1 medium pear, cored and diced
- 1/4 cup pecans, or nut of the day
- 1 cup grapes, seedless
- 1/3 cup canola mayonnaise
- 1/4 cup celery, chopped
- 2 Tablespoons lemon juice

Mix mayonnaise and lemon juice until smooth. Place fruit, nuts and celery into large bowl. Pour mayonnaise mixture over fruit and toss to mix well. Refrigerate and serve cold.

Per serving: 172.4 Calories; 12.6g Fat (63.3% calories from fat); 0.6g Protein; 15.9g Carbohydrate; 4mg Cholesterol; 93mg Sodium

Microwave Baked Apples
Serves 2

- 2 whole apples, washed, cored
- 2 Tablespoons potato starch flour
- 2 Tablespoons beet sugar
- 1 teaspoon cinnamon
- 1 teaspoon allspice
- 1/2 teaspoon nutmeg
- 2 teaspoons canola margarine
- 2 dashes salt

Wash and core apples. Place in individual baking dishes. Place half of each ingredient in the center of each apple. Cover dish. Bake in microwave 4 minutes on high power, or until apple is tender.

Note: Apple may be sliced and layered in baking dish if desired. Sprinkle ingredients over top. Bake as above. Quick and easy dessert-fruit dish kids love to make.

Per serving: 220.0 Calories; 4.5g Fat (17.1% calories from fat); 0.4g Protein; 48.2g Carbohydrate; 0mg Cholesterol; 308mg Sodium

Melon Cup Day 2 C/E
Serves 6

- 2 cups watermelon, pieces
- 2 cups cantaloupe, pieces
- 1 cup honeydew melon, pieces
- 1/2 cup raspberries, fresh or frozen
- 1 cup strawberries, cut in half
- 2 Tablespoons lemon juice, fresh
- 3 Tablespoons apple juice, frozen concentrate, undiluted

Place all melons and strawberries in a large bowl. Toss gently to mix well.
In a blender, puree raspberries on high for 1/2 minute.
In a small bowl, combine raspberry puree, lemon juice, and apple juice concentrate. Stir to mix.
Place melons and strawberries in individual serving cups or wine glasses.
Pour raspberry dressing over melons and strawberries and serve.

For garnish, add a sprig of mint leaves.

For a wonderfully cool dessert in the summer, freeze the melon pieces and strawberries and add the dressing at the last minute.

Per serving: 50.6 Calories; 0.4g Fat (6.2% calories from fat); 0.8g Protein; 12.3g Carbohydrate; 0mg Cholesterol; 7mg Sodium

Hawaiian Fruit Salad
Serves 24

- 2 Tablespoons frozen orange juice concentrate
- 2 Tablespoons lemon juice
- 2 Tablespoons lime juice
- 1/2 cup beet sugar
- 1/2 cup water
- 1 whole watermelon, cut 1 inch cube
- 1 1/2 cups strawberries, halved
- 2 cups cantaloupe
- 1 can pineapple, drained
- 1/2 pound grapes

Mix all juices, sugar, and water and set aside while you prepare fruit. Pour over fruit. Refrigerate.

Variation: This fruity dessert is fun to serve in a carved watermelon shell. Nuts and coconut may be added if desired.

Per serving: 99.2 Calories; 1.0g Fat (7.8% calories from fat); 1.4g Protein; 23.8g Carbohydrate; 0mg Cholesterol; 5mg Sodium

Grape Mango Salad Day 1
Serves 4

- 2 cups seedless grapes, washed
- 2 whole mango, peeled and seeded
- 1/4 cup cashews, unsalted
- 2 Tablespoons maple syrup, or sugar
- 1/4 cup grape juice, white

Split mangos in half lengthwise with a knife and remove the large seed by sliding a large spoon into the fruit and around the seed. Peel the mangos and cut into bite size pieces. To make a dressing: Place approximately 1/2 of one mango into a blender with grape juice and maple syrup. Blend on high for 1/2 minute. Set aside.
Place remaining mango, grapes, and cashews in serving bowls. Spoon maple syrup dressing over salad. Serve as salad or dessert.

Per serving: 177.7 Calories; 4.3g Fat (20.1% calories from fat); 2.4g Protein; 36.1g Carbohydrate; 0mg Cholesterol; 12mg Sodium

Fruit of the Day Salad Day 4
Serves 4

- 1 can pineapple rings in juice
- 2 ripe banana, peeled
- 2 ripe kiwi fruit, peeled
- 1/4 cup peanuts, or pecan pieces

Drain pineapple and reserve juice. Place 2 pineapple rings in each serving plate. Slice bananas and place slices in pineapple juice (this will prevent them from turning brown). Drain the banana slices and arrange on pineapple slices. Slice kiwi and arrange on bananas. Sprinkle with peanuts and serve as a salad or dessert.

Per serving: 146.4 Calories; 4.9g Fat (27.5% calories from fat); 3.4g Protein; 25.6g Carbohydrate; 0mg Cholesterol; 5mg Sodium

Cherry Apple Sauce   Day 2
Serves 8

    6   large apples, of choice
1 1/2   cups cherries, unsweetened
    1   teaspoon cinnamon
    1   teaspoon tapioca flour

Peel, core, and dice apples. Remove pit from cherries and slice in half. In medium sauce pan, heat apples and cherries over low heat until tender, about 15-20 minutes. Add tapioca flour to 1/4 cup water and mix well. Add to apples and cherries and stir well. Allow to simmer until fruit juices becomes thick. Remove from heat and add cinnamon. Serve warm or cold.
May be used as a pie filling or as a topping for cakes and puddings.

Store in the refrigerator and pack in small containers for lunches.

Per serving: 70.5 Calories; 0.5g Fat (5.5% calories from fat); 0.5g Protein; 18.0g Carbohydrate; 0mg Cholesterol; 0mg Sodium

Ambrosia Day 3
Serves 8

- 1 Tablespoon frozen orange juice concentrate, unsweetened
- 1 Tablespoon lemon juice, unsweetened
- 1 Tablespoon lime juice, unsweetened
- 2 Tablespoons honey, room temperature
- 1/4 cup water, room temperature
- 3 medium tangelos, peeled and cubed
- 1 medium grapefruit, pink, peeled and cubed
- 2 medium blood oranges, peeled and cubed
- 1/4 cup coconut, unsweetened
- 1/4 cup pine nuts, optional

Mix orange juice concentrate, lemon juice, lime juice, honey and water together. Set aside. Mix fruit, coconut, and pine nuts together. Stir juice mixture, and pour over fruit. Chill. Stir before serving. Regular oranges may be used instead of blood oranges. Blood oranges add color and a slightly different flavor.

Variation: Hazelnuts may be used in place of pine nuts.

Per serving: 101.8 Calories; 2.6g Fat (19.3% calories from fat); 2.4g Protein; 22.3g Carbohydrate; 0mg Cholesterol; 2mg Sodium

Main Dishes And Entrees

Turkey Tacos
Serves 6

1	pound ground turkey, or chicken
1	medium onion, chopped
2	cloves garlic, minced
2	seeded green chile, minced
2	teaspoons chili powder
1/2	teaspoon cumin
1/4	teaspoon nutmeg
1/2	teaspoon salt
1/2	teaspoon pepper, coarsely ground
1/2	cup chicken broth
3	Tablespoons sun-dried tomato paste
1	Tablespoon oil, oil of the day
1	recipe Quinoa Tortillas

Chop onion, garlic, and chili peppers. In a large skillet, heat oil until hot and saute onion, garlic, and peppers until onion is tender. Do not allow garlic to brown. Add ground meat and cook seperating meat into small pieces as it cooks. Before all the pink is gone from the meat, add chili powder, cumin, nutmeg, salt, and pepper. Stir until all spices are well incorporated into meat mix. Add chicken broth and tomato paste. Stir well and simmer until almost all excess liquid has evaporated. Remove from heat and cover with a lid. Shred lettuce, and nut cheese or rice cheese of choice. Chop onion and tomatoes if desired. Serve with Quinoa tortillas. Or serve meat on a bed of lettuce with cheese, onion, and tomato for Taco Salad.
This recipe is also delicious served with any of the salsas or Avocado Dip.

Serving size: 2 tortllas per person.

Per serving: 212.3 Calories; 11.7g Fat (52.1% calories from fat); 15.4g Protein; 8.8g Carbohydrate; 60mg Cholesterol; 758mg Sodium

Turkey Cutlet Italiano   Day 5
Serves 4

- 4   4 ounce turkey breast cutlets
- 1   cup rice flour
- 1/4 teaspoon salt and pepper
- 2   Tablespoons canola oil
- 2   ounces almond cheese, grated
- 2   cups spaghetti sauce, meatless

Heat oil in nonstick skillet. Combine flour, salt and pepper in a plate. Coat turkey cutlets with seasoned rice flour and place in hot oil. Cook about 4-5 minutes on each side until done (depends on thickness of cutlets). Remove from skillet, drain off excess oil from pan and discard oil. Pour spaghetti sauce into skillet and heat to simmer. Place cutlets in sauce (but do not cover with sauce). Place grated cheese on top of each cutlet and allow cheese to melt. Remove from heat. Serve cutlets with rice or rice pasta.

Per serving: 399.1 Calories; 15.4g Fat (34.6% calories from fat); 12.4g Protein; 53.0g Carbohydrate; 9mg Cholesterol; 1,149mg Sodium

Turkey Cutlet With Gravy C/E
Serves 4

- 3/4 pound turkey breast slices, 4-6 cutlets
- salt and pepper
- 1/4 cup amaranth flour
- 1/4 cup rice flour
- 1 1/4 cups rice milk
- 4 Tablespoons oil

Season turkey with salt and pepper. Combine amaranth flour and rice flour. Coat cutlets with flours. Heat oil in nonstick skillet. Saute cutlets until lightly browned on each side. Do not over cook. Remove from pan. Leave drippings in pan and add remaining flour. Continue to cook the roux over low-medium heat until light brown. Add rice milk and stir constantly until it begins to thicken. Add more milk if desired. Serve over cutlets and mashed potatoes.

Per serving: 333.3 Calories; 16.5g Fat (44.9% calories from fat); 21.8g Protein; 23.8g Carbohydrate; 35mg Cholesterol; 1,249mg Sodium

Quick Turkey Noodle-Day 5
Serves 6

1/2	pound turkey breast, cooked and cubed
1	cup broccoli flowerets, fresh or frozen
7	ounces rice pasta, of choice
3/4	cup turkey broth
2	whole green onion, chopped
	salt and pepper, to taste
1	Tablespoon olive oil, or oil of the day

Boil pasta according to directions. Add broccoli to pasta water for the last 3 minutes of cooking time. Drain pasta and broccoli in colander. Return pasta and broccoli to saucepan and add broth, onion, salt and pepper, oil, and turkey cubes. Toss lightly and serve warm.

Per serving: 189.3 Calories; 5.5g Fat (25.7% calories from fat); 12.9g Protein; 22.9g Carbohydrate; 22mg Cholesterol; 228mg Sodium

Meatloaf
Serves 8

- 3/4 pound ground turkey
- 1/2 pound ground beef
- 1 medium onion, chopped fine
- 1/3 cup green bell pepper, chopped
- 1 1/3 teaspoons egg replacer, =1 egg
- 1/2 teaspoon salt
- 1/4 teaspoon pepper
- 3/4 cup rice crackers, crushed
- 1/2 cup tomatoes, pureed
- 1/2 teaspoon garlic salt

Preheat oven to 350 degrees.
Grease or spray a loaf pan with acceptable oil.
In a large bowl, combine all ingredients and mix well. Press into loaf pan and bake 1 hour. Remove from oven and drain off fat if necessary. Let rest for 10 minutes to cool before turning out onto serving platter. Slice into 8 pieces and serve with vegetables of choice.

Since your oven will be on for 1 hour, why not let it cook the rest of the meal at the same time. Place baking potatoes or sweet potatoes, wrapped in foil, in the oven for 1 hour. Prepare baked apples and place in the oven during the last 30 minutes of the baking time. This saves energy by using your oven efficiently, and cuts down on pots and pans to be washed.

Per serving: 241.3 Calories; 11.2g Fat (41.5% calories from fat); 12.6g Protein; 22.8g Carbohydrate; 58mg Cholesterol; 307mg Sodium

Grilled Sausages and Vegetables
Serves 4

- 1/2 Turkey Breakfast Sausage, recipe
- 1 whole red bell pepper
- 1 whole green bell pepper
- 2 medium eggplant, sliced in 1/3" slice
- 2 medium onions, sliced in half
- 2 medium tomatoes, sliced in half
- 2 cloves garlic, minced
- 1 teaspoon parsley, flakes
- 4 Tablespoons olive oil, or oil of the day

Grill peppers whole until skin is charred black. Remove from heat and allow to cool. Peel, seed, and cut into 8 pieces each. Place in a large bowl and set aside.
Grill eggplant slices, onion halves, and tomato halves. When heated and grill marked, turn to mark other side. Cut tomatoes and onions into wedges and place eggplant, onion, and tomatoes into bowl with peppers.
Sprinkle with garlic, oil, and parsley. Toss lightly and let set until other foods are ready.
Grill sausage patties or links and serve with vegetables.

Nutritional values include meat and vegetables as side dish.

Per serving: 223.5 Calories; 15.1g Fat (57.2% calories from fat); 5.8g Protein; 19.6g Carbohydrate; 8mg Cholesterol; 306mg Sodium

Dirty Rice
Serves 8

1	pound ground turkey, or any ground meat
1	cup onion, chopped
1	cup bell pepper, chopped
1/2	cup banana pepper, any color
2	cloves garlic, minced
1/2	teaspoon garlic salt
3/4	cup carrots, finely chopped
2	Tablespoons cajun seasoning, Chef Paul's
2	cups rice, uncooked
2	cups beef broth, or turkey
2 1/2	cups water
1	teaspoon oregano
1	Tablespoon parsley

Brown ground beef, just until no longer pink, in a large dutch oven with lid. Add onion, carrots, garlic, and peppers to browned beef, stirring frequently, and cook until onions become tender. Add all seasonings and rice. Stir to coat rice with seasonings and beef drippings in pan. Stir in water and broth and stir well. Return to boil, then reduce heat to slow simmer. Cover and cook for 50 minutes until rice is done. Stir occassionally to prevent sticking.

This is a favorite that is even better the next day.
If other cajun seasoning mix is used, instead of Chef Paul's, adjustments may need to be made depending on spices used.

Nutritional analysis is for turkey. Pork and beef values will be higher in fat and calories, while ground chicken will be comparable to turkey.

Per serving: 299.9 Calories; 5.9g Fat (18.0% calories from fat); 17.0g Protein; 43.7g Carbohydrate; 45mg Cholesterol; 692mg Sodium

Best Turkey Burgers
Serves 6

- 1 pound ground turkey
- 1/4 cup onion, chopped
- 1/2 cup rice crackers, crushed (10 cracker)
- 1/4 teaspoon salt and pepper
- 1/4 teaspoon garlic salt
- 1 Tablespoon sesame seeds
- 1 Tablespoon parsley, dried
- 1/2 teaspoon thyme, dried
- 1/2 teaspoon oregano, dried
- 1/2 teaspoon basil, dried

Combine all ingredients and mix well. Hands are the best mixers for this recipe. Form into 6 patties. Heat a large non-stick skillet and cook meat patties until brown on edges, turn and cook on other side. Serve with bread of the day, tomato slices, onion, and nut cheese slices. This recipe makes wonderful meatballs for soups, sauces, and with a dip for appetizers. It is a very versatile recipe.

Nutritional analysis is for burgers only.

Per serving: 136.0 Calories; 7.3g Fat (49.2% calories from fat); 14.0g Protein; 2.8g Carbohydrate; 60mg Cholesterol; 169mg Sodium

Baked Chicken Crunch
Serves 4

- 4 small chicken breast halves, skinless-boneless
- 1 cup dry bread crumbs, bread of the day
- 1 Tablespoon paprika
- 2 Tablespoons parsley, flakes
- 1 teaspoon thyme, dried
- 1 teaspoon garlic salt
- 1/2 teaspoon salt and pepper
- 1/3 cup olive oil

Preheat oven to 350 degrees.

Mix bread crumbs, herbs, and spices on a large plate. Place oil in another plate. Dip chicken in oil to coat completely. Coat with bread crumb mixture. Use remaining oil to grease a nonstick cookie sheet. Place coated chicken breast on cookie sheet and Bake at 350 degrees for 35 minutes.

Per serving: 450.1 Calories; 32.2g Fat (64.7% calories from fat); 31.8g Protein; 7.7g Carbohydrate; 93mg Cholesterol; 336mg Sodium

Baked Oriental Chicken
Serves 4

- 3 Tablespoons tarragon vinegar
- 2 teaspoons sesame oil
- 3 teaspoons soy sauce, wheat free-optional
- 1/2 teaspoon salt
- 1/4 teaspoon thyme
- 1/4 teaspoon ground ginger
- 2 whole chicken breast, skinned
- 4 slices pineapple, fresh

This recipe contains soy and can be omitted if you are allergic to soy.
Mix vinegar, oil, soy sauce, and spices together. Pour over chicken breast and pineapple. Marinate for 2-3 hours. Place in baking dish lightly sprayed with cooking oil. Arrange chicken breasts in baking dish. Place pineapple on top, pour marinade over meat. Cover and bake in oven 350 degrees for 45-60 minutes, or until meat is cooked through. To grill, cook over very low fire. Turn once and place pineapple on top of chicken.

Per serving: 666.2 Calories; 19.1g Fat (24.3% calories from fat); 33.5g Protein; 100.5g Carbohydrate; 93mg Cholesterol; 573mg Sodium

Chicken Artichoke Casserole   Day 1
Serves 8

1	whole chicken, cut up
2	cans artichoke hearts, packed in water
1/4	cup safflower oil mayonnaise
1/4	teaspoon paprika

Preheat oven to 350 degrees.
Grease a large baking dish or spray with oil. Dish should have a lid or cover with foil, and be large enough to hold chicken pieces in a single layer.
Drain artichoke hearts and place on the bottom of the baking dish. It is OK if some liquid is still in the artichoke hearts; it will help steam the chicken as it cooks. Spread mayonnaise over chicken pieces to coat thinly and sprinkle with paprika. Place chicken in a single layer over artichoke hearts. Cover and bake at 350 degrees for 35 minutes. Uncover and bake as additional 15 minutes or until chicken has a golden brown color. Serve hot.

Per serving: 281.3 Calories; 15.0g Fat (49.2% calories from fat); 30.8g Protein; 4.1g Carbohydrate; 95mg Cholesterol; 160mg Sodium

Cashew Chicken Day 1
Serves 4

1 1/2	cups chicken breast, 1/2" cubed
1/2	cup cashews, halves-unsalted
1 1/2	cups chicken broth
1	teaspoon potato starch flour
1/4	cup bell pepper
1	cup mushrooms, sliced
2	teaspoons safflower oil
	salt and pepper, to taste

Heat oil in nonstick skillet or wok. Add chicken and cook just until no longer pink. Add bell pepper and mushrooms and saute until bell pepper is tender.
In a small bowl, combine chicken broth and potato starch flour and stir until mixed well. Pour over chicken and vegetables. Add cashews and stir until broth begins to thicken. Salt and pepper to taste.
Serve over a baked potato for strict rotation diet guidelines.   Serve over rice for liberal rotation diet.

Per serving: 277.0 Calories; 17.7g Fat (57.0% calories from fat); 22.0g Protein; 8.1g Carbohydrate; 46mg Cholesterol; 635mg Sodium

Chicken Oriental Kabobs
Serves 8

- 1/4 cup beet sugar
- 1 teaspoon ground ginger
- 1 1/3 Tablespoons sesame oil
- 1/4 teaspoon garlic powder
- 1/2 cup rice vinegar
- 1/2 teaspoon pineapple juice
- 4 medium chicken breasts without skin, cut in 1" strips
- 1 medium bell pepper, red, cut 1" pieces
- 8 onuces mushroom caps
- 4 small zucchini, quartered
- 1 medium onion, quartered
- 8 ounces cherry tomatoes, whole-optional

Mix marinade and set aside. Prepare meat by cutting boneless, skinless chicken breast into 1 inch strips. Place in large tight sealing plastic dish. Prepare vegetables. Add to container with meat. Pour marinade over the meat and veggies. Mix gently and thoroughly. Let marinate for 1-2 hours or longer. This is easy to do ahead for guests. Alternate meat and desired arrangement of vegetables on skewers. Discard marinade. Cook over low heat on grill or under broiler with broiler pan at most distant position from the broiler.

Note: Substitute wheatfree soy sauce, or liquid amino sauce for the pineapple juice if soy is not being omitted from diet.

Per serving: 198.6 Calories; 4.0g Fat (18.0% calories from fat); 27.8g Protein; 13.3g Carbohydrate; 65mg Cholesterol; 147mg Sodium

Chicken Pizza
Serves 6

1	recipe Pizza Crust
1/2	cup canola mayonnaise
1	whole lemon zest, grated
1/4	pound chicken breast, chopped fine
4	ounces almond cheese, or other cheese
2	medium tomatoes, sliced
	salt and pepper, to taste

Preheat oven to 400 degrees. Bake crust without toppings for 8 minutes. Remove from oven and spread on mayonnaise to edge, sprinkle on lemon zest, chicken, and almond cheese. Place tomato slices over top. Salt and pepper to taste.
Bake in 400 degree oven for 15 minutes or until edges are golden.
Slice and serve with green salad or fruit salad.

Nutritional analysis includes crust and all toppings.
This recipe can also be cut into small squares and served as an appetizer.
This is one of our favorites. Sometimes, we splurge and add 1/4 cup cooked crumbled bacon as an additional topping.

Per serving: 347.8 Calories; 21.2g Fat (56.5% calories from fat); 11.6g Protein; 25.3g Carbohydrate; 16mg Cholesterol; 562mg Sodium

Chicken Stew with Biscuit Tops
Serves 6

- 2 cups chicken, leftover-cubed
- 2 large baked potatoes, leftover-cubed
- 1/2 cup onion, chopped
- 3/4 cup mushrooms, sliced
- 1 cup frozen peas, thawed
- 2 large carrots, sliced thin
- 1 1/2 cups rice milk, or milk of the day
- 1 teaspoon salt
- 1/4 teaspoon pepper
- dash red pepper, optional
- 2 teaspoons potato starch flour
- 1 recipe Drop Biscuits

Preheat oven to 425 degrees.
If you do not have leftover potatoes and chicken on hand, dice two large baking potatoes and boil for 10-15 minutes until tender. Dice two large breast halves and saute in 1 Tablespoon oil.
In a large skillet, combine chicken, onion, mushrooms, and carrots and saute until tender. If needed, add 3 Tablespoons water so the vegetables will not burn. When tender, add potatoes, and peas and heat through. In a large measuring cup, combine milk and potato starch flour and wisk together until thoroughly incorporated. Add to chicken and vegetable mix. Add salt and peppers and stir constantly until liquid begins to thicken. When thick, pour into a large, deep baking dish. Prepare biscuit mix and drop by Tablespoons onto top. Bake at 425 degrees for 12 minutes or until biscuits begin to turn golden.
This is a favorite.
Serve this hearty dish with a salad.

Per serving: 215.5 Calories; 6.2g Fat (25.8% calories from fat); 16.8g Protein; 23.0g Carbohydrate; 43mg Cholesterol; 555mg Sodium

Continental Chicken
Serves 8

3	pounds chicken pieces, bone in, skinless
1/4	cup potato starch flour
1/4	cup rice flour
2	Tablespoons oil
1	can mushrooms, canned, drained, save liquid
1	can tomato wedges, canned, chopped-optional
1	cup onion, sliced
1	clove garlic, minced
1/4	cup pitted black olives, sliced
3	cups white rice, cooked, hot

Stove Top Cooking: Coat chicken with flour and brown in oil, slowly (Save any left over flour). Drain mushrooms. Reserve the liquid. Combine mushroom liquid, tomatoes, and garlic. Add to browned chicken, with onion. Stir to combine. Cover and simmer 45 minutes or til tender. Stir in mushrooms and olives. (If thicker sauce is desired, add remaining flour to browning chicken and stir before adding liquid to chicken. Simmer as above.)

Microwave Cooking: Place oil and onion in large microwave baking dish. Heat 2-3 minutes on high power. Add floured chicken to dish. Cover and return to the microwave. Cook on high power for 16-18 minutes. Add garlic, mushrooms, tomato with juice, and olives. Return to microwave to cook an additional 8-10 minutes, or until chicken is done. Cooking time may vary depending on the size of the individual chicken pieces.

If a more international flavor is desired, add 1/3 cup wheat free soy sauce. Soy should not be used if a soy sensitivity exists.

Per serving: 535.5 Calories; 14.4g Fat (24.7% calories from fat); 28.1g Protein; 70.9g Carbohydrate; 92mg Cholesterol; 363mg Sodium

Grilled Chicken and Vegetables With Taragon   Day 1

Serves 6

- 6 chicken breast halves, skinless-boneless
- salt and pepper, to taste
- 1 Tablespoon tarragon, dried
- 1 1/2 Tablespoons safflower oil, or sunflower oil
- 2 medium eggplant, peeled
- 2 large bell pepper, quartered and seeded
- 4 medium tomatoes, quartered
- 4 ounces mushrooms, any variety sliced

Rub 1 Tablespoon oil over chicken breast and sprinkle with half the salt, pepper, and tarragon. Heat indoor or outdoor grill. When hot, place chicken breasts on grill to cook and leave grill marks. Remove from heat and set aside. Slice eggplant lengthwise in thin slices and quarter bell pepper and tomatoes. Slice mushrooms. Place tomatoes and mushrooms in a saucepan and simmer for 5 minutes. Set aside. Combine remaining 1 Tablespoon oil, salt, pepper, and tarragon. Coat eggplant and bell pepper lightly with seasoned oil. Place on grill and cook for about 5 minutes or until marked well. Place cooked eggplant, bellpepper, tomatoes, and mushrooms in a bowl and mix well. Serve as a side to the chicken.

This is a complete meal served alone.

Per serving: 340.6 Calories; 17.5g Fat (45.7% calories from fat); 32.9g Protein; 13.8g Carbohydrate; 93mg Cholesterol; 103mg Sodium

Layered Chicken-Zucchini Casserole
Serves 6

- 6 small chicken breast halves
- 5 medium zucchini, grated
- 4 medium carrots, grated
- 1 medium onion, sliced into rings
- 1/2 teaspoon salt and pepper
- 1/4 teaspoon garlic salt
- 1 Tablespoon parsley, flakes
- 1 Tablespoon potato starch flour

Preheat oven to 350 degrees.
In small cup, combine salt, pepper, garlic salt, parsley, and potato starch flour. Set aside.
Spray or grease a covered baking dish. Place zucchini on bottom of baking dish. Layer carrots and onions on top of zucchini. Sprinkle with half the spice mixture. Place chicken breast halves on top and sprinkle chicken with the last half of spices. Cover and bake for 1 hour. Remove cover and bake 10 more minutes with lid removed.

For camp-outs: place ingredients in layers in individual aluminum foil pouches and cook on top of the grill away from direct flame. The results are extremely good. One teaspoon of margarine can be used instead of oil. Check one pouch after 45 minutes to determine if chicken is completely cooked. Time will vary according to temperature of the coals or fire.

Per serving: 297.8 Calories; 13.7g Fat (41.5% calories from fat); 32.2g Protein; 11.1g Carbohydrate; 93mg Cholesterol; 323mg Sodium

Lemon Chicken   C/E
Serves 6

- 6 chicken breast halves, skinless-boneless
- 1 medium lemon zest, grated
- salt and pepper, to taste
- 1/4 teaspoon garlic salt

Preheat coals or indoor grill.
Sprinkle chicken breasts with seasonings and lemon zest. Grill over hot coals or on indoor grill about 20 minutes on each side until done or bake at 350 degrees for 45 minutes.

Per serving: 249.1 Calories; 13.4g Fat (49.8% calories from fat); 30.2g Protein; 0.2g Carbohydrate; 93mg Cholesterol; 92mg Sodium

Oven Chicken Casserole
Serves 10

- 2 cups chicken, cooked, cubed
- 2 cups celery, sliced thin
- 1/2 cup almonds, toasted and sliced
- 1/2 teaspoon salt
- 2 teaspoons onion, grated
- 1 cup canola mayonnaise
- 2 Tablespoons lemon juice
- 1/2 cup almond cheese, grated

Mix all ingredients together well, (except cheese). Place in baking dish. Sprinkle cheese on top.
Bake 450 degrees for 10-15 minutes. Done when warmed throughout and cheese is melted.
Serving Suggestion: Serve as a main dish or an appetizer with cracker recipes included in this book.

Per serving: 271.2 Calories; 23.9g Fat (80.5% calories from fat); 10.3g Protein; 2.7g Carbohydrate; 34mg Cholesterol; 369mg Sodium

Pesto Chicken and Pasta
Serves 6

- 2 cups chicken breast, cooked and cubed
- 4 Tablespoons basil pesto
- 1 large carrot, grated
- 4 green onion, chopped fine
- 8 ounces rice pasta, cooked

Cook pasta according to directions.
Warm chicken in microwave (if frozen or refrigerated). Add all ingredients to drained pasta and toss well.
Serve warm with grated almond cheese topping, or serve cold as a chicken pasta salad for picnics.

Per serving: 254.5 Calories; 7.7g Fat (26.8% calories from fat); 18.1g Protein; 29.3g Carbohydrate; 40mg Cholesterol; 72mg Sodium

Portobello Chicken
Serves 6

5	chicken breast halves, skinless-boneless
1/2	teaspoon salt
1/2	teaspoon garlic salt
1/4	teaspoon black pepper
1	medium onion, chopped
7	ounces mushroom, portobello chopped
1	Tablespoon olive oil, or oil of the day
1	cup chicken broth, or wine
1/2	cup almond milk, or rice milk
2	teaspoons potato starch flour

In a large skillet, heat olive oil and saute onion and mushrooms until tender. Place mushrooms and onions in a bowl and set aside.

Cut chicken breasts into small medallions or 1/2" thick strips. Season with salt, pepper, and garlic salt. Saute seasoned chicken in oil remaining in pan until done. Add onion and mushrooms to chicken. Pour chicken broth or wine over chicken and mushroom mix and simmer covered for 10 minutes. In a measuring cup, mix almond milk and potato starch flour until combined. Add milk mixture to chicken and stir into broth. Heat until broth begins to thicken. Remove from heat and serve over pasta, rice, or spaghetti rice.

Per serving: 267.1 Calories; 14.2g Fat (48.6% calories from fat); 28.0g Protein; 5.7g Carbohydrate; 78mg Cholesterol; 617mg Sodium

Savory Meatballs
Serves 8

 1   pound chicken, ground
 1/2 cup onion, finely chopped
 1   Tablespoon parsley, dried
 1/2 teaspoon garlic salt
 1/2 teaspoon oregano, dried
 1/2 teaspoon thyme, dried
     dash red pepper, dried
 10 rice crackers, crushed

Mix all ingredients well and form into small meatballs, patties, or link shapes to use in soups, sauces, or in buns. This recipe makes enough for two meals of meatballs, and links. It makes only one meal for four of patties for use in buns. Freeze half meatballs on waxed paper covered cookie sheet. Transfer to freezer bags and freeze for later use.

Variations: Ground Turkey, Ground Beef, Ground Pork, Ground Venison.

Per serving: 150.8 Calories; 3.7g Fat (23.7% calories from fat); 11.5g Protein; 15.1g Carbohydrate; 31mg Cholesterol; 139mg Sodium

Sundried Tomato Chicken
Serves 6

- 6 chicken breast halves, thawed
- 3 Tablespoons dehydrated minced onion
- 1/4 teaspoon salt
- 1/2 teaspoon pepper, of choice
- 2 Tablespoons olive oil, or oil of the day
- 1/4 cup sun-dried tomatoes, chopped
- 3/4 cup water
- 3 Tablespoons sun-dried tomato paste

Rinse chicken breasts with water. Pat dry with paper towel. Sprinkle dehydrated onion, salt, and pepper on each side of breasts.
Heat oil in large skillet. Add coated chicken to pan and brown lightly on each side. Onions will toast and become browned. Sprinkle sun-dried tomato pieces over chicken. In measuring cup, mix water and sun-dried tomato paste until smooth. Add to chicken. Cover and cook on low another 20-25 minutes until done (depends on thickness of breasts).
Serve sauce over rice or pasta of choice.

Per serving: 327.1 Calories; 20.0g Fat (57.4% calories from fat); 30.7g Protein; 2.6g Carbohydrate; 93mg Cholesterol; 527mg Sodium

Tarragon Chicken Casserole
Serves 8

1 1/2	lb chicken breast, boneless-skinless
6	medium baking potatoes, washed, thin sliced
3	teaspoons canola margarine
6	Tablespoons potato starch flour
1	teaspoon tarragon
1/2	cup rice milk
1/4	teaspoon garlic
1/4	teaspoon parsley
1	teaspoon thyme

Layer about one third of the sliced potatoes in a large covered microwave baking dish. Spinkle 2 Tablespoons of the flour on top; dot with a little of the margarine; sprinkle lightly with salt and pepper. Continue to layer in this manner until all the potatoes have been used. Arrange the chicken breasts on the top layer of potatoes. Pour rice milk over all the chicken to moisten the meat. Lightly spray the meat with cooking oil. Sprinkle lightly with garlic salt and parsley. Top off with tarragon and thyme. Cover and cook on high in the microwave for 35 minutes or until done, or bake covered in a 350 degree oven for 1 hour. The chicken broth makes each layer of the potatoes delicately flavored. The potatoes may be peeled if desired.

Per serving: 247.3 Calories; 7.9g Fat (28.8% calories from fat); 16.1g Protein; 27.8g Carbohydrate; 44mg Cholesterol; 69mg Sodium

Bar-B-Q Cornish Hens
Serves 8

4   whole cornish game hens
1   recipe Bar-B-Que Sauce
3   teaspoons thyme
     salt and pepper, to taste

Heat coals.
Split cornish hens in half down backbone and breast bone. Rinse with water and pat dry. Sprinkle inside of hens with salt, pepper, and thyme. Glaze skin side with Bar-B-Que sauce. Place on the grill skin up. Do not place too close to the heat. Cook about 12-15 minutes. Turn and cook about 10 minutes. Do not let the Bar-B-Que sauce burn. Serve with grilled vegetables of the day.

Per serving: 692.5 Calories; 39.2g Fat (52.5% calories from fat); 77.1g Protein; 3.0g Carbohydrate; 248mg Cholesterol; 897mg Sodium

Sunny Chicken Strips   Day 1
Serves 6

- 1 pound chicken breast halves, skinless-boneless
- 1/4 cup sunflower seeds
- salt and pepper, to taste
- 1/2 cup oat flour
- 1 medium lemon zest, grated
- 4 Tablespoons sunflower oil

Grind oats and sunflower seeds in blender. Place seed and oat mix into plastic bag with lemon zest. Cut chicken into 1/2 inch wide strips, and season with salt and pepper. Add chicken strips to bag one at a time until all strips are coated with mix. Heat sunflower seed oil in skillet until hot. Add chicken strips (one layer) to oil and cook on one side until lightly browned. Turn and brown on other side.
To bake: place 1 Tablespoon of oil on cookie sheet. Layer chicken in one layer on cookie sheet. Spray chicken strips with oil using kitchen sprayer. Bake at 375 degrees for 20 minutes until lightly brown.

3/4 cup rice flour can be substituted for oat flour. Frying results are much better. These are great as appetizers. Prepare them in strips or nuggets, and serve with a dipping sauce.

Per serving: 227.8 Calories; 16.7g Fat (65.8% calories from fat); 14.4g Protein; 5.1g Carbohydrate; 39mg Cholesterol; 106mg Sodium

Tahitian Chicken
Serves 6

6	medium chicken breast halves, skinless-boneless
16	ounces pineapple chunks in juice, reserve juice
1/2	teaspoon ginger, powder
1/2	teaspoon curry powder, mild
1/3	cup honey
1	medium lime, juiced
1/2	cup Italian seasoning

Drain pineapple and use juice in marinade liquid.
After juicing lime, cut lime into 8 pieces and place pieces in marinade for added flavor.
Mix all ingredients except chicken and pineapple. Mix well and pour into large (gallon size) resealable plastic bag. Cut chicken into 1" cubes for kabobs or in strips. Place chicken and pineapple in bag with marinade mix. Chill 2 hours. Chicken may turn lighter color because of acid content of marinade.
Remove chicken and pineapple from marinade and grill or broil for a few minutes on each side or thread on skewers for kabobs.
Marinade can be boiled, strained, and served on the side as a sauce, but the mix must be cooked well because raw chicken has been in contact with liquid.
This dish is my daughter's favorite meal. It is wonderful served with rice and a fresh green salad.

Nutritional analysis includes marinade-actual consumption of marinade is minimal.

Per serving: 368.1 Calories; 13.9g Fat (33.3% calories from fat); 31.1g Protein; 31.6g Carbohydrate; 93mg Cholesterol; 95mg Sodium

Maple Glazed Quail   C/E
Serves 4

- 6   5-6 ounce quail, butterflied
- 6   Tablespoons maple syrup
- 3   Tablespoons orange juice, fresh
       salt and pepper, to taste
- 1   Tablespoon olive oil

Preheat oven to 350 degrees.
Oil a 13" x 9" baking dish with olive oil.
To butterfly quail, cut in half up back bone and snap the breast bone until quail will lie flat in a baking dish.   Place quail in baking dish breast side up. Sprinkle with salt and pepper. In a measuring cup, combine orange juice and maple syrup until mixed well. Pour 1/2 of maple glaze over quail. Cover baking pan with foil and bake for 15 minutes. Uncover, and baste with remaining glaze. Place back in oven and bake for 10 more minutes. Serve with sauted vegetables that you do not eat often.

When basting raw meat and poultry, do not contaminate your marinade base with raw meat juices. Spoon on and then spread over meat, or pour a little marinade into a smaller container to use a basting brush. If you should contaminate the marinade base by dipping back into it with a spoon or brush that has been used on raw meat, you can boil the marinade for several minutes to kill germs that may be present.

Serving size 1 1/2 quail per adult.

Per serving: 428.7 Calories; 23.3g Fat (49.5% calories from fat); 32.4g Protein; 21.0g Carbohydrate; 125mg Cholesterol; 90mg Sodium

Savory Rosemary Game Birds C/E
Serves 4

- 2 large cornish game hens, split in half
- 3 cloves garlic, sliced
- 4 small rosemary, sprigs
- dash salt and pepper
- 2 teaspoons olive oil

Preheat grill or oven to 350 degrees. Split hen down backbone and breast bone. Loosen skin, but do not remove it. Place sliced garlic and rosemary under skin. Smooth skin back down over breast. Lightly rub oil over skin of birds. Sprinkle with salt and pepper. To bake in the oven, place birds, skin side up, in a baking dish. Bake 35 minutes at 350 degrees or until juices run clear.

For grill, place birds on the grill breast side up (about 12" from heat source) for 15 minutes on one side. Turn and cook 10 more minutes on the breast side. If birds are cooking too quickly, move further away from the heat source.

Per serving: 707.3 Calories; 41.1g Fat (53.6% calories from fat); 77.2g Protein; 2.8g Carbohydrate; 248mg Cholesterol; 888mg Sodium

Roasted Duck With Wild Rice Day 5
Serves 8

- 1   5 pound duck
- 1/2   teaspoon black pepper
- 1/2   teaspoon salt
- 1   cup guava juice, or papaya juice
- 1   teaspoon potato starch flour

Preheat oven to 450 degrees. Rinse duck with water and pat dry with paper towels. Season duck, inside and out, with salt and pepper. Place the duck on a rack in a deep roasting pan. The duck will render a large amount of fat. Cook for 15 minutes at 450 degrees, then reduce heat to 350 degrees. Cook an additional 1 1/2 hour at 350 degrees. Carve in the same manner you would a large hen. Discard fat in the pan.

Guava or Papaya Sauce: Wisk juice and potato starch flour together until completely combined. Heat in a small sauce pan until juice begins to thicken. Remove from heat and serve warm with the duck. Serve with wild rice.

Orange juice can be substituted if guava or papaya is not available.
Duck is very high in fat. Some of the fat can be eliminated by removing the skin after cooking.

Per serving: 654.8 Calories; 62.5g Fat (86.5% calories from fat); 18.4g Protein; 3.5g Carbohydrate; 121mg Cholesterol; 235mg Sodium

Aloha Burger
Serves 4

- 1/2 pound ground beef, extra lean, patties
- 4 slices fresh pineapple, 1 inch thick, cored
- 4 dashes garlic powder
- salt and pepper, to taste
- 4 Tablespoons Hot Wing Dip, optional
- 4 leaves lettuce
- 4 slices tomato, optional

Form meat into patties. Sprinkle with garlic, salt, and pepper. Cook on grill. When burger is almost done, place pineapple slices on grill, approximately 2-3 minutes. Serve with our Burger Buns or our Flatbread Medallions. Dress with our Hot Wing Dip, and you will be delighted. This is a favorite at our house!

Per serving: 724.8 Calories; 26.7g Fat (30.6% calories from fat); 19.3g Protein; 117.0g Carbohydrate; 44mg Cholesterol; 222mg Sodium

Beef Burgers Day 2
Serves 4

- 3/4   pound ground beef, extra lean
- 1/2   teaspoon oregano, dried
- 1/2   teaspoon thyme, dried
- 1/4   teaspoon salt
- 1/4   teaspoon pepper
- 2   slices tapioca bread, crumbs

Combine all ingredients in a large bowl and mix well with hands.
Place on a hot grill or skillet and cook until done. (Done when juices run clear)
Serve on tapioca bread with thin cucumber slices instead of lettuce.
Almond cheese is great to make these into cheese burgers. Almond milk is also a part of day 2.

Per serving: 270.6 Calories; 17.5g Fat (60.5% calories from fat); 16.5g Protein; 9.3g Carbohydrate; 59mg Cholesterol; 275mg Sodium

Best Beef Burgers
Serves 6

- 1 pound lean beef, ground
- 1/4 cup onion, finely chopped
- 1/2 cup rice crackers, crushed
- 1/4 teaspoon salt and pepper
- 1/4 teaspoon garlic salt
- 1 Tablespoon sesame seeds
- 1 Tablespoon parsley, dried
- 1/2 teaspoon thyme, dried
- 1/2 teaspoon oregano, dried
- 1/2 teaspoon basil, dried

Combine all ingredients and mix well. Hands are the best mixers for this recipe. Form into 6 patties. Heat a large non-stick skillet and cook meat patties until brown on edges, turn and cook on other side. Serve with bread of the day, tomato slices, onion, and nut cheese slices.

This recipe also makes wonderful meatballs for soups, sauces, and with a dip for appetizers. It is a very versatile recipe.

Nutritional analysis is for burgers with beef.

Per serving: 127.7 Calories; 4.7g Fat (34.3% calories from fat); 17.5g Protein; 2.8g Carbohydrate; 44mg Cholesterol; 141mg Sodium

Beef and Cheddar Pasta
Serves 6

1	pound ground beef, extra lean
1	package rice pasta, cooked, drained
6	ounces almond cheddar cheese, cut in small cubes
1/4	cup rice milk
	salt and pepper, to taste
1	dash garlic powder
1/8	teaspoon oregano
1/8	teaspoon parsley

Brown meat in large sauce pan with seasonings. When meat is cooked all the way through, add cheese and milk. Stir until cheese is melted. Add pasta, mix well and serve.

Substitution: Soy or rice cheese may be used in place of almond cheese.

Per serving: 276.8 Calories; 16.6g Fat (55.4% calories from fat); 21.0g Protein; 9.1g Carbohydrate; 52mg Cholesterol; 337mg Sodium

Beef Strips With Pesto "Pasta"   Day 2
Serves 4

- 2/3 pound beef, cut in thin strips
- 1/3 cup black olives, sliced
- 1 Tablespoon olive oil
- 2 Tablespoons Basil Pesto, recipe
- 2 whole spaghetti squash, cooked

Boil spaghetti squash according to directions in vegetable section. Keep warm.
Brown beef strips (cut into very thin strips-almost shredded) in olive oil. Add black olive slices and pesto. Stir well.
Fluff spaghetti squash with fork and remove from squash shell to individual plates. Top with beef strips and pesto mixture. Toss lightly and serve hot. Top with grated almond cheese if desired.

Per serving: 234.8 Calories; 18.7g Fat (71.6% calories from fat); 12.9g Protein; 3.8g Carbohydrate; 45mg Cholesterol; 152mg Sodium

Coconut Meatballs
Serves 8

- 1 1/2 pounds ground beef, extra lean
- 1/4 cup onion, minced
- 1 teaspoon garlic powder
- 1/2 teaspoon basil, dried
- 1/2 teaspoon parsley, dried
- 2 teaspoons guar gum
- 1/2 teaspoon black pepper
- 1/2 teaspoon salt
- 2 Tablespoons potato starch flour
- 2 Tablespoons rice milk
- 2 Tablespoons safflower oil
- 1 cup chicken broth
- 1 can coconut milk
- 8 ounces mushrooms, sliced
- 2 teaspoons sesame seeds, optional

Mix meat, onions, spices, potato starch flour, and rice milk. Mix well. Form into medium balls. Brown meatballs on all sides in pan with safflower oil. As the meatballs get done, remove from pan and set aside. When all meatballs have been removed from pan, place mushrooms in pan and brown. Add chicken broth simmer for 5 minutes. Add coconut milk and sesame seeds. Add meatballs back into the pan and reduce heat simmer for 10 minutes. Makes 44-48 medium sized meatballs.

Serving suggestions: Serve over piping hot short grain brown rice. May also be served as an appetizer.

Per serving: 338.3 Calories; 26.0g Fat (68.5% calories from fat); 18.9g Protein; 7.9g Carbohydrate; 59mg Cholesterol; 412mg Sodium

Hamburger Stew
Serves 6

- 1 pound ground beef, extra lean, browned and drained
- 1 package baby carrots
- 1 box, 10 oz. frozen peas, with pearl onions
- 1 can, 13 oz. mushrooms, drained, save liquid
- 1 can chicken broth
- 1 teaspoon garlic powder, optional
- 1/2 teaspoon salt
- 1/2 teaspoon black pepper
- 2 Tablespoons potato starch flour
- 2 Tablespoons water

Brown the ground beef. Add onion. Add chicken broth and simmer for 5 minutes. Add vegetables and simmer additional 5 minutes. Mix potato starch and water together. Add this mixture to the simmering beef dish, stirring well. Liquid will thicken. Salt and pepper to taste.

Variations: Great served over baked potatoes, or with our Dumpling recipe.

Per serving: 224.2 Calories; 13.5g Fat (55.1% calories from fat); 17.2g Protein; 7.6g Carbohydrate; 53mg Cholesterol; 561mg Sodium

Meatballs

Serves 8

1 1/2	pounds ground beef, extra lean
1/4	cup onion, minced
1	teaspoon garlic powder
1/2	teaspoon basil
1/2	teaspoon parsley
2	teaspoons guar gum
1/2	teaspoon black pepper
1/2	teaspoon salt
2	Tablespoons potato starch flour
2	Tablespoons rice milk
2	Tablespoons safflower oil

Mix meat, onions, spices, potato starch flour, and rice milk. Mix well. Form into medium balls. Brown meatballs on all sides in pan with safflower oil. Simmer for 10 minutes or until done. Makes 44-48 medium sized meatballs.

May be used with several recipes in this book. Spicy Meatballs served over rice or pasta, or with Tomatoless Pasta Sauce served over spaghetti. The possibilities are endless. Meatballs may also be used in a sauce as an appetizer.

Per serving: 248.1 Calories; 18.0g Fat (66.1% calories from fat); 16.1g Protein; 4.6g Carbohydrate; 59mg Cholesterol; 210mg Sodium

Spicy Meatballs
Serves 8

1 cup salsa, of choice
1 cup Cranberry Sauce
1 recipe Meatballs

Use our recipes for Meatballs and Cranberry Sauce. Combine Cranberry Sauce and salsa and heat in a medium size sauce pan. Brown meatballs and add to the sauce. Allow to simmer a few minutes and serve. May be served over rice, pasta or as appetizers. If you choose to use a commercial salsa or jellied cranberry sauce be sure to read the labels, they may contain corn. May also be used with our Cactus Salsa for a tomatoless version. This is a delightful sweet and sour taste.

Per serving: 96.8 Calories; 3.5g Fat (31.8% calories from fat); 2.2g Protein; 14.7g Carbohydrate; 8mg Cholesterol; 60mg Sodium

Mexican Meat Lovers Pizza
Serves 4

1	recipe Pizza Crust
1/2	can refried beans, all natural
1/2	cup onion, chopped
1	cup fresh mushrooms, chopped or sliced
1/2	pound hamburger, browned and drained
1/2	cup ham, sliced 1/8" thick
1/4	cup broccoli, chopped
1/2	cup Turkey Breakfast Sausage, browned and drained
1/2	pound almond cheese, slice thin, optional

Prepare two small crusts from our pizza crust recipe. Pre bake for 6-7 minutes at 400 degrees. Remove from oven and top with ingredients. Thin the refried beans with 2-3 tablespoons of water. Mix well. Spread half of the thinned refried beans on each of the rice pizza crusts. Sprinkle half of each of the remaining ingredients on each pizza round. Bake at 400 degrees for 10 - 14 minutes or until cheeses are melted.

Almond cheese may be substituted if desired. Serving suggestion. Top with a few small drops of rice vinegar at the table for a new taste in pizza.

Per serving: 607.8 Calories; 20.7g Fat (31.3% calories from fat); 36.4g Protein; 65.7g Carbohydrate; 48mg Cholesterol; 1,630mg Sodium

Spaghetti Sauce With Meat
Serves 8

- 1/2 pound ground beef, extra lean, turkey,chicken,pork
- 4 cups tomatoes, diced
- 2 cloves garlic, chopped fine
- 1 cup onion, chopped
- 3 tablespoons oil
- 1/2 teaspoon oregano, dried
- 1/2 teaspoon thyme, dried
- 1/2 tablespoon parsley, dried
- 1 cup mushroom, chopped
- salt and pepper, to taste

Heat oil in large saucepan. Add onion, garlic, mushrooms and saute on low until tender. Do not let garlic brown. Add tomatoes and spices. Cover and simmer for 1 hour, stirring ocassionally. Taste before adding salt.
Serve over pasta, spaghetti squash, or rice.

Per serving: 136.9 Calories; 10.3g Fat (66.0% calories from fat); 6.5g Protein; 5.5g Carbohydrate; 20mg Cholesterol; 102mg Sodium

Food Allergies, What Do I Eat Now?

Stuffed Peppers with Currants
Serves 4

1	pound ground beef, extra lean
1/4	cup onion, minced
1	teaspoon garlic powder
1/2	teaspoon basil
1/2	teaspoon parsley
2	teaspoons guar gum
1/2	teaspoon black pepper
1/2	teaspoon salt
2	Tablespoons potato starch flour
2	Tablespoons rice milk
1/2	cup dried currants
1/2	cup water, boiling
4	medium bell pepper, topped and cleaned
1/2	cup water

Cover currants with boiling water; let stand for several hours or overnight. Mix meat, onion, potato starch flour, rice milk, and spices thoroughly. Spoon into bell peppers. Spoon currants from water onto tops of stuffed peppers. Drizzle currant juice on top of stuffed peppers. Pour any leftover currant juice into bottom of baking dish. Add 1/2 cup water to bottom of baking dish.
Bake 45 minutes to 1 hr. at 350 degrees.

Hint: Currants may be pureed with own liquid then poured over and around peppers if desired.

Per serving: 374.1 Calories; 19.7g Fat (46.8% calories from fat); 23.0g Protein; 27.4g Carbohydrate; 78mg Cholesterol; 387mg Sodium

Taco Meat
Serves 8

- 1 pound ground beef, extra lean
- 1 teaspoon chili powder
- 1 teaspoon cumin
- 1/2 teaspoon garlic powder
- 1/2 teaspoon paprika
- 1/4 teaspoon celery salt
- 1/4 teaspoon black pepper
- 1/4 teaspoon parsley
- 2 Tablespoons potato starch flour
- 1/2 cup water

Place meat, spices, and potato starch flour. Mix well. Place in skillet that has been lightly sprayed with cooking oil. Cook over medium heat. When almost done, add water and stir well until meat is done. Some meat and spices will stick to the bottom of the pan. Loosen drippings in pan with 1/2 cup water. You may need to add an additional 1/4 - 1/2 cup of water. Stir; remove from heat when pan drippings have released and meat is cook thoroughly. This recipe can be made with ground chicken, turkey or beef. Serve with taco salad, Soft Shell Roll-ups for tacos, or with chips as an appetizer.

Per serving: 150.2 Calories; 9.8g Fat (59.6% calories from fat); 10.8g Protein; 4.2g Carbohydrate; 39mg Cholesterol; 91mg Sodium

Tex-Mex Kabobs
Serves 4

- 1 pound flank steak, thin strips
- 3 medium tomatoes, cut in wedges
- 2 small zucchini, cut in thin slices
- 3/4 cup baby carrots, blanched
- 1 clove garlic, minced
- 4 cloves garlic, left whole
- 1/4 cup maple syrup, natural
- 1 tablespoon canola margarine, melted
- 1 Tablespoon cilantro, finely chopped
- 3/4 teaspoon ground cumin
- 1/8 teaspoon ground red pepper

Soak 8-10 wooden skewers in water for at least 30 minutes.
Heat coals.
Sauce: Mince 1 clove garlic, half remaining garlic cloves and set aside. In a small bowl, combine maple syrup, margarine, cilantro, minced garlic, cumin, and red pepper. Set aside.

Alternately thread sliced meat (accordian style), garlic and vegetables onto skewers. Baste with marinade. Grill or broil kabobs about 6" from heat source for 10-12 minutes, turning and basting with sauce often. Serve with rice, pasta, spaghetti squash, or quinoa.

Per serving: 327.5 Calories; 15.3g Fat (41.7% calories from fat); 24.1g Protein; 24.0g Carbohydrate; 58mg Cholesterol; 138mg Sodium

Rubbed Pork Tenderloin
Serves 4

- 1 pound pork tenderloin
- 4 Tablespoons parsley, flakes
- 1/2 teaspoon sage, rubbed
- 1 teaspoon thyme, dried
- 1 teaspoon oregano, dried
- 1/2 teaspoon garlic salt
- 1/2 teaspoon pepper, coarse ground

This recipe is fabulous when slow cooked in a smoker. One pound tenderloin will take 2 1/4 hour at 200-220 degrees in the smoker.

Preheat oven to 300 degrees. Place a small baking dish with 2" of hot water on the bottom of oven. This will keep the moisture level high in the oven while the tenderloin cooks. Mix all spices and herbs in a bowl. Rub tenderloin with spices until completely covered. Wrap in plastic wrap and refrigerate for 2 hours. In an iron skillet, heat 1 tablespoon oil and sear (lightly brown) tenderloin on all sides. Leave lenderloin in iron skillet, or place in a 9 x 13" x 2" pan. Place in oven and cook for 1 1/2 hour.

To serve, slice tenderloin in 1/2" slices on the diagonal. About 4-5 slices per person. Serve with any vegetable.

Drippings from the pan can make a wonderful sauce. If the pan is dry, add 1/2 cup water and let sit a few minutes, then Scrape off drippings from the bottom of pan. Add 1/4 cup mushrooms and serve with meat.

This is one of my favorites to cook ahead and wrap in foil for family campouts. Very easy--just warm in the foil on the fire.

Per serving: 149.6 Calories; 4.1g Fat (25.3% calories from fat); 24.8g Protein; 2.6g Carbohydrate; 74mg Cholesterol; 77mg Sodium

Rubbed Ribs
Serves 6

- 3 pounds pork center rib
- 1/2 cup parsley, flakes
- 1/4 cup paprika
- 2 Tablespoons pepper
- 2 Tablespoons garlic salt
- 1 Tablespoon onion salt
- 2 Tablespoons oregano, dried
- 2 Tablespoons thyme, dried
- 1 teaspoon red pepper, optional

This is a great substitute for basted Bar-B-Que ribs (most Bar-B-Que sauces contain cane sugar, tomatoes, and corn).

Combine all herbs and spices in a small bowl. Cut ribs into managable size pieces (about 5 ribs per piece). Rinse ribs and pat dry with paper towels. Rub herb and spice mix onto ribs evenly. Place in a large resealable plastic bag and place in the refrigerator to marinate for at least 2 hours. Mix the left over spices with 3 Tablespoons oil of choice if you would like to baste the ribs while they cook. It is not necessary, but will help keep the herbs moist. Remove the ribs from the refrigerator and allow to sit at room temperature for 30 minutes prior to cooking. Heat coals. Place top grill rack about 12" from the heat source. Place ribs in one layer on grill. Turn ribs and brush with marinade and oil if desired. You may turn the ribs as much as you like. This ensures even cooking and prevents burning. Cook until done. These are delicious served with one of our potato salads and crisp bread spread with garlic butter. It just doesn't get any better than this. Forget the fat grams for one special day and enjoy.

Per serving: 350.1 Calories; 21.2g Fat (53.9% calories from fat); 32.1g Protein; 8.7g Carbohydrate; 89mg Cholesterol; 908mg Sodium

BBQ Pork
Serves 8

    1   recipe Mustard n' Spice Barbacue Sauce
    3   cups pork, fat removed, cut
    1/4 cup chicken broth

Perfect recipe for left over pork roast. Follow directions for Mustard and Spice Barbacue Sauce from recipe in this book. Place left over roast in crock pot, add one recipe of Barbacue sauce. Cook all day in crock pot, or over night or in slow oven. Stir occasionally. If your leftover pork still has the bone in, cut off as much meat as possible and place all meat and bone in the crock pot. In several hours meat left on the bone will fall off. Cook covered for 5-6 hours using crock pot auto shift setting, or one hour on high then low setting for duration. After 5-6 hours of cooking time, the pork will have the perfect serving consistency. Add broth if more liquid is required. Remove bones and serve.
Note: 1/4 cup of fruit juice of your choice, or broth reserved form original pork roast with fat removed may be used in place of chicken broth.

Serving suggestion: Serve this hearty meat with our Burger Bun, Soft Taco Shell Roll-up, or Quinoa Tortillas recipes. This makes a very delicious tomatoless BBQ pork sandwich, or southern topping for baked potato. Serve with a few tiny slices of soy cheddar, or almond cheddar on top.

Per serving: 160.5 Calories; 11.0g Fat (62.8% calories from fat); 12.6g Protein; 2.1g Carbohydrate; 45mg Cholesterol; 234mg Sodium

Pork Sausage
Serves 10

- 1 pound ground pork
- 2 teaspoons sage, ground or rubbed
- 1/4 teaspoon nutmeg
- 1 teaspoon marjoram
- 1 teaspoon garlic powder, or salt
- 1/4 teaspoon black pepper
- 2 Tablespoons dried onions
- 1/4 teaspoon salt
- 1/2 teaspoon red pepper flakes, optional

In a large bowl, mix all ingredients together. Hands work best for this. Form sausage mix into desired shapes.
For soups: small 1/2" balls.
For breakfasts: small patties.
For grilling: 4" long link shapes.
Use immediately or freeze.
To freeze: Place the shapes in a single layer on a cookie sheet and place in the freezer for 2 hours until frozen. Place sausages in plastic resealable bags to use later.
For immediate use: sear all sides of sausages in a hot skillet to set shape. Continue to cook until done, or transfer seared sausages to oiled grill basket for last few minutes of cooking. Grilling the sausages with vegetables adds a wonderful flavor your family will love.

Serve these with any of the fruit dips, or any pureed fruit sauce for dipping.

Per serving: 139.1 Calories; 9.5g Fat (62.6% calories from fat); 11.8g Protein; 1.0g Carbohydrate; 43mg Cholesterol; 87mg Sodium

Pork n' Baked Beans

Serves 12

- 1 pound great northern beans, soaked overnight
- 2 pounds pork shoulder roast
- 4 cups water
- 4 Tablespoons Mystic Lake Fruit Concentrate Sweetener
- 1/2 cup beet sugar
- 2 cups peach juice, unsweetened
- 1/2 cup onion, chopped
- 2 teaspoons mustard
- 1/2 teaspoon salt
- 1/2 teaspoon black pepper
- 2 Tablespoons rice vinegar

Soak dry beans over night according to the package. Next day rinse and drain. Place in deep 4-5 qt. baking pan. Add all measured ingredients. Mix well. Rinse roast and place on top of beans. Cover and bake for 2 hours. Uncover, stir, and return uncovered pan to the oven. Continue to bake down the liquid to desired thickness. If too thick you can add a cup of water to get desired thickness. This is a yummy replacement for those with tomato, cane or corn allergies. Two cloves of garlic could be substituted for the onion if desired.

Variation: Use red pepper or hot sauce for pizzazz.

Per serving: 332.4 Calories; 10.7g Fat (28.7% calories from fat); 18.2g Protein; 41.7g Carbohydrate; 40mg Cholesterol; 172mg Sodium

Pineapple Pork Loin (with quinoa)
Serves 4

    4   large pork loin chops, lean-bone removed
    1   cup onions, chopped
1 1/2 cups pineapple chunks in juice, or slices
    2   cups water
    1   cup quinoa

In a large non-stick skillet, brown pork chops on both sides. Remove pork from skillet and place on the bottom of a large crock pot. In same skillet (with drippings), saute onion until beginning to become tender. Reserve 1/4 cup onion for quinoa. Place 3/4 of onion on top of pork chops in crock pot. Drain pineapple and arrange on top of onion and pork chops. Add 1/2 cup of the drained pineapple juice to the crock pot. Cover and cook on low all day or 6 hours.

Quinoa Directions:
Place the quinoa in a wire strainer and rinse thoroughly. Quinoa has a natural bitter coating that needs to be rinsed away before cooking.
  Heat 2 cups water in skillet where pork chops and onion were cooked. This is called deglazing the pan to loosen all the juices and drippings from the cooked meat. Add the reserved 1/4 cup onion to the broth that forms. Bring to a boil and add the quinoa. Cover and simmer for 10-15 minutes. Place in a bowl and cover. Refrigerate until dinner time. The flavors will combine and become delicious. Warm in the microwave at mealtime. Serve as a side dish to the Pineapple Pork dish.

Per serving: 454.4 Calories; 17.3g Fat (34.2% calories from fat); 29.4g Protein; 45.6g Carbohydrate; 74mg Cholesterol; 220mg Sodium

Marinated Pork Chops
Serves 6

- 3 Tablespoons hot pepper sauce
- 2 Tablespoons canola margarine
- 1 teaspoon paprika
- 1 teaspoon garlic powder
- 1 teaspoon tarragon vinegar
- 6 medium pork loin chops

Combine all ingredients. Pour over pork chops in an air tight container or a resealable plastic bag. Allow to marinate for 1 hour or longer. Cook on grill top over low fire or cook indoors in skillet. This is a mild marinade to tantilize the palate with a different flavor. Chops will be tender and moist.

Per serving: 268.3 Calories; 18.4g Fat (63.4% calories from fat); 23.2g Protein; 0.8g Carbohydrate; 74mg Cholesterol; 99mg Sodium

Maple Glazed Pork Tenderloin   C/E
Serves 4

- 1 pound pork tenderloin
- 1/2 teaspoon salt
- 1/2 teaspoon pepper
- 1/4 cup maple syrup

Preheat oven to 350 degrees.
Place tenderloin on a piece of aluminum foil large enough to fold over tenderloin. Brush tenderloin with maple syrup and sprinkle with salt and pepper. Fold foil loosely over tenderloin and seal. Place on a cookie sheet on the middle rack of the oven. Bake for 40 minutes, then unfold foil and bake additional 10 minutes. Remove from oven and let rest for 10 minutes before slicing. Slice into thin diagonal slices. Serve with simple rice for a great cleansing and elimination diet meal.

This dish is also low in fat.

Per serving: 188.5 Calories; 3.9g Fat (19.1% calories from fat); 23.9g Protein; 13.4g Carbohydrate; 74mg Cholesterol; 325mg Sodium

Chinese Apple-Pork   C/E
Serves 6

- 1   pound pork tenderloin, thinly sliced
- 1   Tablespoon oil, of the day
- 3   medium apples, thinly sliced
- 3   Tablespoons honey
- 5   cups chinese cabbage, thinly sliced
- 1/2 cup water
- 6   cups brown rice, cooked

Heat wok or large skillet, add oil and pork. Cook until no longer pink. Add apples, water, and honey. Cook 1 minute, stirring frequently. Add cabbage and stir-fry untill wilted. Serve over rice.

Per serving: 875.0 Calories; 10.3g Fat (10.6% calories from fat); 31.0g Protein; 164.3g Carbohydrate; 49mg Cholesterol; 80mg Sodium

Apple Glazed Pork Roast
Serves 10

- 2 1/2 pounds pork roast, room temperature
- 1 jar apple jelly, fruit sweetened only
- 4 teaspoons dijon-style mustard
- 1 Tablespoon lemon juice
- salt and pepper
- 1 Tablespoon blackberry jam, fruit sweetened only
- 1 Tablespoon chicken broth, rich, cooked down
- 2 Tablespoons lemon juice

Melt apple jelly over medium heat, add mustard and 1 tablespoon of lemon juice. Rinse room temperature roast. Rub generously with salt and pepper. Place on rack. Roast at 350 degrees, 45 minutes. Brush with apple jelly mixture, and return to oven. Brush twice more while roasting an additional 45 minutes or until meat thermometer is 165 degrees. Let stand 10 more minutes or til 170 degrees. Scrape browned areas (not burned) and drippings into remaining basting glaze. Add 2 tablespoons lemon juice and blackberry jam. Stir over low heat. Use chicken broth only if needed to thin mixture. Slice roast thin and top off with sauce. This is a delightful flavor especially when your tastebuds want something different!

Note: Prepared American mustard may be substituted for a dijion-style mustard.

Per serving: 373.0 Calories; 27.5g Fat (67.5% calories from fat); 26.6g Protein; 3.2g Carbohydrate; 102mg Cholesterol; 370mg Sodium

Crock Pot Pork Roast
Serves 14

- 3 pounds pork roast, washed
- 3/4 cup Mustard n' Spice Barbacue Sauce
- 1 cup pineapple chunks in juice
- 1 cup pineapple juice
- 3/4 cup herbal tea
- 1/2 medium onion, quartered
- salt and pepper

Rinse roast and make 2 or 3 large slices with a sharp knife deep into the meat. This will aid in even cooking and blending of flavors. Place roast in crock pot. Add fruit, onion, and liquids. Salt and pepper the top of roast as desired. The Mustard n'Spice Barbacue Sauce recipe can be found in this book. The Barbacue sauce is thick and when added to the roast last will marinate roast as it cooks.

Cover, and cook on auto cook setting if your crock pot has this feature. This will cook roast at a higher temperature for one hour then automatically reduce the heat for the remainder of the cooking time. All day or over night cooking will give the best results. Allow 1 hour per pound in crock pot for tender, moist every time results.

Conventional oven: Bake at 325 degree temperature. Oven bake time is usually 40-45 minutes per pound to reach 185 degrees for thorough cooking.

Per serving: 340.6 Calories; 23.8g Fat (63.6% calories from fat); 23.2g Protein; 7.4g Carbohydrate; 87mg Cholesterol; 442mg Sodium

Shredded Pork Fahitas
Serves 6

1 1/2	cups pork, cooked and shredded
1	cup onion, chopped
1	clove garlic, minced
2	teaspoons canola oil
1	teaspoon jalapeno, chopped
12	Quinoa Tortillas, warmed
3	cups lettuce, shredded
2	cups tomatoes, diced
2	cups almond cheese, shredded

Heat oil in nonstick skillet. Cook onion and garlic over medium-low heat for 5 minutes. Add cooked pork, toss lightly. Heat thoroughly. Stir in jalapeno pepper. Roll warm pork mix, lettuce, tomatoes, cheese, and salsa, if desired, in warm quinoa tortillas.

Per serving: 566.5 Calories; 21.9g Fat (34.3% calories from fat); 24.5g Protein; 69.6g Carbohydrate; 30mg Cholesterol; 1,076mg Sodium

Pigs in a Blanket - Stuffed Cabbage with Tomato
Serves 10

- 1 large head cabbage, blanched
- 3/4 pound pork, lean, ground
- 3/4 pound ground beef, extra lean
- 2 teaspoons guar gum
- 1/4 cup onions, chopped
- 1 teaspoon garlic powder
- 1/2 teaspoon basil
- 1/2 teaspoon parsley
- 1/2 teaspoon black pepper
- 1/2 teaspoon white pepper
- 1/2 teaspoon salt
- 2 Tablespoons potato starch flour
- 2 cups white rice, cooked
- 1 28 oz. can whole tomatoes, drained, save liquid
- 2 cups tomato juice
- 2 Tablespoons potato starch flour

Fill a large dutch oven with water and bring to boil. This will be used for a blanching water bath to aid in easy removal of the cabbage leaves without breaking them. Combine meat, spices, onion, and 2 tablespoons of potato starch flour. Add rice. Mix well. Add 4-5 whole tomatoes; cut into meat and mix well. Set aside. Cut the core from the head of cabbage. Place cabbage, bottom up in hot water and reduce to simmer. Turn cabbage head over in water for a minute then back upside down. Gently, begin removing the outer leaves one at a time. If they do not remove easily, let the cabbage remain another minute, then try again. Use tongs and remove the separated leaves from the water. Place on paper towel to cool and drain. Turn the leaf cup side up and fill with 2 tablespoons of meat mixture. Fold thick end in, then tuck sides in and roll over. Repeat until cabbage and mixture is gone. Arrange rolls in dutch oven. Mash reserved whole tomatoes in their own juice, add 2 cups of tomato juice, and remainder of potato starch flour. Mix and pour over rolls. Cover and bake at 375 degrees for 1 hour.

Per serving: 326.7 Calories; 10.5g Fat (29.1% calories from fat); 15.2g Protein; 42.4g Carbohydrate; 41mg Cholesterol; 351mg Sodium

Tomatoless Stuffed Cabbage
Serves 10

1	large head of cabbage, blanched
3/4	pound pork, ground
3/4	pound ground beef, extra lean
1/4	cup onion, chopped
2	teaspoons guar gum
1	teaspoon garlic powder
1/2	teaspoon basil
1/2	teaspoon parsley
1/2	teaspoon black pepper
1/2	teaspoon white pepper
1/2	teaspoon salt
2	Tablespoons potato starch flour
2	cups white rice, cooked
1	medium green pepper, cored and quartered
2	cups chicken broth
2	Tablespoons potato starch flour
2	teaspoons hot pepper sauce, optional

Fill a large dutch oven with water and bring to boil for blanching cabbage. Combine meat, spices, onion, and 2 Tablespoons of potato starch flour. Add rice. Mix well. Set aside. Cut the core from the head of cabbage. Place cabbage, bottom up, in hot water and reduce to simmer. Turn cabbage head over in water for 1 minute then back upside down. Gently, begin removing the outer leaves one at a time. If they don't remove easily, let the cabbage remain another minute, then try again. Use tongs and remove the separated leaves from the water. Place on paper towel to cool and drain. Turn the leaf cup side up and fill with 2 Tablespoons of meat mixture. Fold thick end in, then tuck sides in and roll over. Repeat until cabbage and mixture is gone. Arrange rolls in dutch oven. Place cut pieces of green pepper on top of completed cabbage rolls. Mix 2 Tablespoons of potato starch flour and hot pepper sauce into chicken broth, and pour over the cabbage rolls and peppers. Cover, bake at 375 degrees for 1 hour.

Per serving: 333.3 Calories; 11.0g Fat (30.0% calories from fat); 17.0g Protein; 40.6g Carbohydrate; 42mg Cholesterol; 487mg Sodium

Avocado-Cucumber Gyro   Day 2
Serves 6

12	buckwheat pancakes, prepared
1	large avocado, peeled and diced
1	medium cucumber, peeled and diced
1/4	cup black olives, sliced
1/4	teaspoon basil, dried or...
3	leaves basil, fresh
	salt and pepper, to taste
1	Tablespoon olive oil
2	ounces almond cheese, grated
1	cup water
1	teaspoon lemon juice

Place 1 cup water and 1 teaspoon lemon juice in a bowl. Soak diced avocado for 1 minute, drain well. This will help prevent the avocado from turning brown after cutting. Place avocado with all other ingredients in a bowl. Toss gently to coat with oil and spices. Place 2 Tablespoons filling into each buckwheat pancake and roll as you would a pita or burrito.

These make a refreshing vegetarian change for a lunch or appetizer.

Serving size is 2 gyroes.

Variations: add cooked, diced beef or lamb for more protein.
Nutritional analysis does not include meat.

Per serving: 227.1 Calories; 12.5g Fat (47.7% calories from fat); 8.0g Protein; 22.9g Carbohydrate; 40mg Cholesterol; 469mg Sodium

Pasta Florentine   C/E
Serves 4

- 8 ounces rice pasta, cooked
- 2 Tablespoons olive oil, or oil of the day
- 2 cloves garlic, chopped fine
- 1 bunch spinach leaves, fresh
  salt and pepper, to taste
- 1 cup chicken, cooked and cubed

Heat oil in large non-stick skillet. Add garlic and suate 1 minute until tender but not brown. Add spinach and toss until wilted. Add salt and pepper if desired and chicken or turkey cubes. Drain pasta and add to skillet. Toss well and serve hot. May top with nut cheese or rice slice.

Per serving: 281.7 Calories; 10.5g Fat (33.7% calories from fat); 14.9g Protein; 31.7g Carbohydrate; 32mg Cholesterol; 39mg Sodium

Vegetarian Lasagna
Serves 6

- 10 ounces rice pasta, lasagna style
- 3 large zucchini, grated
- 3 large carrot, grated
- 1 medium onion, chopped
- 1 stalk celery, chopped
- 4 ounces mushrooms, sliced
- 2 medium tomatoes, sliced
- 2 Tablespoons olive oil, or oil of the day
- 1/4 teaspoon salt
- 1/4 teaspoon pepper, of choice
- 1/2 teaspoon marjoram, dried
- 1/2 teaspoon oregano, dried
- 4 ounces almond cheese, mozzarella flavor

Preheat oven to 350 degrees.
Boil water for pasta with 1 Tablespoon olive oil to prevent sticking. Add pasta and boil 10-15 minutes while you prepare the filling.
Filling: In large skillet, heat 1 Tablespoon oil. Add onion, celery, and mushrooms and saute until tender. Remove from skillet and set aside. Place zucchini and carrots in skillet. Add spices and stir ocassionally to distribute spices evenly. Heat until tender. Turn off heat.
Lightly oil a medium lasagna pan with oil (lid also). Place in layers: 1/3 pasta, 1/2 zucchini and carrots, 1/2 sliced tomatoes, 1/2 onion, celery, and mushroom mix, and 1/2 cheese. Repeat layers and top with remaining 1/3 pasta.
Bake 45 minutes at 350 degrees. Remove from oven and let rest for at least 10 minutes. Cut into 6 servings.

Rice spaghetti noodles or your favorite shaped pasta may be substituted for the lasagna pasta if desired. Omit the top layer of pasta, and use 1/2 pasta in each sequence of layers instead of 1/3.
This recipe is very high in vitamin A.

Per serving: 248.8 Calories; 7.8g Fat (27.4% calories from fat); 9.5g Protein; 36.7g Carbohydrate; 0mg Cholesterol; 393mg Sodium

Veggie Burger
Serves 4

- 1 cup mushrooms, chopped
- 1/2 cup onion, finely chopped
- 1/4 cup bell pepper, finely chopped
- 1/4 cup celery, finely chopped
- 1/4 cup sesame seeds
- 1/2 cup black beans, cooked and drained
- 1/2 cup black beans, pureed
- 2 cloves garlic, finely chopped
- 1 Tablespoon parsley, dried
- 1 teaspoon thyme, dried
- 1 teaspoon oregano, dried
- 1/4 teaspoon salt and pepper
- 1/4 teaspoon red pepper, optional
- 3/4 cup oats, uncooked
- 2 2/3 teaspoons egg replacer, =2 eggs
- 1 Tablespoon oil

Combine all ingredients and let stand for 5 minutes. Heat 1 Tablespoon oil in a skillet. Form small pattie with veggie mix and place in the oiled skillet. Cook over medium heat until edges brown lightly. Turn and cook on other side. Serve warm in pitas, or on the bread of the day. This can also be crumbled and used as a substitute for taco filling or burrito filling.

Serves four: about 2 patties per person.

Note: the egg replacer works better to bind the ingredients than an egg. The egg relacer will supply more calcium to your diet than an egg.

Substitutions for oats: 3/4 cup cooked quinoa (increases protein content), 3/4 cup uncooked kasha (buckwheat), 3/4 cup cooked and chopped brown rice.

Per serving: 671.1 Calories; 11.5g Fat (14.6% calories from fat); 18.9g Protein; 131.8g Carbohydrate; 0mg Cholesterol; 312mg Sodium

Wheat-Corn Free Dressing
Serves 8

16	slices rice bread
2	cans chicken broth, all natural
1	whole onion, chopped
3	stalks celery, chopped
1	teaspoon celery flakes, dried
1	teaspoon garlic salt
1	teaspoon salt
1	teaspoon black pepper
3	Tablespoons sage, dried
1/3	cup Quinoa, seed
3	teaspoons egg replacer, =2 eggs
1/2	cup margarine, melted

The night before preparation: cut slices of bread into small cubes, about 1/2" square. Place in one layer on cookie sheets and dry in 250 degree oven for about 30 minutes. Check to make sure they do not brown. Turn off oven (leave oven light on if you have one to prevent moisture build up during the night). Leave bread in oven over night to completely dry. Crumbs can be stored for later use in an airtight container or thick plastic freezer bag.

Next day: combine all ingredients in extra large bowl or dutch oven. Mix well. Mix will be very wet. Place in lightly oiled baking dish, cover and bake 1 hour at 350 degrees until lightly browned on edges.

I have served this to unsuspecting Thanksgiving guest, and they raved about it. It is even better the next day.

Main dish: Press strips of chicken breast meat into dressing before baking.

Per serving: 561.9 Calories; 17.7g Fat (27.7% calories from fat); 8.8g Protein; 94.9g Carbohydrate; 1mg Cholesterol; 1,045mg Sodium

Garlic Shrimp
Serves 6

1	Tablespoon olive oil, or oil of the day
3	cloves garlic, finely chopped
1	pound shrimp, peeled and deveined
1/2	cup fresh parsley, chopped
1/2	teaspoon salt
1/4	teaspoon pepper
1 1/2	cups almond milk, or rice milk
1 1/2	teaspoons potato starch flour
8	ounces rice pasta, cooked-drained

Place shrimp in a bowl. Add garlic, parsley, and drizzle with oil. Mix well and let set 5 minutes.
Boil water for pasta while shrimp marinates. Cook pasta according to directions. Heat a large nonstick skillet, add shrimp and all contents of bowl. Cook shrimp, stirring frequently for 5 minutes. Wisk nut milk and flour in a medium bowl and pour over shrimp. Stir constantly for 1 minute. Turn heat off and cover pan with lid for another minute. Serve over pasta or rice. Top with a non-dairy cheese ("Rice Slice" or Almond Cheese).

Dried parsley can be substituted for fresh-use 1 Tablespoon.

Per serving: 226.4 Calories; 4.6g Fat (18.5% calories from fat); 18.8g Protein; 26.7g Carbohydrate; 115mg Cholesterol; 318mg Sodium

Lemon Shrimp
Serves 6

- 4 whole green onion, sliced
- 2 Tablespoons olive oil, or oil of the day
- 1 pound shrimp, peeled and deveined
- 1 whole lemon zest
- 1/2 Teaspoon garlic salt
- 2 Tablespoons sesame seeds
- 2 Tablespoons lemon juice, fresh

Place peeled and deveined shrimp on large plate. Sprinkle with onion, lemon zest, garlic salt, and sesame seeds. Drizzle with olive oil. Toss well and cover with plastic wrap. Place in refrigerator for 1 hour. Heat wok or nonstick skillet. When hot, drop all shrimp into pan and cook 5-8 minutes. Do not over cook. It will cause shrimp to become rubbery and tough.
Serve as a main dish over rice or rice pasta or as an appetizer.

Per serving: 170.6 Calories; 7.7g Fat (39.3% calories from fat); 18.0g Protein; 8.7g Carbohydrate; 115mg Cholesterol; 131mg Sodium

Smoked Shrimp with Pasta
Serves 8

1   pound Smoked Shrimp, small
1   Tablespoon Cajun seasoning
2   Tablespoons oil, of choice
8   ounces rice pasta, of choice

Prepare one pound shrimp by using the Smoked Shrimp recipe.
Peel smoked shrimp and place shrimp, 1 Tablespoon of the oil, and cajun spices in a large plastic bag and marinate in the refrgerator for 1 hour.
Cook pasta while shrimp marinates.

Place cooked rice pasta on serving platter. Arrange shrimp on top of pasta. Drizzle with remaining oil.

Per serving: 191.8 Calories; 7.9g Fat (36.8% calories from fat); 13.0g Protein; 17.4g Carbohydrate; 79mg Cholesterol; 162mg Sodium

Shrimp In Saffron Sauce
Serves 6

- 1 pound shrimp, peeled and deveined
- 2 Tablespoons olive oil, or oil of the day
- 2 teaspoons sesame seeds
- 1/2 teaspoon garlic salt
- 1 Tablespoon onion flakes
- 1/4 teaspoon saffron threads
- dash pepper
- 1/2 cup water
- 2 Tablespoons sun-dried tomato paste

Cook 1-1/2 cup brown rice in 3-1/2 cup water until done (about 55 minutes). Toss shrimp to coat with spices and sesame seeds. Saute 2-3 minutes in oil. Add 1/2 cup water and 2 TBS. sundried tomato paste and stir well. cook over low heat for 5 minutes. Remove from heat and serve immediately. You may either toss shrimp and sauce with rice or serve over rice.

Saffron flower pieces may be used (they are less expensive). Increase the amount used to 1 Tablespoon.

May be served without rice as an appetizer.

Per serving: 148.1 Calories; 7.7g Fat (49.9% calories from fat); 15.7g Protein; 1.6g Carbohydrate; 115mg Cholesterol; 268mg Sodium

Coconut Shrimp n' Orange Sauce

Battered

Serves 6

1	cup rice flour
1	teaspoon egg replacer
1/2	teaspoon salt
2	teaspoons baking soda
1	teaspoon guar gum
1	cup rice milk
2	Tablespoons canola oil
36	medium shrimp, shell, tail removed
1	cup coconut, shredded, unsweet
4	ounces canola oil, to cook shrimp in
1	cup orange marmalade, fruit sweetened
1/4	cup horseradish

Mix all dry ingredients together. Combine milk and oil. Slowly add the milk and oil to the dry ingredients. Dredge shrimp in batter, then roll in coconut. Drop into hot canola oil. Cook a couple of minutes on each side. If coconut turns black decrease cooking temperature. If using electric wok, use temperature setting just below that recommended for tempura. When shrimp is done, drain on plate lined with paper towels. Mix dip ingredients together and serve. May be used as a dip or spooned over shrimp. A beautiful and delicious dish to serve.

Note: Read the labels on the horseradish to insure it is a product safe for your diet. Cheaper brands of horseradish tend to be flavorless and woody tasting. White horseradish is usually bottled in vinegar which may contain corn. Red horseradish may be bottled only with beet juice. Read the label, omit horseradish if you can not find it without vinegar to support your gluten free diet.

Per serving: 638.5 Calories; 27.8g Fat (38.3% calories from fat); 18.1g Protein; 82.9g Carbohydrate; 119mg Cholesterol; 803mg Sodium

Fresh Scallops Almondine   C/E
Serves 6

- 3/4   pound sea scallops, fresh
- 3   Tablespoons olive oil, or oil of the day
- 1   teaspoon salt
- 1/2   teaspoon white pepper, or black
- 1/2   cup sliced almonds
- 1   whole lemon zest, grated
- 1   bunch fresh spinach, stems removed
- 1/4   cup chicken broth, or broth of choice

Place scallops on a plate. Sprinkle with 1 Tablespoon oil, lemon zest, salt, and pepper. Let stand 5 minutes.

Heat 2 Tablespoons oil in large skillet. Add almonds and let them heat for about 30 seconds. Add scallops and cook until they turn white. Add spinach leaves and toss just until wilted. Remove from heat and serve with rice, pasta, kasha or quinoa as a side dish.

Per serving: 185.7 Calories; 13.7g Fat (64.5% calories from fat); 12.7g Protein; 4.2g Carbohydrate; 19mg Cholesterol; 518mg Sodium

Jambalaya
Serves 10

- 1/2 pound shrimp
- 4 links Gerhard's Andouille Sausage, or any hot sausage
- 1 whole chicken breast, skinless-boneless
- 2 Tablespoons oil
- 1 cup onion, chopped
- 1 cup celery, chopped
- 3/4 cup bell pepper, chopped
- 1 1/2 cups tomatoes, chopped
- 2 cloves garlic, minced
- 1 1/2 Tablespoons cajun seasoning, Chef Paul's
- 2 Tablespoons parsley, dried
- 2 cups brown rice
- 5 1/2 cups water, for shrimp broth

To make shrimp broth: Peel shrimp and set aside. Place shrimp shells and 5 1/2 cups water in a soup pot and bring to the boil for 5 minutes. Pour broth through a strainer and discard shells. Set broth aside.

Slice Andouille Sausage in 1/4" slices. Dice chicken breast in 1/2" cubes.

In a large dutch oven or soup pot, heat oil and saute onion, celery, garlic, and bell pepper until tender. Add Andouille, chicken, and Chef Paul's seasoning. Stir well, and cook until chicken is no longer pink. Add tomatoes and rice. Stir to coat rice with seasonings. Pour shrimp broth into pot with vegetables, meat, and rice. Cover and cook over low heat (slowly) for 55 minutes. Stir occasionally to prevent sticking. During the last 7 minutes of cooking time, add shrimp and stir well. Do not over cook shrimp. Remove from the heat and let rest for 5 minutes before serving.

This is a hearty meal that works alone or with a salad. The flavors intensify overnight. Jambalaya also freezes well for later meals.

***Andouille contains nitrites. If you would like to prepare your own sausage mix without nitrites, use one of our sausage recipes and make it hot by adding more red pepper or cayenne pepper to the mix.

Per serving: 316.3 Calories; 11.1g Fat (32.5% calories from fat); 18.0g Protein; 33.8g Carbohydrate; 53mg Cholesterol; 368mg Sodium

Smoked Catfish Fillets C/E
Serves 4

1   6 ounce catfish fillets, boneless
1   teaspoon lemon zest
1/2 teaspoon pepper, coarse ground

Preheat grill (coals or lava rock). When coals have a light dusting of white ash, they are ready to cook. Sprinkle fillets with pepper and lemon zest. Place on a wire grid small enough that fish will not fall through when cooked. Soak hickory chips in water for 30 minutes. Drain off water and place wood chips on top of coals. Place a heavy duty disposable aluminum pan on top of the coals and wood chips. Pour in 1 1/2" water. Place grill grid back in place on the grill. Arrange catfish on rack just above the water pan. The water pan will keep the cooking temperature low enough to smoke without over cooking the fish. Cover with lid to grill. Be sure vents are open. Cook for 40-45 minutes. Cooking times will vary depending on the heat source and coal temperatures. Fish is ready when it begins to flake.

These fillets are especially good with Arnaud's Sauce-Original Creole Remoulade. This is a creole sauce that uses no wheat, corn, soy, eggs, milk, or sugar.

Per serving: 38.4 Calories; 1.1g Fat (27.2% calories from fat); 6.6g Protein; 0.3g Carbohydrate; 23mg Cholesterol; 17mg Sodium

Lemon and Chives Fish Fillet   Day 3 C/E
Serves 4

4   6 ounce fish fillets, boneless-skinless
1   lemon, juice & zest
1   Tablespoon chives, finely chopped
1   teaspoon sesame oil
    dash salt

Preheat oven to 400 degrees.
Spread sesame oil on foil lined baking pan. Place fish on foil. Sprinkle with lemon zest, salt, and chives. Cover baking pan with foil and bake for 15-20 minutes depending on the thickness of fillets. Remove foil cover and squeeze lemon juice over fillets. Serve immediately.

You may also make foil pouches and cook on the grill. This is great for fishing trips.

Per serving: 205.1 Calories; 2.8g Fat (12.3% calories from fat); 41.5g Protein;
        2.9g Carbohydrate; 99mg Cholesterol; 126mg Sodium

Jamaican Grilled Fish Fillet
Serves 4

- 4 large fish fillets, of choice-boneless
- 1/2 teaspoon onion powder
- 1/4 teaspoon ground allspice
- 1/4 teaspoon black pepper, ground
- dash cayenne pepper
- 1 teaspoon thyme, dried
- 1/2 teaspoon cinnamon, ground
- 1/8 teaspoon nutmeg, ground
- 1 medium jalapeno pepper, minced-optional
- 1 Tablespoon oil, of the day

Preheat grill.
Lightly oil a wire fish basket or a seafood cooking grill (a grid with smaller holes to prevent cooked fish from falling through the holes.
Rub fish fillets with oil. Set aside. In a small bowl, combine all spices, but not the jalapeno pepper. Sprinkle herb and spice mix over fish fillets. Place fillets, spice side down on fish grill. Sprinkle remaining spice and herb mix over other side of fillets. Sprinkle minced jalapeno pepper over top of fish fillets if desired. Place on the grill directly above the heat source (about 10-12" above coals). Cover lightly with foil. Cook for 12-20 minutes, depending on thickness of the fillets.

Per serving: 226.5 Calories; 5.1g Fat (20.9% calories from fat); 41.4g Protein; 1.7g Carbohydrate; 99mg Cholesterol; 126mg Sodium

Ginger Fish Fillets
Serves 4

- 4 fish fillets, boned
- 1/4 cup green onion, chopped fine
- 1 clove garlic, chopped fine
- 1/2 teaspoon salt
- 1 Tablespoon gingerroot, chopped fine
- 3 Tablespoons oil
- 1 Tablespoon rice vinegar or apple cider vinegar

Place all ingredients except fish fillets in a large resealable plastic bag. Mix well. Add fish fillets to bag, seal, and place in refrigerator for 1 hour.
Preheat oven to 350 degrees. Coat baking dish with oil of the day. Place fish fillets in baking dish and pour marinade over fillets. Cover baking dish with lid or foil and bake for 20 minutes. Check for doneness (fillets should be firm to touch).

Per serving: 287.8 Calories; 11.9g Fat (38.2% calories from fat); 41.4g Protein; 1.8g Carbohydrate; 99mg Cholesterol; 393mg Sodium

Pecan Trout
Serves 4

- 4   4 ounce trout fillet, skin removed
- 3/4   cup pecans, ground coarsley
- 1/2   cup rice flour
- 1   teaspoon salt
- 1/2   teaspoon pepper
- 2   Tablespoons canola oil
- 1   Tablespoon beet sugar, optional

Preheat oven to 375 degrees.
Process pecans in food processor or blender to a coarse meal.
Combine pecan meal, flour, sugar (optional), salt and pepper and mix well. Place in a large plate. Set aside.
Brush baking pan with 1 Tablespoon oil. Brush fillet tops with remaining 1 Tablespoon oil. Dip oiled fillets in pecan flour mixture and place on oiled cookie sheet.
Bake at 375 degrees for 15-20 minutes. Do not over cook fillets. This recipe is also great on salmon.

For campfire cooking: prepare as you would for oven prep, but place in an oiled foil pouch and cook 15-20 minutes over indirect heat (grill).

Per serving: 333.4 Calories; 19.6g Fat (52.7% calories from fat); 18.5g Protein; 21.1g Carbohydrate; 46mg Cholesterol; 574mg Sodium

Pan Fried Trout   C/E
Serves 4

- 4   trout fillets
- 3   Tablespoons olive oil, or oil of choice
- 1   cup rice flour, or flour of choice
-     salt and pepper, to taste
-     dash cayenne pepper, optional

Heat oil in a large skillet.
While oil heats, combine flour, salt, pepper, and cayenne. Stir well with a fork. Dredge trout fillets in flour mix, then place in hot oil, skin side down. When flour begins to turn golden, turn fillet carefully to cook other side. Total cooking time should be about 10 minutes for a fillet, and 15 minutes for whole small trout.

If using whole trout, remove head, scales, and insides of fish. Rinse well with clean water, and pat dry before cooking.

Per serving: 351.0 Calories; 15.9g Fat (41.5% calories from fat); 18.8g Protein; 31.6g Carbohydrate; 46mg Cholesterol; 41mg Sodium

Tuna Skillet
Serves 6

- 2 Tablespoons canola oil, or oil of the day
- 1 large onion, chopped
- 2 large carrots, chopped
- 5 large mushroom, chopped
- 2/3 cup water
- salt and pepper, to taste
- 2 6 ounce cans tuna in water
- 1 teaspoon sesame seeds
- 1/2 teaspoon garlic salt
- 8 ounces rice pasta, spirals
- 2 cups rice milk

Saute onion, carrots, and mushrooms in oil until onions are tender. Add 2/3 cup water and simmer until carrots are tender. Add salt, pepper, sesame seeds, and garlic. Drain tuna and discard liquid from tuna. Add tuna to skillet along with the rice milk. Stir. Add spiral rice pasta or shape of choice. Cook about 15 minutes on low until pasta is tender.
Serve with a green salad.

Per serving: 258.9 Calories; 6.5g Fat (22.5% calories from fat); 17.8g Protein; 32.5g Carbohydrate; 16mg Cholesterol; 316mg Sodium

Tex-Mex Tuna Steak
Serves 6

24 ounces tuna steak, (4 oz. per person)
1 recipe black bean salsa
   salt and pepper, to taste

If you purchase thick tuna steaks, slice each steak into 2 steaks. 4 oz. servings of meat or fish are about the size of a deck of cards, so a 1" thick tuna steak, sliced in half, is perfect.
Make salsa recipe according to directions (appetizer or sauce section). Refrigerate 1 hour.
Grill tuna steaks over coals or on indoor grill. Remove from grill to serving plates and top with salsa.
Serve with mixed green salad or a vegetable.

Per serving: 176.6 Calories; 5.6g Fat (29.8% calories from fat); 27.3g Protein; 2.5g Carbohydrate; 43mg Cholesterol; 48mg Sodium

Salmon With Dill Day 3 C/E
Serves 4

- 4   6 ounce salmon fillets, boneless
- 1   whole lemon, zested and juiced
- 2   Tablespoons fresh dill, chopped coarsely
- salt and pepper, to taste

Preheat oven to 350 degrees or preheat grill.
Line a shallow pan with foil. Lightly oil foil with oil of choice. Place salmon fillets on foil. Sqeeze lemon juice over each fillet. Sprinkle fillets with lemon zest, salt, pepper, and chopped dill. For oven: cover tightly with foil and bake at 350 degrees for 20 minutes. For grill, cover pan lightly with foil (so that fish will absorb that smokey flavor) and cook on the grill for 20 minutes.

Serve with grilled onion halves, carrots and celery for the perfect Rotation Day 3.

Per serving: 206.6 Calories; 6.0g Fat (26.1% calories from fat); 34.5g Protein; 3.7g Carbohydrate; 88mg Cholesterol; 118mg Sodium

Salmon Croquettes   C/E   Baked or Fried
Serves 6

15	ounces canned salmon, skinless-boneless
1 1/3	egg replacer, = 1 egg
1/4	teaspoon salt
	pepper, to taste
1/2	cup rice flour
1/4	teaspoon baking soda
1/4	teaspoon cream of tartar
1/3	cup oil

Check label on salmon to be sure it contains only salmon, water, and salt.
Do not discard liquid of canned salmon.
In a large bowl, mix all ingredients until well incorporated. Heat oil in nonstick skillet. Drop batter by Tablespoonfuls into hot oil. Do not overcrowd skillet. When browned on one side, turn to cook other side. Drain on paper towel.

These can also be placed on greased or oil treated cookies sheet or muffin pan and baked at 375 degrees for 15-20 minutes. When baked instead of fried, the calories =182.1; fat grams=4.4.

Per serving: 331.9 Calories; 16.6g Fat (44.6% calories from fat); 14.8g Protein; 31.5g Carbohydrate; 39mg Cholesterol; 570mg Sodium

Sauces

Homemade Mayonnaise
Serves 32

- 1 whole egg
- 1 cup oil
- 2 teaspoons lemon juice
- 1 teaspoon apple cider vinegar
- 1/2 teaspoon dry mustard
- dash salt

Serving size is 1 Tablespoon.
Place egg in blender and blend on medium. While blender is still on, gradually add oil through center of blender lid. Before mixture gets too thick, add vinegar, mustard, salt, and lemon juice. Store in refrigerator for about 1 week.

Per serving: 62.4 Calories; 7.0g Fat (98.5% calories from fat); 0.2g Protein; 0.1g Carbohydrate; 6mg Cholesterol; 2mg Sodium

Dilled Mayonnaise
Serves 12

- 1/2 cup canola mayonnaise, or mayo of choice
- 1/4 cup dijon mustard
- 1/2 teaspoon fresh dill, minced

Mix mayonnaise, mustard, and dill and place in a covered plastic or glass container. Store in the refrigerator until ready to serve.
Serve with Salmon sandwiches or any fish salad. Also good as a dip for fresh cut vegetables.

Per serving: 77.2 Calories; 8.2g Fat (96.9% calories from fat); 0.3g Protein; 0.3g Carbohydrate; 3mg Cholesterol; 129mg Sodium

Herbed Mayonnaise
Serves 12

- 1/2 cup canola mayonnaise, or mayo of choice
- 1/4 teaspoon garlic salt
- 1/4 teaspoon oregano, dried
- 1/4 teaspoon thyme, dried

Mix all ingredients and place in a covered plastic or glass container. Store in refrigerator until ready to serve.

Per serving: 73.5 Calories; 8.0g Fat (99.8% calories from fat); 0.0g Protein; 0.0g Carbohydrate; 3mg Cholesterol; 67mg Sodium

Brown Steaksauce
Serves 8

- 3/8 cup canola mayonnaise
- 1/2 teaspoon prepared mustard
- 2 teaspoons tarragon vinegar
- 1/4 teaspoon red pepper, ground
- 1/4 teaspoon white pepper
- 1 1/3 Tablespoons soy sauce, wheat free-optional
- 1/4 cup currants, dried
- 1/4 cup boiling water

Cover dried currants with boiling water. Allow to set over night. Puree currants and liquid. Add remaining ingredients to the blender. Process on puree a few more minutes. Refrigerate to allow flavors to blend. Stir and serve.

Per serving: 97.2 Calories; 9.0g Fat (83.5% calories from fat); 0.3g Protein; 3.7g Carbohydrate; 4mg Cholesterol; 218mg Sodium

Cactus Salsa (Tomatoless)
Serves 10

- 15 ounces tender cactus
- 7 ounces jalapeno peppers, canned, drained, save liquid

Tender cactus is a product that is processed cactus in a jar.
Drain cactus and discard liquid. Drain jalapeno peppers and reserve liquid. Chop in food processor or chopper. Combine cactus and peppers. Mix in at least 1/2 of reserved jalapeno liquid. Place in a container and refrigerate. Store in refrigerator up to 2 weeks. Serving suggestion: Use as hot dip, with Taco Salad, Soft Shell Tacos, or in Spicy Meatball recipes.

Per serving: 11.9 Calories; 0.1g Fat (9.6% calories from fat); 0.2g Protein, 2.4g Carbohydrate; 0mg Cholesterol; 1,084mg Sodium

Sweet Mustard Sauce
Serves 6

- 3 Tablespoons canola mayonnaise
- 2 Tablespoons soy sauce, wheat free
- 1 teaspoon prepared mustard
- 2 Tablespoons Mystic Lake Fruit Concentrate Sweetener
- 1 dash garlic powder, optional

Mix all ingredients intil creamy and smooth. Use as desired.
Contains soy. Eliminate soy sauce if you are sensitive to soy.

Per serving: 72.6 Calories; 6.0g Fat (76.0% calories from fat); 0.3g Protein; 4.0g Carbohydrate; 3mg Cholesterol; 337mg Sodium

Bar-B-Que Sauce
Serves 8

- 1 cup onions, chopped fine
- 1/2 cup celery, chopped fine
- 1/4 cup green bell pepper, chopped fine
- 1/4 cup apple cider vinegar
- 1/4 cup oil, of choice
- dash cayenne pepper
- 1/2 cup honey
- 2 cups tomatoes, diced

Heat oil in medium saucepan. Add onion, celery, and green pepper. Saute until tender. When onions are transparent, place vegetables in a blender and blend on high until pureed. Add tomatoes and blend again. Pour puree back into saucepan and turn heat to medium. Add apple cider vinegar, oil, pepper, and honey. Bring to a boil, then turn down to a simmer. Simmer for about 5 minutes. Use immediately or store in an airtight container until ready to use. Will keep for about 1 week.

Per serving: 139.9 Calories; 7.0g Fat (42.1% calories from fat); 0.7g Protein; 21.0g Carbohydrate; 0mg Cholesterol; 84mg Sodium

Mustard n' Spice Bar-B-Que Sauce
Serves 2

- 3/8 cup mustard, prepared
- 2 Tablespoons currants, dried
- 2 Tablespoons boiling water
- 1/3 cup onion, chopped fine
- 3 large garlic cloves
- 1 teaspoon paprika
- 1/2 teaspoon chili powder
- 1/2 teaspoon salt
- 1/4 teaspoon cayenne
- 1/4 teaspoon black pepper
- 2 teaspoons Mystic Lake Fruit Concentrate Sweetener

Cover currants with boiling water and allow to sit over night. Puree garlic cloves, currants with their liquid, and mustard. Add remaining ingredients and blend well. Refrigerate to blend flavors. Mix and serve in desired manner.
Serving suggestion:
Use as you would any BBQ sauce, or use as a dressing on burgers or sandwiches, over roasts.

Per serving: 90.9 Calories; 2.4g Fat (20.9% calories from fat); 3.3g Protein; 16.7g Carbohydrate; 0mg Cholesterol; 1,204mg Sodium

Basil Pesto C/E
Serves 12

- 2 cups basil leaves, washed and dried
- 1/3 cup olive oil, or oil of the day
- 1 Tablespoon pine nuts
- 2 cloves garlic
- 1/4 teaspoon salt
- 1/4 teaspoon pepper
- 1 cup parsley, fresh

Combine all ingredients in a food processor or blender and process until completely pureed and incorporated well. Store in an airtight container in refrigerator, or can be frozen in cubes for up to 3 months.

Use in pasta dishes or spread lightly on toasted bread as appetizer.

Pesto can also be used on pizza instead of tomato sauce. This makes one of the best pizzas we have ever eaten.

Per serving: 77.8 Calories; 6.7g Fat (71.8% calories from fat); 2.0g Protein; 3.9g Carbohydrate; 0mg Cholesterol; 68mg Sodium

Sun-dried Tomato Paste   Day 1
Serves 10

1   cup sun-dried tomatoes, oil-packed, drain off oil

Drain off oil. Pack down tomatoes in the cup, and continue to add more tomatoes until cup is filled. Place tomatoes in a blender or food processor and process until tomatoes are a fine puree. May add 1-2 Tablespoon of oil to obtain the right consistency. Use in recipes as is, or place in airtight container in refrigerator. You may freeze this paste in ice cube trays (about 1 Tablespoon) for use later.

Sun-dried tomato paste adds wonderful flavor to almost any meat or pasta dish.

Per serving: 23.4 Calories; 1.6g Fat (52.7% calories from fat); 0.6g Protein; 2.6g Carbohydrate; 0mg Cholesterol; 29mg Sodium

Meatless Spaghetti Sauce
Serves 10

- 8 cups tomatoes, fresh peeled
- 3 Tablespoons olive oil, or oil of the day
- 1 Tablespoon garlic, minced
- 2 cups onion, chopped
- 1 cup bell pepper, chopped
- 1 teaspoon salt
- 1 teaspoon black pepper
- 2 teaspoons oregano, dried
- 2 Tablespoons parsley, dried flakes

Heat olive oil in large sauce pan. Saute onions and bell pepper. When onions are tender, add garlic and heat through. Do not allow garlic to brown. Add tomatoes, salt, pepper, oregano, and parsley. Simmer, covered at least one hour. Serve over rice pasta, rice, spaghetti squash, or over meat or poultry.

Per serving: 79.4 Calories; 4.6g Fat (47.6% calories from fat); 1.8g Protein; 9.6g Carbohydrate; 0mg Cholesterol; 347mg Sodium

Tomatoless Pasta Sauce
Serves 4

3	medium red bell pepper, cleaned & quartered
1 1/2	cups chicken broth
2	teaspoons Italian seasoning
3/4	teaspoon garlic powder
1/4	teaspoon salt
1/4	teaspoon ground pepper
1/2	pound extra lean ground beef, browned and drained
2	ounces rice cheese, optional
1	ounce almond cheese, optional

Place broth, peppers and seasonings in a medium saucepan. Bring to boil, cover, and simmer approximately 10 minutes or until done. Place in blender or food processor and process on high speed for a few seconds. Strain sauce to remove pepper skins if desired, but not necessary. Combine ground beef and sauce. Serve over rice pasta and top with rice parmesan or almond cheese.

Variations: Serve over rice pasta, rice, spaghetti squash or use in place of tomato paste for tomatoless pizza. The flavor is great.

Ground beef, turkey or chicken can be used in this recipe.

Per serving: 198.1 Calories; 54.2g Fat (50.0% calories from fat); 102.0g Protein; 20.0g Carbohydrate; 40mg Cholesterol; 4,941mg Sodium

Old Fashioned "Milk" Gravy C/E
Serves 8

- 1   Tablespoon drippings from meat preparation, on bottom of pan
- 2   cups almond milk, or milk of day
- 1/2 cup chicken broth, or vegetable broth
  salt and pepper, to taste
- 2   teaspoons potato starch flour

Drain all but one Tablespoon of fat from pan that meat was prepared in.(This can be from frying, sauteing, baking, or broiling)
Heat pan and add 1-1/2 cup almond milk (plain flavored) to drippings in pan. Scrape bottom of pan with heat resistant spatula until most dripping crystals have been incorporated into the milk. In a measuring cup, combines 1/2 cup broth and potato starch flour with fork until mixed well. Stir flour mixture into pan with milk and stir constantly until it begins to thicken. Add salt and pepper to taste. Serve over meats, pasta, rice, spaghetti squash, or mashed potatoes.

Per serving: 46.8 Calories; 2.4g Fat (46.5% calories from fat); 1.2g Protein; 5.1g Carbohydrate; 2mg Cholesterol; 132mg Sodium

Gravy From Drippings
Serves 8

1 Tablespoon drippings from meat or poultry preparation, on bottom of pan
2 cups chicken broth, or vegetable broth
2 teaspoons potato starch flour
  salt and pepper, to taste

Drain all but one Tablespoon of fat from pan that meat was prepared in.(This can be from frying, sauteing, baking or broiling).
Heat pan and add 1-1/2 cup broth to drippings in pan. Scrape bottom of pan with heat resistant spatula until most dripping crystals have been incorporated into broth. In a measuring cup, combine the remaining 1/2 cup broth and 2-1/2 teaspoons potato starch flour and stir with fork until mixed well. Stir flour mixture into pan and stir constantly until it begins to thicken. Add salt and pepper to taste. Serve over meats, pastas, rice, spaghetti squash, or mashed potatoes.

If no fat is present in pan from meat preparation, use 1Tablespoon oil of the day to substitute. The nutritional values will be approximately the same.

Per serving: 38.9 Calories; 2.3g Fat (53.8% calories from fat); 2.8g Protein; 1.7g Carbohydrate; 2mg Cholesterol; 400mg Sodium

Basic White Sauce
Serves 8

  2 Tablespoons canola margarine
  2 teaspoons potato starch flour
 1/4 teaspoon salt
 1/4 teaspoon pepper
1 2/3 cups rice milk, or milk of day

In medium sauce pan, melt canola margarine. Add potato starch flour and stir into a "roux". Add milk a little at a time by whisking in with wire wisk. Continue to stir until sauce begins to thicken. Add salt and pepper and remove from heat when desired thickness is obtained.

Serve over rice, meats, poultry, pasta, and vegetables.
Variations: Add 1 cup grated almond cheese for a creamy cheese sauce for pasta.

Per serving: 54.9 Calories; 3.2g Fat (51.7% calories from fat); 0.2g Protein; 6.5g Carbohydrate; 0mg Cholesterol; 115mg Sodium

Sinful Pecan Sauce
Serves 4

- 1/4 cup canola margarine
- 1/2 cup beet sugar
- 1 teaspoon vanilla, alcohol-free
- 2 Tablespoons rice milk
- 3/4 cup pecans, chopped
- 2 ripe banana, mashed with fork

Melt margarine in a small sauce pan over low heat. Add nuts and allow to heat through. Add sugar, vanilla, and rice milk. Stir. Bring to low boil. Remove from heat. Fold in bananas. Serve over desserts, ice cream, pancakes or waffles. Then don't weigh yourself for about a week.

Per serving: 304.3 Calories; 18.5g Fat (52.4% calories from fat); 1.2g Protein; 36.5g Carbohydrate; 0mg Cholesterol; 123mg Sodium

Cranberry Sauce
Serves 6

1 pound cranberries, washed
1 large orange, zested and sectioned
1 cup beet sugar

Place all ingredients in saucepan and bring to boil for 7 minutes. Cool, cover in airtight container and store in refrigerator overninght. Serve with Turkey, chicken, or pork. Also great on toast for breakfast.

This can also be thinned with apple juice or cranberry juice and used as a sweet sauce for meatballs for appetizers. Heat sauce and serve warm.

Per serving: 167.7 Calories; 0.2g Fat (0.8% calories from fat); 0.4g Protein; 44.3g Carbohydrate; 0mg Cholesterol; 1mg Sodium

Soups

Pork Sausage Soup
Serves 8

- 1 recipe Pork Sausage, meatball shape
- 2 cups onion, chopped
- 2 medium heads Bok choy, sliced
- 5 cups vegetable broth, or chicken broth
- 4 cups water
- 7 ounces rice pasta, small shapes
- 1 teaspoon salt
- 1/2 teaspoon pepper, optional

Cook pasta in water according to directions, drain and cover until ready to use.
In a large soup pot, cook sausages until done (no oil is needed, and drippings add a great flavor to the soup stock). Add onions and saute with sausages until onions are tender, stirring frequently. Pour broth and water into soup pot and bring to boil. Add salt, pepper, and bok choy and gently boil for 5 minutes. Add cooked pasta and stir well. Serve immediately.

This will become a family favorite, and is a quick soup to make with frozen Pork Sausages.
Spinach (one bunch) can be used instead of bok choy.

Per serving: 190.1 Calories; 4.2g Fat (19.6% calories from fat); 6.5g Protein; 32.1g Carbohydrate; 4mg Cholesterol; 1,484mg Sodium

Potato "Bacon" Soup
Serves 8

- 5 pounds potatoes, peeled and chopped
- 1 cup pork tenderloin, smoked naturally
- 2 medium onion, chopped
- 32 ounces rice milk, or milk of day
- 1 teaspoon salt
- 1 teaspoon black pepper
- 1 1/2 Tablespoons oil

For smoked tenderloin, see "Rubbed Tenderloin" recipe.
Wash potatoes and peel (if desired) and chop. Place in a large soup pot and cover with water. Boil for about 35-40 minutes, until tender. While potatoes are boiling, saute onions and smoked tenderloin in oil in a medium skillet. Set aside when onions are tender.
When potatoes are done, drain off liquid, reserving about 4 cups of the liquid. Return potatoes and 4 cups liquid to soup pot. With hand potato masher or hand mixer, process soup until potatoes are about half mashed. The soup needs to have about half of the potatoes chunky. Add onions, tenderloin, salt, pepper, and rice milk. If a thinner soup is desired, add more water or rice milk. Return to heat and simmer for 10 minutes.
This soup is one of our favorites, and with smoked tenderloin in the freezer, I usually have the ingredients on hand.

Per serving: 289.1 Calories; 4.7g Fat (14.4% calories from fat); 11.2g Protein; 51.7g Carbohydrate; 18mg Cholesterol; 473mg Sodium

Smoked Tenderloin and Bean Soup Day 4
Serves 8

- 1   cup pork tenderloin, smoked naturally
- 1   pound dried beans, any variety
- 2   large onion, chopped
- 3   large carrots, diced
- 2   stalks celery, diced
-     salt and pepper, to taste

Smoke one whole pork tenderloin. Dice 1 cup and freeze remainder of meat for later use. See recipe for "Rubbed Tenderloin".

Soak dried beans overnight or for 4 hours. Drain off water. Place dried beans and 1 teaspoon salt in crock pot with 8-10 cups water. Cover with lid and cook on high for 2 hours. Reduce heat to low, and continue to cook for at least 4 more hours. Check occasionally for liquid level. Liquid should always cover beans. If needed, add more water or chicken broth to cover beans. Beans used for soups work best when cooked for long periods of time (at least 8 hours). Add diced pork tenderloin, onion, celery, carrots, and salt and pepper. Cover with lid and cook on med-high for 1 hour.
You may add 2 cups diced tomatoes if desired. Serve hot with crusty bread.

This recipe is very low in fat.

Per serving: 242.9 Calories; 1.8g Fat (6.5% calories from fat); 19.3g Protein; 38.7g Carbohydrate; 18mg Cholesterol; 176mg Sodium

Rice Noodle Soup
Serves 12

- 1 whole chicken, boiled, skinned, boned
- 1 quart water
- 1 dash basil, dried
- 1/4 teaspoon garlic powder
- 1 dash celery salt
- 1 dash marjoram
- 1 quart vegetable broth
- 2 cups frozen carrots
- 2 cups frozen peas, thawed
- 2 small zucchini, sliced 1/3" thick
- 1 cup fresh mushrooms, optional
- 1 medium green onion, thinly sliced
- 1 package 16oz rice noodles, cooked and drained
- 1 teaspoon sesame oil, optional
- 1 teaspoon soy sauce, optional

Place chicken, 1 quart water and seasonings in a dutch oven and bring to boil. Reduce heat and allow to simmer until done, usually 1 hour. Remove skin and bones and discard. Reserve broth for soup. Cook rice noodles in water, drain and set aside. Combine vegetable and chicken broth. Add frozen carrots, mushrooms, zucchini, peas and chicken to broth and cook for 3-5 minutes or until evenly heated without over cooking vegetables. Add sesame oil, soy sauce, sliced onion and stir. Ladle over noodles in bowls and serve.

For lower sodium, substitute liquid amino's for soy, dilute soy or amino's, or omit altogether. Both aminos and soy sauce contain soy. Many oriental noodles are 100% rice. Read the label. "Size L" noodle or wider is best suited for this soup. For zestier flavor, add mongolian fire oil to taste at time of serving.
To reduce fat content, cook chicken ahead of time, cool broth and remove fat before using. This removes more fat than skimming. You can use 2 quarts of chicken broth if desired and omit the vegetable broth. This recipe is great to use leftovers in a flavorful way.

Per serving: 252.0 Calories; 7.9g Fat (28.5% calories from fat); 24.6g Protein; 20.2g Carbohydrate; 63mg Cholesterol; 699mg Sodium

Prudy's Chicken Rice Soup
Serves 6

- 6 cups chicken broth
- 3/4 cup instant rice
- 2 cups chicken, cooked, cubed
- 6 small carrots, baby, sliced thin
- 1/2 cup peas, frozen
- 1 small celery stalk, sliced thin
- 1 small zucchini, sliced thin
- 1/2 teaspoon basil, dried
- 1/4 teaspoon marjoram
- 1 dash garlic powder
- salt and pepper, to taste

Heat broth in large sauce pan. Add instant rice, carrots, celery, chicken, and spices. Cover and cook over medium heat for 10 minutes. Add peas and zucchini. Cover and continue to boil for 2-3 minutes. Do not over cook peas and zucchini. Serve immediately, piping hot. Makes 4-6 servings. Leftover soup freezes well if desired.

Per serving: 240.7 Calories; 7.0g Fat (26.7% calories from fat); 27.0g Protein; 16.1g Carbohydrate; 46mg Cholesterol; 1,617mg Sodium

Chicken Potato Chowder   Day 1
Serves 8

- 2 cups chicken, diced uncooked
- 4 cups potatoes, peeled and diced
- 1/2 cup bell pepper, diced
- 1/4 cup pimiento, diced
- 1 cup mushroom pieces
- 4 cups chicken broth
- 1 Tablespoon potato starch flour
- 1/4 teaspoon chili pepper
- 1 teaspoon salt
- dash tobasco, optional
- 4 cups water

Boil chicken and potatoes just until potatoes are tender. Remove 2 cups of the potatoes, chicken and broth to a blender or food processor. Add 1 Tablespoon potato starch flour and blend on high for about 10 seconds. Return blender portion to the soup pot. Add remainder of the ingredients and cook on low for 20 minutes. Serve hot with oat bread or muffins.

Per serving: 150.0 Calories; 4.5g Fat (27.5% calories from fat); 16.9g Protein; 9.9g Carbohydrate; 34mg Cholesterol; 1,087mg Sodium

Chicken Rice Soup
Serves 8

2	cups chicken breast, cubed
1	cup onion, diced
3/4	cup celery, diced
1	cup carrots, diced
1	cup frozen peas, thawed
4	cups chicken broth
4	cups water
1	teaspoon salt
1/2	teaspoon pepper
1/2	teaspoon garlic
3	cups rice, cooked-leftover

In a large soup pot, heat 1 cup of the broth. When simmering, add onion, carrots, and celery. Cook, stirring occassionally for 5 minutes. Add chicken and cook just until chicken is no longer pink. Add remaining broth and water, salt, pepper, garlic and rice. Bring to a rolling boil, reduce heat and simmer for 10 minutes. Serve with crusty bread or sandwiches.

Per serving: 398.4 Calories; 6.3g Fat (14.5% calories from fat); 21.7g Protein; 61.4g Carbohydrate; 32mg Cholesterol; 1,193mg Sodium

Chicken Soup With Spinach
Serves 8

- 3 cups cooked chicken, cubed
- 5 cups chicken broth, or vegetable broth
- 3 cups water
- 1 teaspoon salt
- 1/2 teaspoon pepper
- 4 ounces rice pasta, small shapes
- 1 bunch spinach leaves, washed-stems removed

This recipe makes good use of leftover chicken when a whole chicken has been cooked and the leftovers frozen for the next chicken rotation lunch.

Cook rice pasta according to directions. Drain and cover until ready to use.
In a large soup pot, combine chicken, broth, water, salt, and pepper. Heat to a boil. Add spinach leaves and pasta and cook for only 3 minutes. Spinach should only become wilted.
Variation: Add mushrooms for more flavor.
This is a refreshing soup that works well with sandwiches. It also is good the next day in lunches.

Per serving: 176.4 Calories; 4.2g Fat (21.9% calories from fat); 24.3g Protein; 9.0g Carbohydrate; 46mg Cholesterol; 1,292mg Sodium

Chicken Tomato Soup   Day 1
Serves 8

- 5   cups tomatoes, peeled and diced
- 2   whole chicken breasts, cubed small
- 1   teaspoon salt
- 1/2 teaspoon pepper
-     dash cayenne pepper, optional
- 3   cups oat milk, or rice milk
- 1   Tablespoon safflower oil, or sunflower oil

Puree 4 cups of the tomatoes (one cup at a time). Reserve 1 cup for a chunky soup consistency. In a large soup pot, heat oil and saute chicken with spices until done. Add pureed tomatoes and 1 cup diced tomatoes. Bring to the boil and add oat milk. Cover and simmer for 15 minutes, stirring frequently. Serve hot with toasted bread.

Per serving: 189.7 Calories; 9.2g Fat (43.8% calories from fat); 17.1g Protein; 9.4g Carbohydrate; 46mg Cholesterol; 398mg Sodium

Turkey Cabbage Soup   Day 5 C/E
Serves 8

- 2   cups turkey breast-skinless and boneless, uncooked diced
- 2   Tablespoons canola oil
- 6   cups chinese cabbage, sliced thin
- 6   cups turkey broth
- 3   cups rice, cooked
       salt and pepper, to taste
- 2   teaspoons dry mustard

Heat canola oil in soup pot. Coat turkey meat with salt, pepper, and mustard. Cook on medium-high heat until no longer pink. Add broth and cooked rice to pot. Bring to a boil, then reduce heat to simmer. Cook for 10 minutes. Add cabbage and cook an additional 10 minutes. Serve hot with crusty or toasted bread.

Per serving: 432.8 Calories; 9.8g Fat (20.8% calories from fat); 25.7g Protein; 58.0g Carbohydrate; 36mg Cholesterol; 1,238mg Sodium

Italian White Bean and Savory Meatball Soup
Serves 4

1/2	recipe Savory Meatballs
2	16 oz. cans Navy beans, in water
2	Tablespoons olive oil
3	medium tomatoes, chopped
2	cloves garlic, chopped fine
1	large onion, chopped
2	medium carrot, chopped
1/2	teaspoon oregano, dried
1/2	teaspoon black pepper
1/2	Tablespoon parsley, dried
2	cups chicken broth

Saute onion, garlic, and carrots in oil in large soup pot. Remove from pan. Brown meatballs in pot. Remove from pan. Add chicken broth to pan scraping bottom of pan while broth heats. Add onion, garlic, carrots, and meatballs back to pot. Add beans, tomatoes, and seasonings to soup. Stir well and lower heat to a slow simmer. Stir ocassionally and cook for 1 hour. Serve immediately.

Per serving: 506.2 Calories; 10.2g Fat (17.7% calories from fat); 31.8g Protein; 75.3g Carbohydrate; 5mg Cholesterol; 970mg Sodium

Turkey Noodle Soup
Serves 8

- 3 cups cooked turkey, leftover-cubed
- 5 cups turkey broth, or vegetable broth
- 3 cups water
- 1 small onion, chopped
- 3 large carrots, chopped
- 1 cup frozen peas
- 4 ounces rice pasta, small shapes
- water, to cook pasta
- salt and pepper, to taste

Cook pasta according to directions, drain, and cover until needed.
In a large soup pot, heat 1 cup of the broth. Add onions, carrots, and peas and cook about 10 minutes until tender. Add remaining broth, water, and turkey meat. Heat to boiling. Add rice pasta. Salt and pepper to taste. Serve hot with bread and salad or with sandwiches.

Per serving: 173.4 Calories; 3.7g Fat (19.6% calories from fat); 19.9g Protein; 14.4g Carbohydrate; 29mg Cholesterol; 1,103mg Sodium

Turkey Rice Soup   Day 5   C/E
Serves 8

- 2 cups turkey breast, uncooked diced
- 1 1/2 cups brown rice, uncooked
- 4 cups turkey broth
- 6 cups water
- 2 teaspoons salt
- 1 teaspoon pepper

Place water and turkey broth in large soup pot. Add all other ingredients and bring to the boil. Turn heat down to low and continue to cook for 1 hour, covered. Serve hot. This recipe freezes well.

Per serving: 252.0 Calories; 6.0g Fat (21.9% calories from fat); 19.9g Protein; 28.3g Carbohydrate; 36mg Cholesterol; 1,354mg Sodium

Vegetable Meatball Soup
Serves 8

- 1/2 recipe Savory Meatballs
- 1 Tablespoon oil
- 1 cup carrots, sliced
- 1 cup broccoli, chopped
- 1 cup celery, chopped
- 1 large onion, chopped
- 24 ounces chicken broth
- 4 ounces rice pasta, style of choice
- 3 cups water
- 1 teaspoon salt

In large dutch oven, brown meatballs in oil. Add vegetables and toss to coat with meat drippings. Add chicken broth, water, and salt. Cook 30 minutes until carrots are tender. Add pasta and cook until pasta is beginning to soften (about 12-15 minutes). Serve hot with toasted bread.

Substitute sliced Bok Choy for broccoli for a milder flavor.

Per serving: 98.6 Calories; 3.0g Fat (27.4% calories from fat); 6.2g Protein; 11.9g Carbohydrate; 3mg Cholesterol; 896mg Sodium

Beefy Tomato Soup
Serves 8

- 1 pound beef steak, cut into 1/2" cubes
- 1 cup rice flour
- 3 cups onions, coarsely chopped
- 6 cups tomatoes, coarsely chopped
- 1 teaspoon salt
- 3/4 teaspoon pepper
- 2 cups cooked rice
- 3 cups water
- 2 Tablespoons olive oil

This classic Greek soup is simply delicious!

In a medium bowl, add flour, salt, and pepper. Mix well. Add beef cubes and mix until coated. Dust off excess flour.

Heat oil in the bottom of a large soup pot. When hot, add 1/2 of the beef and cook until browned. Remove from pan and cook remaining beef cubes until brown. Add back all of the beef to pan. Reduce heat to medium-low. Add the onions, one cup of the water, and the rest of the seasoned flour if any remains. Stir well and cook until onions begin to become tender. Add tomatoes and remaining water. Stir well and cook for 20 minutes, stirring occassionally to prevent sticking. Add cooked rice and cook another 10 minutes. Serve hot with toasted bread or fococcia.

Per serving: 330.6 Calories; 14.2g Fat (38.8% calories from fat); 12.3g Protein; 38.4g Carbohydrate; 32mg Cholesterol; 525mg Sodium

White Chili
Serves 8

- 2 cans great northern beans, canned
- 1 can dark kidney beans, with liquid
- 1 small whole onion, chopped
- 2 Tablespoons chili powder
- 1/2 teaspoon cayenne
- 1/2 teaspoon cumin
- 1 cup chicken broth
- 1 Tablespoon canola oil
- 1 pound ground beef
- 1 teaspoon hot sauce, optional

Saute onion in oil. Add spices and ground beef. Cook until meat is done. Add remaining ingredients. Bring to a boil, reduce heat to simmer 5 to 10 minutes. Salt and pepper to taste.
Serving Suggestion: Serve piping hot over short grain brown rice.
Note: Canned dark red kidney beans may contain corn syrup. If you have corn or cane allergies, substitute an additional can of northern beans, or purchase dry red beans and cook in advance. Can be divided into portions and frozen for future meals. If lunch packing, remove from freezer and place directly in lunch bag. It will not require refrigeration. At lunchtime, simply reheat in microwave. Seasonings can be altered for preference. Ground chicken or turkey may also be used in place of ground beef. This is a family favorite.

Per serving: 363.0 Calories; 18.0g Fat (44.2% calories from fat); 21.5g Protein; 29.7g Carbohydrate; 49mg Cholesterol; 332mg Sodium

Salmon Gumbo
Serves 8

1	medium green pepper, chopped
3/4	cup onion, chopped
2	Tablespoons canola margarine
3	cups tomato juice
1	cup clam juice
1	15 oz. can tomatoes, chunked
1	cup chicken broth, rich, cooked down
2	Tablespoons parsley
1	package frozen okra, 10 oz
1	can salmon, pink, 12 1/2 oz
4	ounces mushrooms

In large skillet or dutch oven, saute green pepper and onion in margarine for 5 minutes. Add tomato juice, tomatoes, clam juice, chicken broth, and parsley to green pepper and onion. And bring to boil. Add frozen okra and return to boil. Drain pink salmon and remove skin and bones. Fold salmon into mixture. Reduce heat, simmer 10 minutes. Serve over rice with hot sauce to taste at the table.

Per serving: 95.1 Calories; 3.7g Fat (33.4% calories from fat); 5.5g Protein; 11.3g Carbohydrate; 6mg Cholesterol; 746mg Sodium

Vegetarian Bean Soup   Day 4
Serves 8

- 1 can black beans, all natural
- 1 1/2 cups frozen lima beans
- 1 can pinto beans, all natural
- 1 1/2 cups frozen peas
- 1 can white beans, all natural
- 2 bunches spinach leaves, washed-stems removed
- salt and pepper, to taste
- water, to make soupy

Any combination of beans can be used.
Place at least 3 cups of water in a large soup pot with frozen limas, and peas. Bring to a boil, and cook, covered for 20 minutes. Add all other beans, and enough water to make the soup as thick or thin as you want, and bring back to the boil for 10 minutes. Add spinach and cook for 5 minutes. Salt and pepper to taste.

If desired, this bean soup can be made from dried beans soaked over night and cooked in the crockpot (on high) the next day. Add spinach leaves 10 minutes before serving.

Per serving: 312.4 Calories; 1.1g Fat (3.1% calories from fat); 20.2g Protein; 57.4g Carbohydrate; 0mg Cholesterol; 62mg Sodium

Tomato Basil Soup
Serves 8

- 8 cups tomatoes, peeled and seeded
- 1 cup water
- 1 teaspoon salt
- 24 ounces almond milk, or milk of day
- 10 medium basil leaves, chopped

Puree 8 cups tomatoes (one cup at a time) with basil leaves in blender or food processor. Place tomatoes with basil in soup pot with water and salt. Bring to boil, then turn down heat to simmer, covered, for 20 minutes. Stir occasionally. Add almond milk and simmer for additional 5 minutes. Serve hot with toasted bread.

This is a delicately flavored soup that is good enough for company. Extremely low in fat, it is an excellent choice over canned soups. Some people are highly allergic to tomatoes; if this is the case, do not prepare this recipe.

Per serving: 68.5 Calories; 1.5g Fat (17.7% calories from fat); 2.2g Protein; 13.3g Carbohydrate; 0mg Cholesterol; 320mg Sodium

Sweet Potato Soup   Day 5
Serves 6

- 4 large sweet potatoes, with peel
- 3 cups water
- 4 cups rice milk
- 4 Tablespoons rice syrup
- 1 teaspoon allspice
- 1 teaspoon cloves

Boil sweet potatoes (whole) in water to cover until a knife can pierce through easily(about 20 minutes). Drain off water and reserve one cup of liquid. Peel potatoes, be careful, they will be hot. Return to soup pot. Add 3 cup water and use hand mixer to mash completely until potatoes are smooth. Add rice milk, rice syrup, and spices. Mix with hand mixer about one minute longer. Return to heat and heat just until warm. This soup may also be served cold as a summer appetizer.
It is like having sweet potato pie as a nutritious soup with only 1.6 grams of fat per serving.

Per serving: 175.9 Calories; 1.6g Fat (8.2% calories from fat); 1.7g Protein;
   39.3g Carbohydrate; 0mg Cholesterol; 74mg Sodium

Squash Soup   Day 2
Serves 4

10	medium yellow squash, cubed
	water, to cover squash
1	large onion, chopped fine
	salt and pepper, to taste
3	cups almond milk, or milk of day
2	ounces almond cheese, grated

Place squash and onion in large soup pot and just cover with water. Boil, covered with a lid, for 20 minutes. When squash is tender, use a hand electric mixer to partially puree cooked squash. Leave chunky. Add almond milk and season to taste with salt and pepper. Bring back to the boil. Place in individual serving bowls and top with almond cheese.

This is a delicious soup that is very satisfying. Serve with crusty bread.

Per serving: 171.7 Calories; 4.3g Fat (21.2% calories from fat); 8.5g Protein; 27.7g Carbohydrate; 0mg Cholesterol; 360mg Sodium

Split Pea Soup
Serves 8

- 1 pound split peas, dried
- 1/2 teaspoon salt
- 3 medium potatoes, diced small
- 2 medium carrots, diced small

Soak split peas covered in water for 3-4 hours, or overnight. In morning, drain and place in large crock pot with 1-1/2 quart water (8 cups). Add 1/2 teaspoon salt and cook 2 hours. Add potatoes and carrots to crockpot. Salt and pepper to taste. Cook one hour until vegetables are tender.

When done, place about 1/2 soup in blender to blend-- one cup at a time. This will thicken the soup and give it a creamy consistency. Return to the crock pot and stir to mix. Serve hot.

Per serving: 225.3 Calories; 0.7g Fat (2.8% calories from fat); 14.7g Protein; 41.5g Carbohydrate; 0mg Cholesterol; 149mg Sodium

Potato Soup
Serves 6

- 8 large potato, washed and cubed
- 1 large onion, chopped
- water, to cover potatoes
- 3/4 teaspoon salt
- 1/4 teaspoon pepper, black or white
- 2 cups nut milk, or rice milk

Place cubed potatoes in large pot and just cover with water. Boil about 30 minutes or until tender. Drain off enough water so that top layer of potatoes is exposed. Add chopped onion and 2 cups nut milk. Boil 10 minutes or until onions are tender. Add salt and pepper to taste. Remove from heat and carefully mash potatoes coarsely with hand masher. (may use hand mixer to coarsely blend, leaving chunky potatoes). Serve hot in bowls.

Per serving: 123.4 Calories; 1.0g Fat (6.8% calories from fat); 3.2g Protein; 26.2g Carbohydrate; 0mg Cholesterol; 398mg Sodium

Potato Leek Soup
Serves 8

- 7 large potatoes, washed and diced
- 3 cups leeks, washed and sliced
- 2 cups chicken broth, or vegetable broth
- 2 cups almond milk, or rice milk
- 1 teaspoon salt
- 1/2 teaspoon white pepper, or black pepper
- 1 Tablespoon oil

Place diced potatoes in water to cover. Boil for 30 minutes. Slice leeks (white part and tender part of green stem). In nonstick skillet, saute leeks in oil. Drain water off potatoes, and return to saucepan. Add leeks, broth, salt and pepper. Stir well mashing some of the potatoes. Add nut milk or rice milk. Bring back to boil and serve hot.

Per serving: 125.9 Calories; 3.1g Fat (21.7% calories from fat); 5.1g Protein; 20.0g Carbohydrate; 1mg Cholesterol; 691mg Sodium

Golden Mushroom Soup
Serves 4

- 1/2 pound fresh mushrooms, sliced
- 1 quart chicken broth
- 1/2 teaspoon salt
- 1/2 cup white bean flour
- 1 cup milk
- 1/2 small carrot, finely shredded
- salt and pepper, to taste

Place mushrooms in large sauce pan. Add broth. Cover and simmer for 20 minutes. Remove from heat and allow to cool to room temperature. Add bean flour to the cooled mushroom broth mixture. Mix well with wire wisk. Return to heat until thickens. Stirring constantly. Thin with rice milk if needed. Double mushrooms for more robust mushroom flavor!

Variation: Use portabella mushrooms. Cook uncovered slowly to reduce volume by half. Add two cups milk. Bring to boil. Add white bean flour. Stir until thickens. Subtitution: May omit white bean flour and use potato starch flour to thicken. Use 2 tablespoons potato flour mixed with 2 tablespoons of water. Add to cooled mushroom broth as above.

Per serving: 204.9 Calories; 5.2g Fat (22.7% calories from fat); 15.5g Protein; 24.0g Carbohydrate; 11mg Cholesterol; 1,867mg Sodium

French Onion Soup Day 3
Serves 6

- 2 Tablespoons canola margarine, or oil of the day
- 5 cups onion, chopped
- 1 teaspoon salt
- 1/2 teaspoon pepper, of choice
- 32 ounces beef broth, chicken or vegetable
- 6 slices rice bread, or bread of the day
- 6 ounces Almond cheese, or cheese of the day

Heat margarine or oil in large sauce pan. Add onion and cook over medium-low heat stirring frequently until most of the onions have become caramel colored. Add salt, pepper, and broth. Bring to a boil for about 5 minutes. Serve in bowls with a piece of the toasted bread and 1 ounce cheese substitute on top.

Per serving: 296.7 Calories; 11.4g Fat (35.1% calories from fat); 15.9g Protein; 31.6g Carbohydrate; 2mg Cholesterol; 2,122mg Sodium

Broccoli Soup   Day 5   C/E
Serves 8

- 3 cups broccoli, finely chopped
- 2 1/2 cups turkey broth
- 2 Tablespoons rice flour
- 4 Tablespoons canola oil
- 4 cups rice milk
- salt and pepper, to taste

In soup pot, cook broccoli 20 minutes in turkey broth, covered, until tender. Do not discard liquid from soup pot, it will become part of the soup stock. In a blender, puree 2 cups of the cooked broccoli. Return to soup pot with liquid. Set aside.

In a medium sauce pan, heat oil. Add rice flour to make a roux (a paste that is the base for many creamy soups and sauces). Allow the roux to bubble for about 30 seconds. Add rice milk slowly and let mixture come to a boil until it begins to thicken. Add the creamy sauce to the ingredients in the soup pot. Bring back to a slow boil and boil for 5 minutes, stirring frequently. Serve hot with sandwiches or alone.

Per serving: 162.7 Calories;   8.8g Fat (47.5% calories from fat);   5.1g Protein;   16.8g Carbohydrate;   1mg Cholesterol;   543mg Sodium

Asparagus Soup   C/E
Serves 8

- 1 pound asparagus, fresh
- 6 cups low sodium chicken broth, natural
- 4 cups rice milk, or milk of choice
- salt and pepper, to taste

Clean asparagus tips and remove tough ends. Cut into 1" length pieces. Place asparagus in large soup pot and add the chicken broth to pot. Bring broth to boil and cook asparagus for 15 minutes. Remove asparagus from chicken broth with ladle. Reserve chicken broth. Puree asparagus in blender or food processor until smooth. Return asparagus puree to chicken broth. Add salt and pepper to taste. Stir in rice milk and bring soup to boil. Simmer for 5 minutes and serve hot.

Per serving: 80.1 Calories; 1.1g Fat (8.8% calories from fat); 9.5g Protein; 15.3g Carbohydrate; 0mg Cholesterol; 434mg Sodium

Vegetables

Baked Potato Skins
Serves 16

- 8 medium baking potatoes
- 2 Tablespoons olive oil
- 2 Tablespoons cajun seasoning, seasoning of choice
- 4 green onion, sliced
- 3/4 cup Rice Slice, cheese of choice
- 1/4 cup bell pepper

Bake potatoes at 350 degrees for 45 minutes. Cut into halves and then quarters lengthwise. Scoop out potato to leave about 1/4"-1/2" on the shell. Reserve the scooped out potatoes for another use in soups or as sauce thickener.

Brush potato skin and pulp side with oil. Lay skin side down on a cookie sheet. Sprinkle with seasonings, bell pepper, onion, and cheese. Place cookie sheet under broiler or on top of the grill for 2-3 minutes or until cheese is melted.

Serve as a vegetable to compliment an outdoor meal, or as an appetizer.

Serving size: 2 quarters per person.

Per serving: 75.2 Calories; 2.5g Fat (24.5% calories from fat); 3.1g Protein; 14.0g Carbohydrate; 0mg Cholesterol; 144mg Sodium

Twice Baked Potatoes
Serves 4

- 4 large baking potatoes
- 1/4 cup onion, minced
- 2 Tablespoons canola margarine
- 1 cup almond milk, regular flavor
- 1/2 teaspoon salt
- 1/4 teaspoon pepper
- 4 ounces almond cheese, grated

Preheat oven to 375 degrees. Place potatoes on oven rack to bake for 1 hour (Do not wrap with foil. The skins need to be dry and stiff). Remove potatoes from oven and allow to cool just enough to be able to handle them. Slice 1/3 of potato off. Scoop the potato pulp out of the top slice and scoop out inside of potato shell. Place pulp in a large bowl with margarine, almond milk, onion, salt and pepper. Whip with hand mixer until smooth. Stir in almond cheese with spoon. Spoon mashed potato mix into potato shells. Place under broiler or in the toaster oven until golden brown. Serve hot.

Per serving: 234.5 Calories; 9.8g Fat (37.6% calories from fat); 9.0g Protein; 27.5g Carbohydrate; 0mg Cholesterol; 679mg Sodium

Potato Cakes
Serves 4

2	large potatoes, leftover baked
1/2	cup onion, chopped fine
3	teaspoons egg replacer, =2 eggs
1/2	teaspoon salt
1/4	teaspoon pepper
1 1/4	cups rice milk, or milk of the day
2/3	cup rice flour
2	Tablespoons olive oil, or oil of choice

Chop fine or grate potatoes and place into a large bowl. Add onion, egg replacer, salt, pepper, rice flour, and rice milk. Mix well with a spoon. Heat oil in a large skillet. Spoon about 1/4 cup batter into hot skillet (these will be similar to thick pancakes). Turn with spatula when golden around the edges. Serve hot as a side dish.

Per serving: 554.3 Calories; 7.8g Fat (12.1% calories from fat); 2.9g Protein; 124.2g Carbohydrate; 0mg Cholesterol; 519mg Sodium

Mashed Potatoes   Day 1
Serves 6

- 7 large potatoes, washed and diced
- 1 teaspoon salt
- water, to cover potatoes
- 1 Tablespoon canola margarine, or oil of the day
- 1 cup chicken broth
- salt and pepper, to taste

Place potatoes in large sauce pan with 1 teaspoon salt and cover with water. Boil until tender, about 30 minutes. Drain off water. Place potatoes back in saucepan. Add broth, margarine, salt and pepper. Mix with hand mixer or potato masher. May require more broth to obtain desired consistency.

Per serving: 107.0 Calories; 2.4g Fat (19.5% calories from fat); 3.9g Protein; 17.9g Carbohydrate; 0mg Cholesterol; 642mg Sodium

Baked Sweet Potatoes   Day 5   C/E
Serves 4

- 4 large sweet potatoes
- 1 teaspoon cinnamon, optional
- 4 Tablespoons rice syrup, optional
- 1 teaspoon canola margarine, optional

Wash sweet potatoes with water. Preheat oven to 350 degrees. Wrap sweet potatoes in foil and place wrapped potatoes in a baking pan with 1-2" of water in the pan. Bake at 350 degrees for 1 hour. Remove foil and cut potato down the center. Spread the potato open and add rice syrup and cinnamon if desired. Sweet potatoes are sweet enough as is, but my family loves to add the cinnamon and sweetener. A large sweet potato is nutritious and is almost a meal by itself.

Sweet potatoes are comparable to carrots in Vitamin A. They are very low in fat (about 0.3 gms per cup) and high in potassium.

Sweet potatoes also are a favorite for camping. Wrap the potato in heavy duty foil and place in hot coals of a fire for 1-1/2 hour or until tender. Do not place directly in the fire.

Per serving: 150.6 Calories; 1.2g Fat (7.2% calories from fat); 1.6g Protein; 33.7g Carbohydrate; 0mg Cholesterol; 24mg Sodium

Sweet Potato Bake With Cranberries Day 5 C/E
Serves 6

- 6 small-medium sweet potatoes
- 1/2 cup dried cranberries
- 1 cup water, boiling
- 1/2 cup rice syrup

Preheat oven to 350 degrees. Peel and cut sweet potatoes into 1-2" cubes. Place dried cranberries in 1 cup boiling water for 15 minutes. Drain and reserve liquid. Spray a glass casserole dish with oil. Place cubed sweet potatoes in oiled baking dish. Sprinkle with cranberries. Pour drained cranberry liquid over all. Drizzle with rice syrup. Cover with lid or foil and bake at 350 degrees for 45 minutes.

Serve hot with a turkey dinner. This dish makes a fabulous substitute for the high calorie Sweet Potato Casserole that is usually served with Thanksgiving dinner. This one is much lower in calories and fat.

Per serving: 164.1 Calories; 0.3g Fat (1.7% calories from fat); 1.6g Protein; 39.1g Carbohydrate; 0mg Cholesterol; 15mg Sodium

Sesame Asparagus C/E Day 3
Serves 4

- 1 pound asparagus
- 1 teaspoon sesame oil
- 1 Tablespoon olive oil
- 1 clove garlic, minced
- 1 Tablespoon sesame seeds

Wash asparagus and remove any tough ends. You may cut asparagus in half to make tossing easier. Place about 1" of water in a nonstick skillet. Arrange asparagus in water evenly and turn heat to medium high. When water begins to boil, turn down to simmer. Cover with lid and cook for 7 minutes. Check to make sure water does not completely evaporate. Drain off water and remove asparagus from pan. Place oils in skillet with garlic and heat until warm, about 1 minute. Place asparagus back in skillet and toss with oils and garlic. Sprinkle with sesame seeds and serve immediately.

Per serving: 68.5 Calories; 5.9g Fat (71.9% calories from fat); 2.0g Protein; 3.2g Carbohydrate; 0mg Cholesterol; 2mg Sodium

Broiled Tomatoes
Serves 4

- 4 medium tomatoes
- 1 slice rice bread, dried-crumbs
- 1/2 teaspoon oregano, dried
- salt and pepper, to taste
- 2 ounces almond cheese, grated

Preheat oven to 375 degrees.
Hint: Use a muffin tin to hold tomatoes upright and prevent them from rolling to the side.

Cut tomatoes in half and arrange on muffin tin, cut side up. Sprinkle with salt and pepper if desired.
In a small bowl, combine bread crumbs and oregano. Sprinkle over tomatoes. Top tomatoes with grated cheese and bake at 375 degrees for 10 minutes. Then, place under broiler or in toaster oven until cheese is bubbly and beginning to turn golden.
Serve hot with grilled chicken or other meat.

Serving size: 2 halves.

Per serving: 89.5 Calories; 2.8g Fat (27.1% calories from fat); 4.5g Protein; 12.3g Carbohydrate; 0mg Cholesterol; 153mg Sodium

Green Bean Stir-Fry
Serves 6

- 1 pound green beans, washed and dried
- 4 whole green onion, chopped
- 3 Tablespoons oil, of choice
- 1/2 cup chicken broth, natural
- 1/2 teaspoon salt

Heat oil and green onions until tender. Add green beans to pan and toss to coat with oil. Continue to toss over medium heat until beans turn bright green (about 3-5 minutes). Reduce heat and cover with lid. Simmer for 10 minutes. Beans will be crispy-done. This is a delicious side dish that is high in vitamin A and Folacin.

This recipe will be a C/E recipe by omitting the onion.

Per serving: 118.3 Calories; 7.3g Fat (50.8% calories from fat); 3.9g Protein; 12.0g Carbohydrate; 0mg Cholesterol; 328mg Sodium

Honeyed Carrots   C/E
Serves 4

- 1 pound carrots, peeled and sliced
- water, to cover carrots
- 1/4 cup frozen orange juice concentrate
- 1/3 cup honey

Place carrots in medium sauce pan and cover with water. Place lid on pan and bring to boil over medium heat. Boil for 20-30 minutes until tender. Remove from heat and drain off water. (You may wish to save the carrot broth for soup stock) Place hot carrots back in saucepan. Add orange juice concentrate and honey. Gently stir to coat with honey and juice. Serve hot as a side dish with any meal. This is a crowd pleaser! This recipe is extremely high in vitamin A and low in fat and calories.

Per serving: 157.5 Calories; 0.2g Fat (1.2% calories from fat); 1.6g Protein; 40.3g Carbohydrate; 0mg Cholesterol; 37mg Sodium

Wilted Spinach C/E

Serves 4

- 2 bunches spinach, wash twice
- 1 Tablespoon olive oil, or oil of the day
- 1 clove garlic, minced
- 1/3 cup chicken broth

Wash spinach and remove stems. Set aside to drain off as much water as possible.
In large non-stick skillet, heat oil and garlic for about 1 minute over medium heat. Do not let garlic brown.
Add about 1/2 of spinach leaves, cover and cook down for 2 minutes. Add remaining spinach leaves and toss with spinach already in the pan. Cover and cook about 4 minutes on low heat. Add chicken broth and cook 2 minutes. Serve hot. Spinach cooked in this manner retains more of its vitamins and minerals than boiling.

Spinach is a good source of Vitamin A.

Per serving: 41.7 Calories; 3.7g Fat (75.9% calories from fat); 1.5g Protein; 1.1g Carbohydrate; 0mg Cholesterol; 146mg Sodium

Rice Pilaf
Serves 6

- 1 1/2 cups brown rice, or rice of choice
- 3 1/2 cups chicken broth, or vegetable broth
- 2 teaspoons olive oil, or oil of choice
- 1/2 cup onion, diced
- 1/2 cup celery, diced
- 1/2 cup carrots, diced
- 1/4 cup bell pepper, diced
- 1 cup mushrooms, chopped
- 1 teaspoon minced garlic

In a large sauce pan with lid, heat oil. Saute vegetables in oil for 5 minutes. Add rice and stir to coat rice with vegetables and oil. Add chicken broth and stir well. Bring to boil, then reduce heat to slow simmer. Cover with lid and cook for about 55 minutes or according to package directions. Check frequently and stir occassionally to prevent rice from sticking to the bottom of the pan. Serve as a side dish to any meat, fish or seafood dish.

Per serving: 243.5 Calories; 4.4g Fat (16.3% calories from fat); 10.6g Protein; 40.1g Carbohydrate; 1mg Cholesterol; 975mg Sodium

Quinoa Pilaf
Serves 6

- 2 cups chicken broth
- 1 cup quinoa, rinsed
- 1/2 cup carrots, shredded
- 1/2 cup celery, chopped fine
- 1/2 cup onion, chopped fine
- 1/2 cup green beans, chopped
- 1/4 cup red bell pepper, chopped fine
- 1 Tablespoon olive oil, or oil of choice
- 1/2 teaspoon garlic salt

In a large skillet, heat oil and saute carrots, onion, celery, beans, and bell pepper until tender. Add chicken broth and bring to a boil. Add quinoa and garlic and stir. Turn heat to simmer and cover skillet for 12-15 minutes. Check to see if all liquid has been absorbed. If not, remove lid and simmer until liquid is gone. Serve as you would Rice Pilaf.

I find that this dish resembles couscous in taste and texture.

Per serving: 162.8 Calories; 4.8g Fat (26.2% calories from fat); 7.8g Protein; 22.7g Carbohydrate; 1mg Cholesterol; 590mg Sodium

Spanish Rice
Serves 6

- 1 cup long-grain brown rice
- 1 cup chicken broth
- 1 1/2 cups water
- 1 teaspoon salt
- 1/2 teaspoon pepper
- 1 teaspoon chili powder
- 1/4 teaspoon cumin
- 1 small onion, chopped
- 2 medium green chile, chopped fine
- 1 Tablespoon oil
- 1 small tomato, chopped-optional

In medium sauce pan, saute onion and green chilis. When onion is tender, add chopped tomato (optional). Add all spices and dry rice. Stir well to coat rice with spices and oil. Add chicken broth and water. Stir and cover with lid. Cook over very low heat until all liquid has absorbed (about 45-50 minutes). Stir frequently to prevent sticking.

Per serving: 162.1 Calories; 3.8g Fat (20.9% calories from fat); 5.0g Protein; 27.4g Carbohydrate; 0mg Cholesterol; 718mg Sodium

Brazil Nut Risotto Day 5 C/E
Serves 6

- 2 cups turkey broth
- 2 cups rice milk
- 1 1/2 cups risotto, or rice of choice
- 1/2 teaspoon salt
- 1/4 teaspoon pepper
- 4 ounces rice slice, (cheese)
- 1/3 cup brazil nuts, chopped

Place risotto in a nonstick skillet with 1 cup broth. Heat over low heat, stirring constantly, until risotto absorbs almost all of the broth. Add 1 cup rice milk and stir until most of the liquid is absorbed. Add remaining 1 cup of broth, salt, pepper, and brazil nuts and stir until liquid is mostly absorbed. Add last cup of rice milk and continue to stir. When liquid is almost completely absorbed and rice is desired doneness. Add rice cheese and stir well. Serve as a main dish or side.

This creamy Italian rice dish is worth the time it takes to prepare.
If using brown rice, the cooking time will be longer and may require more liquid.
Risotto usually cooks in 20-25 minutes.

Per serving: 259.4 Calories; 61.0g Fat (42.4% calories from fat); 121.3g Protein; 65.4g Carbohydrate; 1mg Cholesterol; 6,213mg Sodium

Grilled Portobello Mushrooms
Serves 4

- 4 medium portobello mushrooms, stems removed
- 2 Tablespoons Basil Pesto, recipe
- 2 Tablespoons sun-dried tomato paste
- 4 Tablespoons almond cheese, grated

Heat outdoor or indoor grill. Remove and discard stem of mushrooms. Turn mushrooms over so that smooth top side is on the bottom. Spread on a thin layer of tomato paste (1/2 Tablespoon per mushroom). Then, spread on a thin layer of pesto sauce (about 1/2 Tablespoon per mushroom). Top with grated cheese.
Place mushrooms, topping side up, on grill surface. Grill only until cheese begins to melt. Remove from heat.

This is my personal favorite. Portobello mushrooms are large enough that this can be served as a side dish. Many times, I have used large portobello mushrooms as a meat substitute. Its flavor is similar to a choice cut of meat.

Per serving: 63.0 Calories; 3.9g Fat (64.8% calories from fat); 2.2g Protein; 2.6g Carbohydrate; 0mg Cholesterol; 310mg Sodium

Mushroom Macaroni Casserole
Serves 8

- 10 ounces rice pasta, elbow shaped
- 1 medium bell pepper, chopped
- 1 large onion, chopped
- 1 cup mushrooms, chopped
- 1 cup Creamy Mushroom Soup, Imagine brand
- 10 rice crackers, crushed
- 2 Tablespoons olive oil

Preheat oven to 350 degrees.
Cook elbow pasta and drain.
While pasta is cooking, saute onion, mushrooms, and bell pepper in oil until beginning to become tender. Add sauted vegetables to drained pasta. Stir in almond cheese and soup. Place in a large casserole dish and top with cracker crumbs. Bake at 350 degrees for 25-30 minutes.

Per serving: 218.3 Calories; 5.6g Fat (23.8% calories from fat); 4.5g Protein; 35.6g Carbohydrate; 0mg Cholesterol; 267mg Sodium

Braised Celery   C/E

Serves 4

- 10 stalks celery, about 1 bunch
- 1 cup pork broth, fat removed

Preheat oven to 350 degrees or bake in microwavable dish.

Wash celery stalks, cut in half and remove 1/2" of root end. Place in a baking dish. Pour pork broth over celery. Cover dish with lid. Bake at 350 degrees for 20 minutes or microwave on high for 10 minutes and let rest for 5 minutes. Serve hot.

Per serving: 33.6 Calories; 0.8g Fat (19.5% calories from fat); 3.4g Protein; 3.7g Carbohydrate; 1mg Cholesterol; 469mg Sodium

Ratatouille
Serves 4

1	pound eggplant, 1/2" cubes
1	medium onion, diced
3/4	pound yellow squash, 1/2" cubes
3/4	pound zucchini, 1/2" cubes
1	cup tomatoes, diced
3	cloves garlic, minced
	salt and pepper, to taste
1	teaspoon oregano
1	Tablespoon parsley
1	teaspoon basil
2	Tablespoons olive oil, or oil of the day

Peel and cube eggplant (select smallest eggplant available, this cuts down on bitterness), cube yellow squash and zucchini. Dice onion, tomatoes, and mince garlic.
Heat oil in a large skillet with lid. Saute onion and garlic (do not let garlic brown). Add eggplant, squash and zucchini. Saute for about 5 minutes, then add tomatoes and herbs. Cover and simmer on low heat for 20 minutes. Salt and pepper to taste.

Serve as a side dish for pasta or grilled meats.

Per serving: 134.3 Calories; 7.5g Fat (45.3% calories from fat); 3.9g Protein;
    16.4g Carbohydrate; 0mg Cholesterol; 153mg Sodium

Stuffed Zucchini Squash Day 2 C/E
Serves 6

```
4     medium Zucchini squash
2     Tablespoons olive oil
2     slices tapioca bread, crumbs
1     teaspoon marjoram, dried
2     ounces almond cheese, grated
1/2   teaspoon salt
```

Peheat oven to 350 degrees.
Dry bread crumbs overnight on the counter or in oven for 1 hour at 200 degrees. Chop or crush into fine crumbs. Place in a bowl and sprinkle with marjoram, salt, and cheese. Cut zucchini in half lenthwise. Boil in a large pot for about 10 minutes. Gently remove from the water and scoop out seeds with a spoon. Reserve scooped out seeds, chop, and place in the bowl with the bread crumbs. Mix well. Place zucchini halves in a baking dish. Stuff squash halves with bread crumb mixture and bake 15 minutes at 350 degrees until cheese melts.

These are great with Beef Burgers Day 2.

Per serving: 121.9 Calories; 7.8g Fat (57.9% calories from fat); 3.3g Protein; 9.5g Carbohydrate; 0mg Cholesterol; 331mg Sodium

Baked Squash Casserole
Serves 6

- 2 pounds yellow squash, washed and cubed
- 1 cup onion, chopped
- 8 ounces almond cheese, grated
- 1 teaspoon oregano, dried
- 1 teaspoon basil, dried
- 1/2 tea salt
- 15 rice crackers, crushed
- water, to cover squash

Place cut up squash in large sauce pan and cover with water. Boil for 10 minutes. Drain off water and place back into sauce pan.
Preheat oven to 350 degrees.
In sauce pan with squash, add onion, almond cheese, spices, and salt. Place squash mixture in a greased 9" x 9" baking dish and sprinkle cracker crumbs over top. Bake at 350 degrees for 20 minutes. Serve hot.

If rice crackers are not available, use bread crumbs from 2 slices of rice bread.
Rice or soy cheese can be substituted for almond cheese.

Per serving: 279.7 Calories; 6.3g Fat (21.6% calories from fat); 12.6g Protein; 39.2g Carbohydrate; 0mg Cholesterol; 795mg Sodium

Spaghetti Squash   Day 2 C/E
Serves 4

- 1 large spaghetti squash
- water
- 1/2 teaspoon salt

Cut spaghetti squash in half lengthwise. Put about 3" of water in two large dutch ovens. Place squash cut side down in water. Boil on medium (uncovered) for 20 minutes. Do not let all the water evaporate. Remove squash and drain. Fluff flesh portion with fork and remove to plate. When handled gently, the strands will resemble spaghetti. The taste is a sweet alternative to pasta.

Per serving: 5.9 Calories; 0.1g Fat (14.2% calories from fat); 0.1g Protein; 1.2g Carbohydrate; 0mg Cholesterol; 270mg Sodium

Zucchini Patties
Serves 4

- 2 pounds zucchini, grated
- 1/2 cup onion, chopped
- 3 teaspoons egg replacer, =2 eggs
- 1 teaspoon salt
- 1/4 teaspoon pepper
- 1/4 teaspoon garlic salt
- 1/2 teaspoon marjoram, dried
- 1 cup rice flour
- 1/2 teaspoon baking soda
- 1/2 teaspoon cream of tartar
- 1/4 cup rice milk, or milk of the day
- 1 Tablespoon olive oil, or oil of the day

Grate zucchini and squeeze in a cloth towel to remove excess water. Place zucchini in a large bowl. Add onion, egg replacer, salt, pepper, garlic salt, marjoram, baking soda, cream of tartar, rice flour, and milk. Stir well until all ingredients are incorporated. Heat oil in non-stick skillet and drop about 1/4 cup batter in non-stick skillet. Cook until lightly brown around edges. Turn with spatula and cook on other side. Cook several at one time if there is room in the pan for easy turning.

Per serving: 540.8 Calories; 4.4g Fat (6.9% calories from fat); 5.1g Protein; 127.5g Carbohydrate; 0mg Cholesterol; 926mg Sodium

Food Allergies, What Do I Eat Now?

Appendix

Food Allergies, What Do I Eat Now?

Product List

The Pampered Chef™ - "The Kitchen Store That Comes To Your Door"™ - The Pampered Chef carries a complete line of superior kitchen and food preparation aids for busy cooks. Many items speed food preparation, such as the *Food Chopper*, and the *Apple Peeler/Corer/Slicer*. Other items that I have found invaluable are *The Family Heritage*™ *Stoneware Collection*. My baked goods turn out better when I use these stoneware products. They are perfect for cookies, crackers, biscuits, and pizza crusts.

A product that is especially tailored for people with food allergies is the *Kitchen Spritzer* – It is designed to spray oil and other liquids with a fine mist. This allows you to use oils of choice to spray cookie sheets and baking pans without the additives present in commercial cooking sprays. It also reduces the amount of oil you use in other types of food preparation. I use it to spray over baked homemade French fries before cooking. It is also useful to spray pasta with olive oil instead of "drizzling" with Tablespoons of oil.

Another of my children's favorites is the *Ice Shaver*. You can create sorbets, snow cones, and slush drinks in seconds by using frozen juice and fruits to shave with the *Ice Shaver*.

To contact The Pampered Chef representative in your area, call 1(800)-266-5562. All their products are guaranteed, and they do mean it! You can also get many items free by hosting a demonstration.

Food Allergies, What Do I Eat Now?

Food Product List

Annie's Wild Herbal Organics™
Foster Hill Road
North Calais, VT   05650

    A variety of organic salad dressings. Check label for ingredients that may effect you.

Arnaud's Sauce™
Arnaud's Food Co., Inc.
813 Bienville Street
New Orleans, LA 70112
(504) 523-5433

    Original Creole Remoulade-No wheat, corn, soy, eggs, dairy or tomato.

Arrowhead Mills, Inc.   phone # 1-806-364-0730
Box 2059
Hrerford, TX   79045-5802

    Flours, baking mixes, & soups

Barbara's Bakery, Inc.   phone # (707)-765-2273
3900 Cypress Drive
Petaluma, CA   94954-5694

    Line of cereals, & mashed potatoes

Big Chief Sugar™   phone # (517)-686-0161
Monitor Sugar, Co.
Att. Cher Beiser
P.O. Box 39
Bay City, MI 48707-0917

Internet address: http:\\www.monitorsugar.com
E-mail: bigchief@monitorsugar.com

    Beet sugar- pure beet sugar granulated (confectioner's sugar contains 3% wheat starch)   2- 5 lb. bags = $9.60, which includes S&H. Make check payable to Monitor Sugar Co.

Food Allergies, What Do I Eat Now?

Bob's Red Mill-Natural Foods, Inc.   phone # (503)-654-3215
5209 S.E. International Way
Milwaukie, OR 97222   For free catalogue

     Specializing in mail-order alternative foods. About half of the products listed contain wheat, corn, or soy. Read ingredients list for each item carefully.
     Many exotic bean flours, quinoa, amaranth, buckwheat, rice, millet, unsweetened coconut.
     Good assortment of books.

Ceres Fruit Juices (PTY) LTD.
Bon Chretien Street, Ceres.
South Africa

     Medley of fruit juices- mango, papaya, guava, pineapple, & passion fruit. Great for freezing for Italian Ice.

Conrad Rice Mill, Inc.   (318)-364-7242
307 Ann Street
New Iberia, LA 70560-4719

     Rice crackers & bran products

Chef Paul Prudhomme's® Magic Seasoning Blends   phone # (504)-731-3590
842 Distributors Row
P.O. Box 23342
New Orleans, LA 70183-0342

Internet address http://www.chefpaul.com   E-mail info@chefpaul.com

     An extensive line of all-natural spice blends for cooking Cajun style foods. All of Chef Paul's seasoning mixes contain no MSG, no additives, & no preservatives.
     Most contain no sugar- just natural spices. Read labels carefully.

Chicago Dietetic Supply, Inc.

     Featherweight baking powder (cereal-free)

Debole's Rice Pasta   phone # 1-800-749-0730
Debole's Nutritional Foods
Arrowhead Mills, Inc.
P.O. Box 2059
Hereford, TX 79045-2059

Earth's Best, Inc. phone # 1-800-442-4221
Boulder, CO 80301

    Organic baby foods, no sugar, salt-fillers, preservatives.

Edward & Sons Trading Co., Inc.
P.O. Box 1326
Carpinteria, CA 93014

    Brown Rice Snaps- crackers

Ener-G Foods, Inc. phone # 1-800-331-5222
P.O. Box 84487
Seattle, WA 98124-5787

Internet address: www.ener-g.com

    Ener-G Foods, Inc. products can be found in all health food stores and some large grocery stores. They have a complete line of flours & baking mixes, as well as egg replacement products (egg-free). They also provide a line of wheat- free baked products, including breads, buns, cakes, cookies, and snacks. Rice pastas, soup mixes, cereals, and books on allergies.

Enrico's
Ventre Packing Co., Inc.
Syracuse, NY 13206

    Ketchup, bean dips, salsa, all natural, no sugars, preservatives, artificial flavors, additives, or fillers.

Fantastic Foods, Inc. phone # (707)-778-7801
1250 N. McDowell Blvd
Petaluma, CA 94954-1113

    Hummus

Food For Life Baking Co., Inc.
2991 E. Doherty Street
Corona, CA 91719

Frontier™ Natural Flavors   phone # 1-800-669-3275
Frontier Co-op
Box 299
Norway, IA   52318

Internet address: www.frontiercoop.com

    Alcohol-free flavors contain glycerin & oils

Galaxy Foods Company   phone # (800)-808-2325
2441 Viscount Row
Orlando, FL   32809

Internet address: http://www.galaxyfoods.com

Gerhard's
Napa Valley Sausage Co.
Napa Valley, CA   94558

Health Valley Co, Inc.   phone # 1-800-432-4846
16100 Foothill Blvd.
Irwindale, CA   91706-7811

    A variety of cereals & snacks- a crispy rice bar made without wheat, corn, or oats. Sweetened with fruit & rice syrup.

Imagine Foods, Inc.
350 Cambridge Ave, Suite 350
Palo Alto, CA   94306

Internet address: info@imaginefoods.com

    Rice milks, creamy puddings, & delicious soups.

Jennie's® coconut macaroons   phone # (718)-384-2150
Red Mill Farms®, Inc.
290 S. 5th Street
Brooklyn, NY. 11211-6214

    Macaroon cookies sweetened with honey, contains egg white

The Kroger Company phone # (800) 632-6900
Cincinnati, OH 45202

Growing health foods departments with personnel willing to assist with special orders. Many products made by Kroger are acceptable to special dietary needs. Jams and jellies sweetened with fruit juices, and sauerkraut without vinegar for example.

McCutcheon Apple Products, Inc.
Historic Frederick, MD 21701

Apple butter sweetened with fruit juice.

Mystic Lake Dairy™
Mystic Lake Dairy, Inc.
24200 N.E. 14th St.
Redmond, WA 98053

100% Fruit sweetener, made with pineapple syrup, with pear and peach concentrate without preservatives.

New England Cranberry Co. phone # (617)-237-2892
4 Bishop Street
Framingham, MA. 01701

Dried cranberries

Organic Baby™
United Natural foods
P.O. Box 999
260 Lake Road
Dayville, CT 06241-1537

20 varieties with no salt, sugar, fillers, or preservatives

Pacific Foods of Oregon, Inc. phone # 1-503-692-9666
19480 S.W. 97th Ave.
Tualatin, OR 97062

Chicken Broth (Free-range Chickens), vegetable broth, almond milk, vanilla flavored almond milk, and other non-dairy beverages.

Perdue Farms Incorporated
P.O.Box 1655
Horsham, PA 19044-6655
E-mail www.perdue.com

    Quality poultry products without hormones, feeding grains free of pesticides and comtaminants to flocks.

Quinoa Corporation
P.O. Box 1039
Torrance, CA 90505

    Quinoa grain and meal (flour).

Rice Innovations, Inc.
Pickering Postal Station
P.O. Box 16
Pickering, Ontario
Canada Liv 2R2

    Pastariso- One of the best rice pastas, all shapes and sizes.

Season's Enterprises, Ltd.
P.O. Box 965
Addison, IL 60101-0965

    Michael Season's Potato Chips- Flavor variety no corn oil or soybean oil used.

Stretch Island Fruit, Inc.
Grapeview, WA 98546

    Fruit Leathers in a variety of fruits. Grape, apple, cherry, strawberry, tropical fruit, raspberry, apricot, etc (less expensive than making it in the dehydrator).

Thai Kitchen
Epicurean International, Inc.
P.O. Box 13242
Berkeley, CA 94712-4242

Internet address: www.thaikitchen.com
E-mail: info@thaikitchen.com

    Pure coconut milk "lite" no additives or preservatives

Food Allergies, What Do I Eat Now?

Trademark List

Ritalin™

Imitrex™

Kamut™

Spelt™

NutQuik™

Rice Slice™

Rice Dream™

Crisco™

Jolly Joan Egg Replacer™ by EnerG

Egg Replacer™ by EnerG

Egg White Replacer™ by EnerG

Egg Beater™

Mystic Lake Dairy Sweetener™

Ovaltine™

Imagine™ - puddings, broths, and soups

Postum™

Bibliography

Braly, James, M.D. <u>Dr. Braly's Food Allergy and Nutrition Revolution.</u> New Canaan, Connecticut: Keats Publishing, Inc. 1992.

Brostoff, Johathan. <u>Food Allergies and Intolerances.</u> Philadelphia, PA: Butler and Tanner, Ltd.

Carper, Jean. <u>Food - Your Miracle Medicine.</u> New York: Harper Perennial 1993.

Cataldo, Corinne Balog; Rolfes, Sharon Rady; Whitney, Eleanor Noss. <u>Understanding Clinical Nutrition.</u> st. Paul, MN: West Publishing Company. 1991.

Crook, William G., M.D. <u>Detecting Your Hidden Food Allergies.</u> Jackson, TN: Professional Books. 1988.

Crook, William G., M.D. <u>The Yeast Connection.</u> Jackson, TN: Professional Books. 1988.

Dixon, Hamilton S., M.D.; Trevino, Richard J., M.D., F.A.C.S., <u>Food Allergy.</u> New York: Theini. 1997.

Dorfman, Kelly, M.S., L.N. "Improving Cognitive Functioning with Nutrient Therapy," <u>New Developments</u>, Vol. 3, No. 2, Fall 1997. Published by the Developmental Delay Registry.

Dorfman, Kelly, M.S., L.N. "Improving Detoxification Pathways," <u>New Developments</u>, Vol. 2, No. 3, Published by Developmental Delay Registry.

Gaby, Alan R., M.D. "Preventing and Treating Ear Infections," <u>New Developments,</u> Vol. 3, No. 2, Fall 1997. Published by the Developmental Delay Registry.

Gates, Donna. "The Body Ecology," <u>World Health News,</u> Vol 2, No. 1, Winter 1998. World Health News, Inc.

Gioannini, Marilyn. <u>The Complete Food Allergy Cookbook.</u> Rocklin, CA: Prima Publishing. 1996

Gilman-Lacy, Janice; Kaufman, Peter B. <u>Botany Illustrated-Introduction to Plants.</u> New York; Van Nostrand Reinhold. 1984.

Hagman, Bette. More From the Gluten-Free Gourmet. New York: Henry Holt and Company. 1993.

Johns, Stephanie Bernardo. The Allergy Guide to Brand-Name Foods and Food Additives. New York: New American Library, A Plum Book. 1988.

Mansfield, John, (Dr.). Arthritis, the Allergy Connection. Wellingborough, England: Thorsons Publishing Group. 1990.

The Merck Manual, Merck and Co., Inc., 3rd printing of 15th edition. New Jersey: Rahway, 1989.

Moore, David M. ed., The Marshall Cavendish Illustrated Encyclopedia of Plants and Earth Sciences. New York: Marshall Cavendish.

Randolph, Theron G., M.D.; Moss, Ralph W., Ph.D. An Alternative Approach to Allergies. New York; Harper and Row, Publishers. 1989.

Rea, William J. "Chemical Sensitivity," Vol. 1. Boca Raton, FL: Lewis Publishers, 1992.

Rowe, Katherine S., B.A., M.Sc. "Synthetic Food Coloring and Behavior: A dose response effect in a double blind, placebo-controlled, repeated-measures study." The Journal of Pediatrics, November, 1994.

Sheinkin, David, M.D.; Schlacter, Michail, M.D., Hutton, Richard. The Food Connection-How the Things You Eat Affect the Way You Feel-And What You Can Do About It. New York: The Bobbs-Merrill Company, Inc. 1979.

Taylor, John. Helping Your Hyperactive/ADD Child. Rocklin, CA: Prima Publishing.

Went, Frits W. The Plants. New York: Time-Life Books. 1969.

Food Allergies, What Do I Eat Now?

Allergen, 20
Allergic responses, 42
Amaranth, **24**
Antibodies, 42
Antigen, 42
Appendix, 457
Appetizers and Dips, 107
    Apricot Dipping Sauce C/E, 108
    Avocado Dip/Salsa, 114
    Avocado Quesadillas, 118
    Black Bean Salsa, 115
    "Cheese" Straws and Crackers, 119
    Cranberry Dipping Sauce, 109
    Cucumber Rounds with "Cheese" and Dill, 111
    Dill Dip, 116
    Herbed Savory Bread, 120
    Honey Mustard Dip, 110
    Hot Wing Dip, 111
    Humus and "Bacon" Spread, 117
    Humus Dip, 117
    Mini Pizzas, 121
    Mustard Dip Day 5, 110
    Orange Dipping Sauce, 108
    Quinoa Chips C/E, 122
    Quinoa Rounds (crackers) C/E, 123
    Raspberry Dipping Sauce, 108
    Sesame Amaranth Crackers Day 3, 124
    Shrimp Butter, 113
    Spicy Chicken Wings, 112
    Spicy Humus, 117
Arrowroot, 25
Arthritis, 17
  Caffeine, 18
  Milk, 18
Baking powder/soda, 21, 36
Beverages, 125
    Almond Tea, 128
    Banana Shake, 133
    Cranberry Delight C/E, 132
    Frostee, 134
    Fruit Punch, 130
    Fruited Ice Ring For Punch, 131
    Hot Cocoa, 127
    Lemonade, 129
    Mango Smooth Day 1, 135
    Mulled Cranberry-Apple Cider, 126
    Peach Float Punch, 136
    Peach Strawberry Freeze Day 2, 135
    Pina Colada Shake, 134
    Raspberry Chill Day 2 C/E, 137
    Red, White, and Blue Freeze Day 5 C/E, 138
    Russian Tea, 127
    Sunny Shake Day 3, 137
    Tropical Delight Shake Day 4, 138
Breads and Baked Goods, 139
  Introduction to, 140
  Recipes, 143
    Almond Poppyseed Muffins, 157
    Amaranth Bread Day 3, 146
    Apple-Almond Buckwheat Muffins Day 2, 154
    Banana Nut Bread, 147
    Bean Bread, 148
    Blackeyed Pea Bread, 149
    Blueberry Rice Muffins Day 5 C/E, 159
    Brown Rice Flour Bread, 145
    Burger Bun, 160
    Carrot Coconut Muffins, 156

Breads and Baked Goods, continued
    Cranberry Rice Muffins Day 5 C/E, 158
    Crumble Biscuits, 161
    Dumplings, 162
    Flatbread Medallions, 163
    Focaccia, 164
    Granola Muffins with Raisins, 155
    Individual Pizza Crusts, 165
    Oat Muffins With Cashews Day 1, 153
    Pizza Crust, 166
    Pumpkin Bread, 150
    Pumpkin Quick Bread C/E, 151
    Quinoa Bread (Mock Cornbread) C/E, 144
    Quinoa Tortillas C/E, 167
    Raisin Oat Muffins Day 1, 152
    Rice Potato Bread, 143
    Soft Shell Taco Roll-up, 168
Breakfast Foods, 169
    Banana Nut Pancakes, 179
    Blackberry Syrup Day 2 C/E, 171
    Blueberry Syrup Day 5 C/E, 173
    Breakfast Granola, 181
    Breakfast Rice Day 5 C/E, 183
    Buckwheat Pancakes, 177
    Citrus Sauce Day 3, 172
    Company Waffles C/E, 180
    Cranberry Syrup Day 5 C/E, 173
    Drop Biscuits C/E, 184
    Hazelnut Pancakes with Citrus
        Sauce Day 3 C/E, 176
    Mango Syrup, 170
    Maple Raisin Syrup Day 1, 170
    Oat Granola With Raisins and Sunflower
        Seeds Day 1 C/E, 182
    Oat Pancakes With Maple
        Syrup Day 1 C/E, 175
    Pancakes C/E, 174
    Pecan Pancakes, 178
    Prudy's Turkey Breakfast Sausage, 186
    Raspberry Syrup Day 2, 171
    Stir Fry Breakfast Medley, 185
    Tropical Syrup, 172
Buckwheat, **25**
Campfire Cooking, 187
    Alternate Fruit and Nut Mix Day 2 C/E, 189
    Best Trail Mix C/E, 188
    Breakfast Taco, 204
    Burger Pouch, 203
    Cajun Jerky, 196
    Chicken Pouch, 203
    Dried Cinnamon Apples, 195
    Dried Cranberries C/E, 192
    Dried Honey Carrots, 194
    Dried Mushroom Soup, 197
    Dried Mushrooms, 193
    Dried Sweet Potatoes C/E, 192
    Dried Trail Soup Mix, 198
    Dry Fruit and Nut Mix Day 5 C/E, 190
    Dry Fruit and Nut Mix Day 4 C/E, 189
    Dry Fruit and Nut Mix Day 3 C/E, 190
    Dry Fruit and Nut Mix Day 2 C/E, 190
    Dry Fruit and Nut Mix Day 1 C/E, 189
    Fresh Fish Pouch, 202
    Grill Top Potato Medley, 200
    Honey Banana Chips, 191
    Jerky and Rice Soup, 199
    Sombrero Bundles, 201

Food Allergies, What Do I Eat Now?

"C/E", Cleansing/Elimination Recipes
- Alternate Nut and Fruit Mix, Day 2 C/E, 189
- Apricot Dipping Sauce C/E, 108
- Asparagus Soup C/E, 431
- Baked Pears C/E, 241
- Baked Sweet Potatoes Day 5 C/E, 437
- Basic Tapioca C/E, 208
- Basil Pesto C/E, 394
- Best Trail Mix C/E, 188
- Blackberry Syrup Day 2 C/E, 171
- Blueberry Cobbler Day 5 C/E, 253
- Blueberry Rice Muffins Day 5 C/E, 159
- Blueberry Syrup Day 5 C/E, 173
- Braised Celery C/E, 450
- Brazil Nut Risotto Day 5 C/E, 447
- Breakfast Rice Day 5 C/E, 183
- Broccoli Soup Day 5 C/E, 430
- Chinese Apple-Pork C/E, 359
- Company Waffles C/E, 180
- Cranberry Delight C/E, 132
- Cranberry Rice Muffins Day 5 C/E, 158
- Cranberry Syrup Day 5 C/E, 173
- Crunchy Topping for Cobblers Day 5 C/E, 256
- Dried Cranberries C/E, 192
- Dried Sweet Potatoes C/E, 192
- Drop Biscuits C/E, 184
- Dry Fruit and Nut Mix Day 5 C/E, 190
- Dry Fruit and Nut Mix Day 2 C/E, 189
- Dry Fruit and Nut Mix Day 3 C/E, 190
- Dry Fruit and Nut Mix Day 4 C/E, 190
- Dry Fruit and Nut Mix Day 1 C/E, 189
- Fresh Scallops Almondine C/E, 375
- Hazelnut Pancakes with Citrus Sauce Day 3 C/E, 176
- Honeyed Carrots C/E, 442
- Lemon and Chives Fish Fillet Day 3 C/E, 378
- Lemon Chicken C/E, 324
- Mandarin Orange Salad C/E, 276
- Maple Glazed Pork Tenderloin C/E, 358
- Maple Glazed Quail C/E, 334
- Melon Cup Day 2 C/E, 299
- Oat Granola with Raisins and Sunflower Seeds Day 1 C/E, 182
- Oat Pancakes with Maple Syrup Day 1 C/E, 175
- Old Fashioned "Milk" Gravy C/E, 398
- Pan Fried Trout C/E, 382
- Pancakes C/E, 174
- Pasta Florentine C/E, 366
- Peach Crisp C/E, 258
- Pumpkin Pie Filling Day 2 C/E, 251
- Pumpkin Quick Bread C/E, 151
- Quinoa Bread (Mock Cornbread) C/E, 144
- Quinoa Chips C/E, 122
- Quinoa Rounds (crackers) C/E, 123
- Quinoa Tortillas C/E, 167
- Raspberry Chill Day 2 C/E, 137
- Raspberry Dipping Sauce C/E, 108
- Raspberry Dressing C/E, 276
- Red, White and Blue Freeze Day 5 C/E, 138
- Salmon Croquettes C/E (Baked or Fried), 386
- Salmon Salad C/E, 272
- Salmon With Dill Day 3 C/E, 385
- Savory Rosemary Game Birds C/E, 335
- Sesame Asparagus C/E Day 3, 439
- Shrimp Salad with Dill C/E, 273
- Smoked Catfish Fillets C/E, 377

"C/E", continued
- Spaghetti Squash Day 2 C/E, 454
- Spinach Salad With Chickpeas Day 4 C/E, 283
- Stuffed Zucchini Squash Day 2 C/E, 452
- Sweet Potato Bake With Cranberries Day 5 C/E, 438
- Tuna Salad C/E, 274
- Turkey Cabbage Soup Day 5 C/E, 413
- Turkey Cutlet With Gravy C/E, 308
- Turkey Rice Soup Day 5 C/E, 416
- Wilted Spinach C/E, 443

Celiac disease, **17**
Challenge testing, **44**
Children, 48
- Additives and preservatives, 48
- Attention defecit, 52, 53
- Babies, 50
- Behavioral problems, 49
- Breast feeding, 50
- Convenience foods, 48
- Cows' milk, 51
- Delayed reaction, 50
- Diaper rash, 51
- Feingold Association, 52
- Food diary, 49, 50
- Food sensitivities, 48
- Formula, 51
- Headaches, 49
- Hyperactivity, 52
- Impulsive behavior, 52
- IgE, IgG, 53
- Inattention, 52
- Nutritional deficiencies, 53
- Pediatric resource guide, 54, 55
- Ritalin™, 48, 52

Cleansing/Elimination, 43, **56**
- Additives, 56
- Alcohol, 56
- Allergens, 56, 57
- "C/E", **58**
- Caffeine, 56
- Fasting, 57
- Few foods diet, 57
- Five day rotation plan, 58
- Food cleansing choices, 59
- Fruits, 59
- Grains and seeds, 59
- Industrial toxins, 56
- Milk substitute, 60
- Narcotics, 56
- Nicotine, 56
- Nuts, 59
- Oils, 59
- Protein, 59
- Rare foods diet, 57
- Sweeteners, 60
- Toxins, 56
- Vegetables, 59

Cookbook
- Introduction, 104
  - Additives, 104
  - "C/E", 104
  - Preservatives, 104

Corn, **31**
- Gluten, 31
- Foods containing, 31

Corn, continued

Food Allergies, What Do I Eat Now?

Aspartame/corn, 32
Delayed/masked reactions, 42
Desserts, 205
    Any Berry Cobbler, 252
    Applesauce Cake, 225
    Baked Apples, 239
    Baked Pears C/E, 241
    Banana Boats, 240
    Basic Sugar Cookies, 211
    Basic Tapioca C/E, 208
    Black Cherry Sherbert, 259
    Blueberry Cobbler Day 5 C/E, 253
    Boiled Cookies, 212
    Bread Pudding, 206
    Brown Honey Cake, 227
    Chocolate Nut Bars, 221
    Chocolate Rice Milk Ice Cream, 261
    Coconut Cream Pie Filling, 246
    Coconut Frosting, 229
    Coconut Pie Crust Day 3, 245
    Coconut Snowballs, 218
    Crunchy Amaranth Cobbler Topping Day 3, 255
    Crunchy Cobbler Topping Day 1, 254
    Crunchy Topping for Cobblers Day 5 C/E, 256
    Deep Dish Blueberry Pie, 249
    Dutch Pear Pie Filling, 247
    Fresh Apple Cake, 226
    German Chocolate Cake, 228
    Ginger Cookies Day 3, 217
    Golden Pound Cake, 232
    Granola Oat Cookies, 216
    Hazelnut Cake, 235
    Heavenly Chocolate Frosting, 231
    Heavenly Chocolate Fudge Brownie Cake, 230
    Homemade Chocolate Chips, 210
    Lemon Ice Day 3, 264
    Lemon Lime Sherbert, 264
    Mocha Rice Milk Ice Cream, 263
    Oat Pie Crust, 243
    Oat Squares, 224
    Old Fashion Apple Pie, 248
    Orange Cake, 233
    Orange Filled Crepes, 209
    Orange Sherbert, 259
    Peach Crisp C/E, 258
    Peaches and Cream Rice Milk Ice Cream, 260
    Peanut Butter Cookies, 219
    Pecan Cake, 234
    Pecan Pie Filling, 250
    Pineapple Upside-Down Cake, 237
    Plain Pastry, 242
    Pumpkin Cookies, 215
    Pumpkin Pie Filling Day 2 C/E, 251
    Pumpkin Rice Milk Ice Cream, 262
    Raisin Peanut Butter Bars or Cookies, 220
    Raspberry Cake with Sauce, 236
    Rice Coconut Pie Crust, 244
    Rice Fruit Bars Day 5, 222
    Rice Granola Bars Day 5, 223
    Rice Pecan Cookies, 214
    Rice Pudding Day 5, 207
    Southern Pecan Cookies, 213
    Strawberry Banana Sherbert, 259
    Strawberry Dessert, 238
    Strawberry Rhubarb Cobbler, 257

Dressings,
    See Fruits, Salads, and Dressings, 265
Eating away, 87
    Air travel, 89
    Auto travel, 90
    Camping, 90
    Fast foods, 90
    Food sensitivities, 87
    Helpful tips, 91, 92
    Recreation, 90
    Restaurant foods, 87 – 89
    Vacation, 90
Eczema, 5, 9, 17
    Milk, 18, 27
Elimination diet, 6
Eggs, **36**
    Products containing, 37
    MMR Vaccine, 37
    Substitute for, 36
    Egg Replacer™, 36
Entrees,
    See Main Dishes and Entrees, 305
Fast Food, 10
Fibromyalgia, 6, 10, **16**
Five day rotation plan, **70**
    Day one, 72 – 74
    Day two, 75 – 77
    Day three, 78 – 80
    Day four, 81 – 83
    Day five, 84 - 86
Flours
    Amaranth, **24**
    Buckwheat, **25**
    Exotic flours, **26**
    Millet flour, **26**
    Potato starch flour, **25**
    Quinoa flour, **25**
    Rice flour, **24**
    Soybean flour, **26**
    Tapioca flour, **25**
FDA,
    Food and drug administration, 20
Food additives, 20 - 22
Food allergy, 13, **15**
Food Classifications, 61
    Amaranth, 67
    Apple, 63
    Arum, 66
    Arrowroot, 64
    Banana, 64
    Bean and Pea, 62
    Berry, 63
    Birch, 65
    Brazil nut, 67
    Buckwheat, 63
    Cabbage/mustard, 62
    Cactus, 67
    Carrot, 62
    Cashew, 64
    Chestnut, 67
    Chocolate, 67
    Citrus, 63
    Coffee, 67
    Cucumber, 63
    Currant, 64
    Daisy, 63

Food Allergies, What Do I Eat Now?

Food Classifications, continued
  Date, 64
  Fish/shellfish, 69
  Flax, 67
  Fungi, 66
  Ginger, 64
  Grape, 64
  Grass, 62
  Heath, 65
  Kiwi, 66
  Laurel, 65
  Lily, 63
  Macadamia, 66
  Mallow, 65
  Maple, 66
  Meats, 68
  Mint, 65
  Morning Glory, 65
  Mulberry, 64
  Myrtle, 65
  Nightshade, 62
  Nutmeg, 66
  Olive, 66
  Palm, 64
  Papaya, 67
  Passion fruit, 67
  Peppercorn, 66
  Persimmon, 67
  Pine, 65
  Pineapple, 66
  Plum, 63
  Poppyseed, 67
  Poultry/eggs, 68
  Saffron/iris/crocus, 67
  Sesame, 66
  Seaweed, 68
  Spinach, 63
  Spurge, 66
  Tea, 65
  Vanilla, 66
  Walnut, 64
  Waterchestnut, 67
  Yams, true, 67
Food diary, 43, **45**, 46
  Sample diary, 47
Food intolerance, 13
Food product list, 459
Food starch, 20
Food sensitivity, 13
Fruits, Salads, and Dressings, 265
  Ambrosia Day 3, 304
  Black Bean Quinoa Salad, 292
  Carrot-Raisin Salad, 291
  Cherry Apple Sauce Day 2, 303
  Chicken Cashew Salad Day 1, 266
  Chicken Salad Day 1, 266
  Chinese Salad Dressing, 277
  Company Chicken Salad, 268
  Cool Cucumber Salad, 290
  Dirty Potato Salad, 287
  Donna's Coleslaw, 289
  Flavored Oils, 282
  Fruit of the Day Salad Day 4, 302
  Fruited Vinegars, 281
  Grape Mango Salad Day 1, 301
  Hawaiian Fruit Salad, 300
  Herbed Vinegars, 280

Fruits, Salads, and Dressings, continued
  Honey Carrot Raisin Salad, 288
  Honey Mustard Dressing, 279
  Hot German Potato Salad, 286
  Italian Dressing, 278
  Mandarin Orange Salad C/E, 276
  Melon Cup Day 2 C/E, 299
  Microwave Baked Apples, 298
  Mustard Potato Salad, 285
  Pasta Salad, 295
  Prudy's Chicken Salad, 267
  Raspberry Dressing C/E, 276
  Rice Salad, 294
  Rice-Black Bean Salad, 293
  Rice-Broccoli-Turkey Salad Day 5, 271
  Salmon Salad C/E, 272
  Savory Croutons, 275
  Seven Layer Salad, 284
  Shrimp Salad With Dill C/E, 273
  Spinach Salad With Chickpeas Day 4 C/E, 283
  Tuna Salad C/E, 274
  Turkey Taco Salad, 269
  Turkey-Rice-Cranberry Salad Day 5, 270
  Waldorf Salad, 297
  Zucchini Relish, 296
Gluten, 18
Gluten intolerance, **14**
Headaches, 6, 27
Hectic lives, tips, 98
Indirect food additives, **20**
Immune system, 42
Joint pain, 6
Lunches, 93
  Lunch menus,
    Day one, 95
    Day two, 95
    Day three, 96
    Day four, 96
    Day five, 97
Main Dishes and Entrees, 305
  Aloha Burger, 337
  Apple Glazed Pork Roast, 360
  Avocado-Cucumber Gyro Day 2, 365
  Baked Chicken Crunch, 314
  Baked Chicken Oriental Chicken, 315
  Bar-B-Q Cornish Hens, 331
  BBQ Pork, 353
  Beef and Cheddar Pasta, 340
  Beef Burgers Day 2, 338
  Beef Strips With Pesto "Pasta" Day 2, 341
  Best Beef Burgers, 339
  Best Turkey Burgers, 313
  Cashew Chicken Day 1, 317
  Chicken Artichoke Casserole Day 1, 316
  Chicken Oriental Kabobs, 318
  Chicken Pizza, 319
  Chicken Stew with Biscuit Tops, 320
  Chinese Apple-Pork C/E, 359
  Coconut Meatballs, 342
  Coconut Shrimp n' Orange Sauce, 374
  Continental Chicken, 321
  Crock Pot Pork Roast, 361
  Dirty Rice, 312
  Fresh Scallops Almondine C/E, 375
  Garlic Shrimp, 370
  Ginger Fish Fillets, 380

Food Allergies, What Do I Eat Now?

Main Dishes and Entrees, continued
    Grilled Chicken and Vegetables with
        Tarragon Day 1, 322
    Grilled Sausages and Vegetables, 311
    Hamburger Stew, 343
    Jamaican Grilled Fish Fillet, 379
    Jambalaya, 376
    Layered Chicken-Zucchini Casserole, 323
    Lemon and Chives Fish Fillet, 378
    Lemon Chicken C/E, 324
    Lemon Shrimp, 371
    Maple Glazed Pork Tenderloin C/E, 358
    Maple Glazed Quail C/E, 334
    Marinated Pork Chops, 357
    Meatballs, 344
    Meatloaf, 310
    Mexican Meat Lovers Pizza, 346
    Oven Chicken Casserole, 325
    Pan Fried Trout C/E, 382
    Pasta Florentine C/E, 366
    Pecan Trout, 381
    Pesto Chicken and Pasta, 326
    Pigs in a Blanket-Stuffed
        Cabbage with Tomato, 363
    Pineapple Pork Loin (with quinoa), 356
    Pork n' Baked Beans, 355
    Pork Sausage, 354
    Portobello Chicken, 327
    Quick Turkey Noodle Day 5, 309
    Roasted Duck With Wild Rice Day 5, 336
    Rubbed Pork Tenderloin, 351
    Rubbed Ribs, 352
    Salmon Croquettes C/E (Baked or Fried), 386
    Salmon with Dill Day 3 C/E, 385
    Savory Meatballs, 328
    Savory Rosemary Game Birds C/E, 335
    Shredded Pork Fahitas, 362
    Shrimp In Saffron Sauce, 373
    Smoked Catfish Fillets, 377
    Smoked Shrimp with Pasta, 372
    Spaghetti Sauce With Meat, 347
    Spicy Meatballs, 345
    Stuffed Peppers with Currants, 348
    Sundried Tomato Chicken, 329
    Sunny Chicken Strips Day 1, 332
    Taco Meat, 349
    Tahitian Chicken, 333
    Tarragon Chicken Casserole, 330
    Tex-Mex Kabobs, 350
    Tex-Mex Tuna Steak, 384
    Tomatoless Stuffed Cabbage, 364
    Tuna Skillet, 383
    Turkey Cutlet Italiano Day 5, 307
    Turkey Cutlet With Gravy C/E, 308
    Turkey Tacos, 306
    Vegetarian Lasagna, 367
    Veggie Burger, 368
    Wheat-Corn Free Dressing, 369
Migraine, 10, **18**, 19
  Vascular headache, 18
  Imitrex™, 10
  Nausea/vomiting, 18
Milk, **27**
  Breast feeding, 27
  Calcium, 27
  Electrolyte imbalance, 28
  Gastrointestinal distress, 27

Milk, continued
  Lactose, 27
    Intolerances, 27
  Nausea/vomiting, 27
  Pregnancy, 27
  Skin reactions
    Eczema, 27
    Itching, 27
  Milk alternatives, 28
    Nut, 28
    Rice, 28
    Soy, 28
Milk,
  Foods containing, 28
Milk Reactions, 27
    Congestion, 27
    Cough, 27
    Eczema, 27
    Fatigue, 27
    Headache, 27
    Irritability, 27
    Otitis media, 27
    Runny nose, 27
    Sluggish feeling, 27
    Thickened mucus, 27
    Watery eyes, 27
Milk substitution, 29
Millet, **26**
MSG, 22
  Monosodium glutamate, 22
Nightshades, 17
Nutritional values, 106
Potato starch flour, 25
Product list, 458
Quinoa flour, **25**
Reaction time, **17**
    Type I – immediate, 17
    Type II – cytotoxicity, 17
    Type III – immune complex, 17
    Type IV – delayed sensitivity, 17
Rice, **24**
Salads,
  See Fruits, Salads and Dressings, 265
Sauces, 387
    Bar-B-Que Sauce, 392
    Basic White Sauce, 400
    Basil Pesto C/E, 394
    Brown Steaksauce, 390
    Cactus Salsa (Tomatoless), 391
    Cranberry Sauce, 402
    Dilled Mayonnaise, 389
    Gravy From Drippings, 399
    Herbed Mayonnaise, 389
    Homemade Mayonnaise, 388
    Meatless Spaghetti Sauce, 396
    Mustard n' Spice Bar-B-Que Sauce, 393
    Old Fashioned "Milk" Gravy C/E, 398
    Sinful Pecan Sauce, 401
    Sundried Tomato Paste Day 1, 395
    Sweet Mustard Sauce, 391
    Tomatoless Pasta Sauce, 397
School lunch programs, 13
Self test, 11
Self test responses, 44
  Gastrointestinal distress, 44
  Headaches, 44
  Irritability, 44

Self test responses, continued
  Lack of energy, 44
  Shakiness, 44
Signs and symptoms, **15**
  Cardiac symptoms, 16
  Gastrointestinal, 16
  General symptoms, 16
  Mood alterations, 16
  Musculo-skeletal, 16
  Respiratory, 16
  Skin conditions, 16
Soups, 403
      Asparagus Soup C/E, 431
      Beefy Tomato Soup, 418
      Broccoli Soup Day 5 C/E, 430
      Chicken Potato Chowder Day 1, 409
      Chicken Rice Soup, 410
      Chicken Soup With Spinach, 411
      Chicken Tomato Soup Day 1, 412
      French Onion Soup Day 3, 429
      Golden Mushroom Soup, 428
      Italian White Bean and
           Savory Meatball Soup, 414
      Pork Sausage Soup, 404
      Potato "Bacon" Soup, 405
      Potato Leek Soup, 427
      Potato Soup, 426
      Prudy's Chicken Rice Soup, 408
      Rice Noodle Soup, 407
      Salmon Gumbo, 420
      Smoked Tenderloin and Bean Soup Day 4, 406
      Split Pea Soup, 425
      Squash Soup Day 2, 424
      Sweet Potato Soup Day 5, 423
      Tomato Basil Soup, 422
      Turkey Cabbage Soup Day 5 C/E, 413
      Turkey Noodle Soup, 415
      Turkey Rice Soup Day 5 C/E, 416
      Vegetable Meatball Soup, 417
      Vegetarian Bean Soup Day 4, 421
      White Chili, 419
Soy, **34**
  Foods containing, 34
  Soy flour, 26
  Substition for, 35
Sugar, **38**
  Forms of, 38, 39
  Products containing, 39
  Substitute for, 40
Tapioca flour, **25**
Testing, **41**
  IgE, IgG, 42
  RAST, 41
  Self test, 43, 44
  Skin test, 43
    False negative, 43
Vegetables, 432
      Baked Potato Skins, 433
      Baked Squash Casserole, 453
      Baked Sweet Potatoes Day 5 C/E, 437
      Braised Celery C/E, 450
      Brazil Nut Risotto Day 5 C/E, 447
      Broiled Tomatoes, 440
      Green Bean Stir-Fry, 441
      Grilled Portobello Mushrooms, 448
      Honeyed Carrots C/E, 442
      Mashed Potatoes Day 1, 436

Vegetables, continued
      Mushroom Macaroni Casserole, 449
      Potato Cakes, 435
      Quinoa Pilaf, 445
      Ratatouille, 451
      Rice Pilaf, 444
      Sesame Asparagus Day 3 C/E, 439
      Spaghetti Squash Day 2 C/E, 454
      Spanish Rice, 446
      Stuffed Zucchini Squash Day 2 C/E, 452
      Sweet Potato Bake With
           Cranberries Day 5 C/E, 438
      Twice Baked Potatoes, 434
      Wilted Spinach C/E, 433
      Zucchini Patties, 435
Weight loss, 6
Wheat, 21, **23**
  Barley, 21, **24**
  Celiac sprue, 21
  Gastrointestinal distress, 21
  Gluten, 21
  Kamut, 21, **23**
  Oat, 21, **24**
  Rye, 21, **24**
  Spelt, 21, **23**
  Teff, 21, **23**
  Triticali, 21, **23**
Wheat free flours, **21**
Wheat products, 22

Order Form

Food Allergies, What Do I Eat Now?
Coping and Cooking Day to Day

To order, mail check or money order in the amount of $49.95 for each book requested. Georgia residents add 6% sales tax. Add $4.00 shipping and handling for each book. Please complete the shipping form below. Please include a phone number in case we have questions about your order.

Ship to:

Company Name _____

Name _____

Address _____

City _____ State _____ Zip _____ -- _____

Telephone _____

Number of copies _____ @ $49.95 each = _____

Georgia residents sales tax 6% = _____

Shipping and handling add $4.00 each book _____

Total _____

Please make check payable to:

Food Allergy Solutions, Inc.

Mail all requests with check or money order to the following address.

Attn: Mail Orders

Food Allergy Solutions, Inc.,

2995 Johnson Ferry Road, Suite 250-802

Marietta, GA 30062

We also may be reached by e-mail:
food_allergy_solutions@yahoo.com

Order Form

Food Allergies, What Do I Eat Now?
Coping and Cooking Day to Day

To order, mail check or money order in the amount of $49.95 for each book requested. Georgia residents add 6% sales tax. Add $4.00 shipping and handling for each book. Please complete the shipping form below. Please include a phone number in case we have questions about your order.

Ship to:
Company Name _____
Name _____
Address _____
City _____ State _____ Zip _____--_____
Telephone _____

    Number of copies _____ @ $49.95 each = _____
    Georgia residents sales tax 6% = _____
    Shipping and handling add $4.00 each book _____
                                         Total _____

<u>Please make check payable to:</u>

        Food Allergy Solutions, Inc.

Mail all requests with check or money order to the following address.

Attn: Mail Orders
Food Allergy Solutions, Inc.,
2995 Johnson Ferry Road, Suite 250-802
Marietta, GA 30062

We also may be reached by e-mail:
food_allergy_solutions@yahoo.com